FOREVER L.A.

A Field Guide to

Los Angeles Area Cemeteries

& Their Residents

Douglas Keister

GIBBS SMITH
TO ENRICH AND INSPIRE HUMANKIND

To Kay and Carl Keister, for
    giving me the gift of life,

to Bill W and Dr. Bob, for
    giving it back to me, and

to Sandy, for making the present
    a wonderful adventure.

First Edition
14 13 12 11 10   5 4 3 2 1

Text and photographs © 2010 Douglas Keister
Map © 2010 Marianne Govan

Published by
Gibbs Smith
P.O. Box 667
Layton, Utah 84041

1.800.835.4993 orders
www.gibbs-smith.com

Designed and produced by Kurt Wahlner
Printed and bound in Hong Kong

Gibbs Smith books are printed on either recycled, 100% post-
consumer waste or on FSC-certified papers or on paper produced
from a 100% certified sustainable forest/controlled wood source.

Library of Congress Cataloging-in-Publication Data

Keister, Douglas.
  Forever L.A. : a field guide to Los Angeles area cemeteries &
their residents / Douglas Keister ; map by Marianne Govan ;
photographs by Douglas Keister. — 1st ed.
      p. cm.
  Includes index.
  ISBN-13: 978-1-4236-0522-5
  ISBN-10: 1-4236-0522-5
  1. Cemeteries—California—Los Angeles—Guidebooks.
2. Sepulchral monuments—California—Los Angeles—
Guidebooks. 3. Los Angeles (Calif.)—Biography. 4. Los Angeles
(Calif.)—Genealogy. I. Govan, Marianne. II. Title. III. Title:
Forever Los Angeles.
  F869.L8K45 2010
  929'.5--dc22
                                2009046618

Page 2: Hollywood Forever Cemetery

Contents

About L.A.

Los Angeles, L. A., City of Angels, la-la-land, The Big Orange, Lotusland—few cities are as diverse and mystifying as Los Angeles, California. It was founded on September 4, 1781, by Spanish governor Felipe de Neve as El Pueblo de Nuestra Señora la Reina de los Ángeles de Porciúncula (The Village of Our Lady, the Queen of the Angels of the Little Portion). The official name was El Pueblo de la Reina de Los Angeles and, as the years ticked on, eventually became known simply as Los Angeles.

Close to four million Angelenos are corralled within five hundred square miles that is the City of Los Angeles. However, most people know Los Angeles as a rather amorphous blob comprising the City of Los Angeles and bits and pieces of neighboring communities. Los Angeles *County* is over 4,750 square miles and contains over 125 incorporated and unincorporated communities that, including the City of Los Angeles, are home to over 10 million souls. Around 200 of them die every day, about 60,000 in a calendar year: 20,000 from heart disease, 55,000 from cancer, 10,500 from accidents 4,000 from cirrhosis of the liver, and 700 by suicide. All of the dead need to be tended to.

The first formal burials in the Los Angeles area were in small churchyards (known as God's Acre) around Mission San Gabriel Arcángel (established 1771 in San Gabriel) and Mission San Fernando Rey de España (established 1797 in San Fernando). The area around the Plaza Church at 521 North Main Street is said to have been the principal burial ground for Los Angeles from 1826 to 1844. In 1837, the parish priest warned that the burial ground was insufficient, and in 1842, Calvary

Angelus Rosedale Cemetery

Cemetery was established (it was formally designated as the first official cemetery of Los Angeles in 1962). As Los Angeles grew, specialty cemeteries sprang up for secret societies like the Freemasons and Odd Fellows and for ethnic groups like the Chinese and Jews. The Los Angeles City Council outlawed burials within the city in 1879 except for the use of plots already purchased. This led to the development of dozens of cemeteries in Los Angeles suburbs.

When a cemetery was closed, that did not necessarily mean that all of the bodies were exhumed and buried elsewhere. In many cases, streets, buildings, and then parking lots were constructed over the area with little regard for what had been there. This often resulted in the discovery of human remains when there was an excavation where a cemetery had been. However, there are dozens of cemeteries that are well known and are well tended. Others have not fared so well. A complete list of all cemeteries in Los Angeles County is found on page 244.

Nowadays, some of the dead are buried in the county cemetery, others are cremated and scattered, but the majority are interred in the dozens of cemeteries that dot the landscape. Although most modern burials are marked with rather pedestrian flat markers, there is still much to see in Los Angeles cemeteries. Architecture and art abound. Who knows? You may even run into one of your favorite celebrities. Better yet, unlike most entertainment and exploration options in modern-day America—it's all free! Pack a lunch, a map or a GPS device, and a copy of *Forever L.A.* You'll be rewarded with a whole new perspective on art, architecture, symbolism, and stargazing. Indeed, where else can you easily get within six feet of your favorite celebrity?

Valhalla Memorial Park

Forest Lawn Memorial Park– Glendale

1712 South Glendale Avenue
Glendale, California 91205
800-204-3131
⊛ 34 07 30 N 118 15 10 W
www.forestlawn.com/
Maps in office

With all due respect, Forest Lawn (and Forest Lawn–Glendale in particular) is the Disneyland of cemeteries. It's only fitting that it is in Los Angeles, which is one of the bastions of artifice, thanks to the film industry. The immaculate grounds, spic-and-span monuments, and informative exhibits almost make one forget that there are over a quarter million bodies reposing underground and in mausoleums. Forest Lawn was famously skewered in Evelyn's Waugh's darkly comedic novel *The Loved One* (1948) and later in a movie of the same name (1965), with a cast of some of Hollywood's finest stars, including Jonathan Winters playing the dual role of an owner of a Forest Lawn–like cemetery (Whispering Glades) and his hapless twin brother who operates a pet cemetery (Happier Hunting Grounds). In truth, Forest Lawn established a trend in making the modern-day memorial park a place that softens the impact of death.

The Mystery of Life

Forest Lawn began simply enough in 1906 as a 55-acre nonprofit, nonsectarian cemetery founded by a group of San Francisco business-men. The landscaping and funerary architecture and monuments were in keeping with the garden/rural cemetery esthetic of winding roads, lush landscaping, and a hodgepodge of individualized monuments. In 1912, Hubert Eaton and C. B. Sims (who had developed the idea

No.555.
Forest Lawn Mausoleum
Forest Lawn Memorial Park, Glendale, California.

Prior to the opening of Disneyland, Forest Lawn–Glendale was the #1 tourist attraction in the Los Angeles area. A number of postcard views were produced, which were gobbled up by visitors.

of selling "pre-need" cemetery plots) purchased the cemetery, and by 1917, Eaton took over its management. Eaton had no cemetery experience, but he was a businessman with an entrepreneurial spirit. Previously, he had been involved in a number of business ventures, most notably as a developer of mining property in Nevada. After Eaton took over Forest Lawn Cemetery (which he soon renamed Forest Lawn Memorial Park), he implemented his idea of designing a cemetery where all of the markers were at ground level and is thus credited with establishing the "memorial park." He felt that most other cemeteries were too haphazard and depressing, especially when the monuments aged and became tarnished and tilted. Although Forest Lawn does not have many upright grave markers (the ones it does have are leftovers from the original cemetery), it does have a smattering of gleaming private mausoleums and flawless statuary.

Much of the Forest Lawn aesthetic has little or nothing to do with death. Like all cemeteries, Forest Lawn has a definite religious aspect with lots of fluttering angels and evocatively hopeful statuary, but the most interesting aspects of Forest Lawn–Glendale are its tributes to great artists and architecture. There are exact replicas of Michelangelo's *David, Moses,* and *La Pietà;* an enormous stained glass re-creation of da Vinci's *Last Supper;* and a museum chock-full of rare paintings, coins, jewelry, sculpture, and stained glass. And for the thrifty traveler, it's all free. Modern-day travelers may find it hard to believe, but before the official opening of Disneyland in 1955, Forest Lawn was the #1 tourist destination in the Los Angeles area.

Entrance Gates

🌀 34 07 30 N 118 15 10 W

This postcard view illustrates the English Renaissance–style entrance gates to the 300-acre cemetery. The gates, which are 25 feet high and built in seven sections, are the largest wrought-iron gates in the world.

Wee Kirk o' the Heather

🌀 34 07 38 N 118 14 54 W

One of the most popular Los Angeles postcards in the 1950s was a depiction of the Wee Kirk o' the Heather chapel, which is nestled in a hillside on Cathedral Drive. The diminutive stone chapel, built in 1929, is modeled after the village church in Glencairn, Scotland, that was attended by Annie Laurie of Scottish lore. The chapel, which seats 85, is very popular

with couples looking for an unusual (and economical) venue in which to say their wedding vows. Indeed, Ronald Reagan and Jane Wyman were married there on January 6, 1940.

Church of the Recessional

🌀 34 07 45 N 118 14 38 W

This replica church, across from the Hall of The Crucifixion–Resurrection, was modeled after Rudyard Kipling's home church in Rottingdean, England; the name was inspired by his poem "Recessional":

> God of our fathers, known of old—
> Lord of our far-flung battle line
> Beneath whose awful hand we hold
> Dominion over palm and pine—
> Lord God of Hosts, be with us yet,
> Lest we forget—lest we forget!

FOREST LAWN MEMORIAL PARK, GLENDALE, CALIFORNIA

The tumult and the shouting dies;
The captains and the kings depart:
Still stands Thine ancient sacrifice,
An humble and a contrite heart.
Lord God of Hosts, be with us yet,
Lest we forget—lest we forget!

Far-called, our navies melt away;
On dune and headland sinks the fire:
Lo, all our pomp of yesterday
Is one with Nineveh and Tyre!
Judge of the Nations, spare us yet,
Lest we forget—lest we forget!

If, drunk with sight of power, we loose
Wild tongues that have not Thee in awe—
Such boasting as the Gentiles use
Or lesser breeds without the law—
Lord God of Hosts, be with us yet,
Lest we forget—lest we forget!

For heathen heart that puts her trust
In reeking tube and iron shard—
All valiant dust that builds on dust,
And guarding, calls not Thee to guard—
For frantic boast and foolish word,
Thy mercy on Thy people, Lord!

The Little Church of the Flowers

34 07 27 N 118 15 04 W

The Little Church of the Flowers, dedicated in 1918, was the first replica church built at Forest Lawn. It was modeled after a church in the village of Stoke Poges, Buckinghamshire, England, where famed English poet Thomas Gray (1716–1771) wrote "Elegy Written in a Country Churchyard." The last section, The Epitaph, of the 128-line poem reads as follows:

Here rests his head upon the lap of Earth
A youth to Fortune and to Fame unknown.
Fair Science frown'd not on his humble birth,
And Melancholy mark'd him for her own.

Large was his bounty, and his soul sincere,
Heav'n did a recompense as largely send:
He gave to Mis'ry all he had, a tear,
He gain'd from Heav'n ('twas all he wish'd) a friend.

No farther seek his merits to disclose,
Or draw his frailties from their dread abode,
(There they alike in trembling hope repose)
The bosom of his Father and his God.

In unpoetic language, The Epitaph can be summarized in the following way: Here lies a humble and common man who was not blessed with fame, fortune, or education. He had his ups, his downs, and was generous and sensitive to the needs of others. No need to know more about him. He was judged and now resides in heaven.

Hall of the Crucifixion–Resurrection

✳ 34 07 41 N 118 14 44 W (auditorium housing Jan Styka's painting)

At the top of the hill stands the Hall of the Crucifixion–Resurrection and an adjacent museum and gift shop. The main purpose for the hall and the huge parking lot to accommodate tour buses is for the display of two enormous paintings. *The Crucifixion* is said to be the largest framed and mounted canvas painting in the world. At 195 feet long and 45 feet high, it is twice the size of a basketball court. In 1894, Polish statesman Ignacy Padrewski commissioned Polish painter Jan Styka to execute a painting titled *Golgotha*

A postcard view of the auditorium that houses Jan Styka's painting

(the Aramaic name for the site of the Crucifixion). Styka journeyed to Jerusalem to make preliminary drawings and stopped on the way back to Poland to have the project blessed by Pope Leo XIII. The enormous painting made its debut in Warsaw in June 1897 and then toured Europe before being packed up and sent to America, where it was to be featured at the 1904 Louisiana Purchase Exposition in St. Louis. Apparently it never made it to the Exposition since no suitable building could be found, and Styka's American partners neglected to pay the customs taxes. The painting was rolled up on a telephone pole and ended up in the basement of the Chicago Civic Opera Company. It was there that Forest Lawn founder Hubert Eaton found it. The badly damaged painting was restored with the help of Jan Styka's son, Adam Styka. A more extensive restoration occurred during 2005–2006 as part of Forest Lawn's 100th anniversary celebration.

The Crucifixion shares space with The Resurrection, completed in 1965 by American painter Robert Clark. That painting is a mere 70 by 51 feet.

Gates of Paradise
Florence, Italy

✺ 43 46 23 N 11 15 18 E

Museum and Gift
Shop

✺ 34 07 41 N 118 14 44 W

Next to the Hall of the Crucifixion–Resurrection is a museum and store. The museum has a permanent collection and a series of changing exhibitions. The permanent collection features items that founder Hubert Eaton collected in his travels and a replica of the doors, known as the Gates of Paradise, from the Battistero di San Giovanni (Baptistery of St. John) in Florence, Italy.

Gates of Paradise, Florence, Italy

Arcade, Campo Santo, Genoa, Italy

✳ 44 25 47 N 8 57 02 E

The Great Mausoleum

✳ 34 07 21 N 118 14 54 W

Arcade, Campo Santo, Genoa, Italy

The architectural inspiration for Forest Lawn's Great Mausoleum comes from the Campo Santo in Genoa, Italy, According to Forest Lawn, the Great Mausoleum has been called the "New World's Westminster Abbey" by *Time* magazine. Inside the Great Mausoleum are some of Hollywood's greatest (and most private stars). Their privacy is still guarded long after their deaths, since access to their crypts is severely limited. The Memorial Court of Honor, which contains reproductions of some of Michelangelo's most recognized works, is somewhat reminiscent of the galleries at Campo Santo except that the galleries of Campo Santo have a much more obvious mortality theme.

The Builder's Creed

✳ 34 07 21 N 118 14 54 W
(in front of the Great Mausoleum)

Forest Lawn developer Hubert Eaton referred to himself as "The Builder." Eaton's manifesto, *The Builder's Creed*, which explains the design aesthetic of Forest Lawn, was penned by Eaton on January 1, 1917. It is on the exterior wall of the Great Mausoleum. The Builder's Creed says, in part, "I shall try to build at Forest Lawn a great park, devoid of misshapen monuments and other customary signs of earthly death, but filled with towering trees, sweeping lawns, splashing fountains, singing

birds, beautiful statuary, cheerful flowers, noble memorial architecture with interiors full of light and color, and redolent of the world's best history and romances." No visitor to Forest Lawn will doubt that Eaton fulfilled his promise.

The Last Supper

This stained glass interpretation of Leonardo da Vinci's *Last Supper* was crafted in Italy by Rosa Caselli Moretti, using Leonardo's original sketches. When the Last Supper window was created, it was rightly billed by Forest Lawn as more evocative than the original since the original, which is painted on the walls of the Convent of Santa Maria del Grazie in Milan, Italy, had faded and flaked away. A major and somewhat controversial renovation of the original was completed in 1999. Forest

Lawn's stained glass re-creation is covered by drapes, but it is displayed every half-hour, from 9:30 a.m. through 4:00 p.m., 365 days a year. The drapes are automatically drawn and a narration complete with music tells the story of the construction of the Last Supper window.

The Memorial Court of Honor

✦ **34 07 21 N 118 14 54 W (mausoleum entrance)**

The Memorial Court of Honor is Forest Lawn's answer to Westminster Abbey. It is lined with reproductions of sculptures of Michelangelo's *Twilight and Dawn* and *Night and Day* (both originals in the Medici Chapel in Florence, Italy), *La Pietà* (original in the Vatican), *Madonna of Bruges* (original in the Cathedral of the Holy Savior in Bruges, Belgium), and

Madonna and Child (original also in the Medici Chapel in Florence). Like Westminster Abbey, the Memorial Court of Honor contains the remains of notable citizens. However in the case of Forest Lawn, their notability is determined by the Forest Lawn Council of Regents. Among those spending eternity there are sculptor Gutzon Borglum (1871–1941), most noted for his plus-size granite carving of four United States presidents at Mount Rushmore; Nobel Prize–winning physicist Robert Andrews Millikan (1896–1953); composer Carrie Jacobs-Bond (1862–1946), who wrote "I Love You Truly"; and Jan Styka (1858–1925) who painted *The Crucifixion*, which resides in Forest Lawn's Hall of the Crucifixion–Resurrection.

David

✳ 34 07 32 N 118 14 26 W

A reproduction of Michelangelo's *David* stands 16 feet 9 inches tall and was carved from brilliant white Carrara marble. The Forest Lawn version originally had a fig leaf in the usual place. Forest Lawn says that founder Hubert Eaton wanted the David statue to be sans fig leaf, but he was overruled by the "Victorian influenced art committee." The current leafless version was installed in 1971 after the original was destroyed in an earthquake. The sculpture stands on a four-foot pedestal in the Court of David.

The Mystery of Life

✳ 34 07 32 N 118 14 24 W

This gleaming marble statuary group was carved for Forest Lawn by Ernesto Gazzeri. Another copy is in Forest Lawn–Cypress in Cypress,

The Mystery of Life (detail)   *The Finding of Moses*

California. It depicts the meaning of life as interpreted by 18 life-sized figures, from youth to old age to the clueless agnostic. A legend guides the viewer through the various mysteries of life.

The Finding of Moses
✳ 34 07 34 N 118 14 57 W

Down the hill from the Wee Kirk o' the Heather is a fountain with a sculpture of *The Finding of Moses.* The original, which is a representation of Pharaoh's daughter finding Moses in the bulrushes, is at the Pincio Gardens in Rome.

Court of Freedom—The Republic
✳ 34 07 22 N 118 14 10 W

The Republic is an 18-foot-high (24 feet with base) sculpture crafted in bronze and marble by Daniel Chester French (April 20, 1850–October 7, 1931). French's first *Republic* was the colossal centerpiece of 1893s World's Columbian Exposition in Chicago. Another version similar to Forest Lawn's is in Chicago. French is best known as the sculptor of the *Lincoln Memorial* in Washington, D.C.

Court of Freedom— *George Washington*

✳ 34 07 20 N 118 14 06 W

Across from *The Republic* is a sculpture titled *George Washington* by John Quincy Adams Ward. According to Forest Lawn, it is the finest sculptural likeness of Washington. It was originally commissioned by Congress for the Capitol, but due to a bureaucratic mix-up, the appropriation was never made, so Forest Lawn obtained it. The sculpture is fronted by seven links of a chain that was strung across the Hudson River in New York to prevent British warships from attacking the river forts. Each link in the chain, which was originally 1,800 feet long, weighs 350 pounds.

Court of Freedom—*The Signing of the Declaration of Independence*

✳ 34 07 22 N 118 14 10 W

The Signing of the Declaration of Independence is a mosaic reproduction of the famous painting by John Trumbull in the Capitol rotunda in Washington,

D.C. Composed of 700,000 pieces of Venetian glass tile, it is three times the size of the 12 x 18-foot oil-on-canvas original that is titled *Declaration of Independence*, often mistakenly called *The Signing of the Declaration of Independence*. It only shows the presentation of the draft, not the signing. Forest Lawn also mistakenly calls it *The Signing of the Declaration of Independence* in its materials.

Freedom Mausoleum

✳ 34 07 20 N 118 14 04 W (entrance)

The other community mausoleum in Forest Lawn–Glendale is the blue-granite-pillared patriotic-themed Freedom Mausoleum. A number of

celebrities reside inside. Although red velvet ropes discourage access to some of the galleries, many of the crypts can be easily seen with a bit of neck-craning.

Labyrinth
Chartres, France

✳ 48 26 51 N 1 29 15 E

Labyrinth

✳ 34 07 18 N 118 14 02 W

Located down the hill and to the right of the Freedom Mausoleum is the Labyrinth, which is modeled after one located in the cathedral at Chartres, France. The labyrinth at Chartres, was built around 1200 in a medieval pattern. The labyrinth was meant to be walked as a kind of a pilgrimage or for repentance. When used for repentance, pilgrims often walk on their knees.

Lullabyland

✳ 34 07 17 N 118 14 44 W

Babyland

✳ 34 07 23 N 118 14 37 W

Capping off the Disney-esque ethos is the fairytale-themed Lullabyland; Babyland is nearby. "Lullabyland" verses, penned by noted cowboy poet E. A. Brininstool, are carved on a plaque there.

You strain your ears to catch a note
That drifts in cadence soft and low,
From out the Heaven Land remote,
Where all the little children go.

And often in your dreams you hear
In echoes gently, sweetly flung,
Some simple song, in accents clear,
Your little one has often sung.

And so from out the Shadow-Shore,
God hands to you the golden key,
With which you may unlock the door
Of sacred, hallowed memory.

And from within, a smiling face
Before your eager vision stands,
And you may feel the glad embrace
Of dimpled, loving baby hands.

Notable Residents

The list of notable permanent residents of Forest Lawn is encyclopedic. There are literally hundreds, and we can only list a few here. For an exhaustive and ever-expanding list, go to the excellent database maintained at findagrave.com.

Casey Stengel

✴ 34 07 21 N 118 14 14 W
(southwest corner)
Court of Freedom

Casey Stengel was the colorful and irascible manager of the New York Yankees and the New York Mets. Although he steered the Yankees through a number of American League titles and World Series victories, he is perhaps best remembered as one of the early managers of the hapless New York Mets. Commenting on the 1962 team, he said, "The Mets have shown me more ways to lose than I even knew existed."

Nat "King" Cole

March 17, 1919–February 15, 1965
✴ 34 07 20 N 118 14 04 W (mausoleum entrance)
Freedom Mausoleum, Sanctuary of Heritage

Nat "King" Cole (Nathaniel Adams Coles) first came to prominence as a leading jazz pianist. Although an accomplished pianist, he owes most of his popular musical fame to his soft baritone voice, which he used to perform in big band and jazz genres. Despite the segregationist policies at the time, he broke many color barriers, most notably when, on November 5, 1956, *The Nat King Cole Show* became the first mainstream television program hosted by an African-American. He is the father of Natalie Cole.

Francis X. Bushman

January 10, 1883–August 23, 1966

✳ 34 07 20 N 118 14 04 W (mausoleum entrance)

Freedom Mausoleum, Sanctuary of Gratitude

Robustly fit and handsome, Francis Xavier Bushman appeared in over 200 films plus stage and television performances. He was named the "Handsomest Man in the World," thanks to his roles in manly films like *Ben-Hur* (1925) and an aggressive public relations agent.

Jean Hersholt

July 12, 1886–June 2, 1956

✳ 34 07 22 N 118 14 53 W

(across from the courtyard of the Great Mausoleum)

Danish-born actor Jean Hersholt appeared in 140 films (75 silent; 65 sound). He usually played sympathetic roles, best typified as Shirley Temple's kindly grandfather in *Heidi* (1937). In 1939, Hersholt helped found the Motion Picture Relief Fund. To honor that accomplishment, The Academy of Motion Picture Arts and Sciences (Academy Awards) established the Jean Hersholt Humanitarian Award in 1956. Hersholt's memorial is a bronze figure of Klods Hans (Clumsy Hans), a character from a Hans Christian Andersen fairy tale.

Michael Jackson

August 29, 1958–June 25, 2009

✳ 34 07 21 N 118 14 54 W (mausoleum entrance)

Great Mausoleum, Holly Terrace (locked Area)

Michael Jackson was born in Gary, Indiana, to Joseph Walker Jackson and Katherine Esther Scruse Jackson. When Michael was eight years old, he joined his four brothers—Jermaine, Jackie, Marlon, and Tito—to form The Jackson 5. The group was an immediate success. Michael Jackson's 1982 breakthrough solo album *Thriller* is the all-time best-selling album worldwide. His untimely death rocked the whole world and was the subject of media conversation for many months. He was laid to rest on September 3, 2009, more than two months after his death.

Entrance to Holly Terrace

Alan Ladd

September 3, 1913–
January 29, 1964
⌖ 34 07 20 N 118 14 04 W
(mausoleum entrance)
Freedom Mausoleum, Sanctuary of Heritage

Alan Walbridge Ladd was the actor best remembered for his 1953 role of a gunfighter named Shane in the western movie of the same name. He appeared in over ninety feature films. His last film was *The Carpetbaggers* (1964).

Aimee Semple McPherson

October 9, 1890 d. September 27, 1944

✹ **34 07 22 N 118 14 50 W**

Sunrise Slope (low marble exedra-like monument near the Great Mausoleum)

Flamboyant evangelical preacher Aimee Semple McPherson has one of the more ostentatious monuments at Forest Lawn. The thrice-married McPherson was one of the pioneers of over-the-top ministries. She conducted services complete with bands, huge choirs, and theatrics. She was a glutton for publicity and was said to have faked her own death as a publicity stunt. She died for good after overdosing on Seconal. Over 60,000 attended her funeral.

George Burns and Gracie Allen
See page 174.

Joe Cobb (Fat Kid in Our Gang)
See page 151.

Larry Fine (Larry of The Three Stooges)
See page 145.

Mary Pickford
See page 181.

Spencer Tracy
See page 158.

Joe E. Brown
See page 159.

Maxene Anglyn Andrews

January 3, 1918–October 21, 1995

✺ 34 07 21 N 118 14 54 W (mausoleum entrance)

Great Mausoleum, Columbarium of Memory (niche 20390)

Maxene Andrews and her sisters, Laverne and Patty, formed the singing trio The Andrews Sisters, which was enormously popular during World War II. They were known as America's Wartime Sweethearts. Two of their best-known songs are *Beat Me Daddy, Eight to the Bar* and *Boogie Woogie Bugle Boy*. As a group, the Andrews Sisters sold between 75 and 100 million records.

Humphrey Bogart

December 25, 1899–January 14, 1957

✺ 34 07 38 N 118 14 31 W

Garden of Memory, Columbarium of Eternal Light (locked area)

Humphrey DeForest Bogart starred in a number of classic films, including *The Maltese Falcon* (1941), *Casablanca* (1942), and *To Have and Have Not* (1944). He won a Best Actor Academy Award for *The African Queen* (1951). The American Film Institute considers Bogart the Greatest American Male Screen Legend of all time. He married starlet Lauren Bacall in 1945, when he was 46 and she was 21.

Clara Bow

July 29, 1905–September 27, 1965

✺ 34 07 20 N 118 14 04 W (mausoleum entrance)

Freedom Mausoleum, Sanctuary of Heritage

Clara Gordon Bow was one of Hollywood's first sex symbols. She was vaulted to fame in the silent film era of the 1920s. Despite of (or because of) an abusive childhood, she blossomed on the screen. Her raw sexual magnetism and high-spirited personality gave her the title of "The It Girl." She also became known as the quintessential flapper. Her abusive childhood eventually caught up with her, and memories came flooding back. Electroshock and psychotherapy helped little, and she was under constant care during the last few years of her life.

William Boyd

June 5, 1895–September 12, 1972

✺ 34 07 21 N 118 14 54 W (mausoleum entrance)

Great Mausoleum, Sanctuary of Sacred Promise

William Lawrence Boyd is best known for his role as cowboy hero Hopalong Cassidy. In 1935, he starred in the movie *Hopalong Cassidy*. He turned the character into the classic western good guy with strong moral values who didn't smoke, drink, or cuss, and never started a fight. In all, Boyd starred in 66 Hopalong Cassidy movies, eventually purchasing rights to the Hopalong Cassidy character as well as the movies. Boyd was quite adept at marketing Hopalong Cassidy and his image-emblazoned watches, comic books, mugs, and clothing. The Hopalong Cassidy lunchbox was the first one created with a celebrity decal. Boyd's horse Topper is interred at the Los Angeles Pet Memorial Park in Calabasas (see page 126).

Sam Cooke

January 22, 1931–December 11, 1964

⊛ 34 07 34 N 118 14 27 W

Garden of Honor (locked private area)

Samuel Cooke was a gospel, R&B, soul, and pop singer, a songwriter, and an entrepreneur. In his brief career, which spanned from 1957 to 1965, he had 29 Top 40 hits, including *You Send Me, Chain Gang, Wonderful World, Another Saturday Night,* and *Bring It on Home to Me.* His best-crafted song, *A Change Is Gonna Come,* was released posthumously. Sam Cooke was shot to death by a motel clerk following an altercation. The death was ruled justifiable homicide, but like many cases where a celebrity dies young, the actual circumstances remain controversial.

Sammy Davis Jr.

December 8, 1925–May 16, 1990

⊛ 34 07 34 N 118 14 27 W

Garden of Honor (locked private area)

Samuel George Davis Jr. was a multitalented dancer, singer, instrumentalist, impressionist, and comedian. He won a posthumous Lifetime Achievement Grammy (2001), was posthumously inducted into the Grammy Hall of Fame in 2002 for his 1962 song *What Kind of Fool Am I,* won an Emmy for *Sammy Davis Jr.'s 60th Anniversary Special* (1990), and received a Kennedy Center Honor in 1987. Davis broke many racial barriers, most notably as a member of the 1960s Rat Pack.

Walter Elias Disney

December 5, 1901–
December 15, 1966

⊛ 34 07 20 N 118 14 05 W

Freedom Mausoleum (small private garden to the left of the entrance)

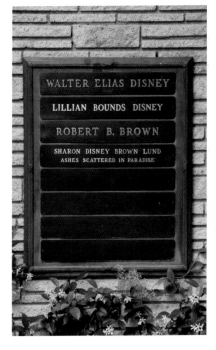

Walt Disney created the "Happiest Place on Earth": Disneyland. There is perhaps no place more associated with the California Dream than this world-famous amusement park. He won multiple Academy Awards, Emmys, and other honors as a film producer, director, screenwriter, voice actor, animator, entrepreneur, and philanthropist. The Walt Disney Company, the corporation he co-founded with his brother, Roy Disney, has annual revenues of approximately $35 billion.

Ralph Edwards

June 13, 1913–November 16, 2005

✳ 34 07 35 N 118 14 31 W

Ascension Plot (lot 7190)

Ralph Edwards was a game show host and producer. He created and hosted the game show *Truth or Consequences*, which first aired on the radio in 1940 and then transitioned to television. The radio and television versions ran for a combined 38 years. He is also well remembered for creating and hosting the program *This is Your Life*, which ran on the radio from 1948 to 1952 and on television from 1952 to 1961. He helped develop the television programs *The Cross-Wits*, *About Faces*, *Knockout*, *Name that Tune*, and *The People's Court*.

W. C. Fields

January 29, 1880–December 25, 1946

✳ 34 07 21 N 118 14 54 W (mausoleum entrance)

Great Mausoleum, Hall of Inspiration, Columbarium of Nativity

Young W. C. Fields (William Claude Dunkenfield) left his Pennsylvania home at age 11 to find his success in vaudeville. By age 21, he put together an act called The Eccentric Juggler. He changed his name to Fields because it was shorter and easier to pronounce. He soon found his way into movies, where he truly hit his stride. His character was a hapless drunken huckster, and he did it well. Unfortunately, the drunken part followed him into real life. Despite his voluminous consumption of spirits, he starred in a number of enormously successful shorts and movies, including *The Golf Specialist* (1930), *My Little Chickadee* (1940), *The Bank Dick* (1940), and *Never Give a Sucker an Honest Break* (1941).

Errol Flynn

June 20, 1909–October 14, 1959

✳ 34 07 21 N 118 14 07 W

Garden of Everlasting Peace (located under a statue of a woman)

Errol Leslie Thomson Flynn, an Australian-born actor, was most famous for his romantic swashbuckler roles in a series of films, including *Captain Blood* (1935), *The Adventures of Robin Hood* (1938), and *The Adventures of Don Juan* (1948). He appeared in 62 films from *In the Wake of the Bounty* (1933) to *Cuban Rebel Girls* (1959). His devil-may-care lifestyle, which included the liberal use of alcohol and narcotics, womanizing, and brawling no doubt led to his premature demise from a massive heart attack. His exploits with women supposedly resulted in the phrase "in like Flynn."

Clark Gable

February 1, 1901–November 16, 1960

✳ 34 07 21 N 118 14 54 W (mausoleum entrance)

Great Mausoleum, Sanctuary of Trust

In his heyday, William Clark Gable was nicknamed "The King of Hollywood." He is best known for his portrayal of Rhett Butler in the 1939 Civil War epic film *Gone with the Wind*. In 1999, the American Film Institute named him number seven on the list of Greatest Male Stars of All Time. He won the Academy Award for Best Actor for his performance in *It Happened One Night* (1934). In total, he appeared in 67 feature films, from *The Painted Desert* in 1931 to *The Misfits* (which was also Marilyn Monroe's last film) in 1961, released after Gable's death.

Jean Harlow

March 3, 1911–June 7, 1937

✳ 34 07 21 N 118 14 54 W (mausoleum entrance)

Great Mausoleum, Sanctuary of Benediction (private family room #34, crypt B)

Jean Harlow (Harlean Harlow Carpenter) was Hollywood's best-known sex symbol of the 1930s. She was known as the "Platinum Blonde" and the "Blonde Bombshell," due to her famous bleached locks and stunning beauty. She appeared as an uncredited extra in a number of films in 1928 and 1929, then burst to stardom in the 1930 film *Hell's Angels*, where she uttered the now famous line "Would you be shocked if I changed into something more comfortable?" When Harlow signed on with MGM, her career soared, and any film she appeared in was a guaranteed money-maker. Alas, she suffered from kidney disease and ultimately died of renal failure when she was only 26 years old. Her funeral took place at the Wee Kirk o' the Heather Chapel. It was rumored that William Powell paid for her $25,000 private room in the Great Mausoleum.

Louis L'Amour

March 22, 1908–June 10, 1988

✳ 34 07 21 N 118 14 54 W (mausoleum entrance)

Great Mausoleum (just outside the entrance)

Louis L'Amour (LaMoure) was one of America's most prolific Western fiction writers. He penned over 100 novels, many of which were in series format. They have sold over 225 million copies and have been translated into dozens of languages. His first novel was *Westward the Tide*, published in 1950. His last was *The Haunted Mesa*, published in 1987. L'Amour also wrote scripts for movies and television. In 1982, he won the Congressional Gold Medal; then in 1984, President Ronald Reagan awarded him the Presidential Medal of Freedom.

Carole Lombard

October 6, 1908–January 16, 1942

✳ 34 07 21 N 118 14 54 W (mausoleum entrance)

Great Mausoleum, Sanctuary of Trust

Carole Lombard (Jane Alice Peters) made her film debut in the 1921 film *A Perfect Crime*, where she was cast as a tomboy. She soon blossomed, and her good looks secured her a number of eye-appeal roles meant largely to bolster the careers of her leading men. She found success of her own in the mid-1930s when she was cast in the 1934 film *Twentieth Century* opposite John Barrymore, and in 1935 in *Hands Across the Table* opposite Fred MacMurray. Her most well known role was in the 1936 film *My Man Godfrey*, where she was nominated for a Best Actress Academy Award. After a failed marriage to William Powell, she wed Clark Gable in 1939. Lombard died tragically in an airplane accident while on a war bond tour. She is listed as number 23 on the American Film Institute's list of Greatest Female Screen Legends, just after Jean Harlow (Katherine Hepburn is number 1).

Tom Mix

January 6, 1880–October 12, 1940

✳ 34 07 30 N 118 14 58 W

Whispering Pines (lot 1030, space 8, at the top of the hill)

Tom Mix (Thomas Hezikiah Mix) was one of the silent film era's first stars, and he was known as the "King of the Cowboys." Mix got his start as a supporting cast member and cattle wrangler for the Selig Polyscope Company and soon found himself in leading roles. He made over 100 short films for Selig, most of which were shot in New Mexico, before moving to Fox Film Corporation in Los Angeles. While at Fox, he made more than 160 cowboy films, and his salary skyrocketed to $17,500 a week. During his career, he made over 300 movies before retiring to perform in circuses and other exhibitions. When USC football player John Wayne got injured and was unable to play, Mix got Wayne a job as a prop man at Fox Studios.

Clayton Moore

September 14, 1914–December 28, 1999

✵ 34 07 21 N 118 14 07 W

Garden of Everlasting Peace (lot 5492)

Handsome lantern-jawed Jack Carlton Moore was a circus acrobat and male model in his youth. Producer Edward Small convinced him to change his name to Clayton. His big break came in 1949 when he was spotted on the movie *Ghost of Zorro* and was asked to try out as the lead in the television version of *The Lone Ranger*; it was already a successful radio program, but the producers needed someone with Moore's physique for the television version. With the addition of Jay Silverheels as Tonto and voice lessons to lower Moore's baritone even more, *The Lone Ranger* became a hit. With one break during a contract dispute, Moore played the Lone Ranger until the series ended in 1956. However, he never really quit playing the Lone Ranger. For over 40 years, he continued to wear the Lone Ranger outfit to hundreds of events, despite a lawsuit by the owner of the Lone Ranger image. Moore became the Lone Ranger, saying he had "fallen in love with the Lone Ranger character" and lived by the Lone Ranger's creed.

Alfred Newman

March 17, 1901–February 17, 1970

✵ 34 07 21 N 118 14 54 W (mausoleum entrance)

Great Mausoleum, Sanctuary of Eternal Prayer

Alfred Newman was a music prodigy who began studying piano at age 5. By age 20, he was conducting musicals for George Gershwin, Richard Rodgers, and Jerome Kern. Hollywood beckoned, and at age 31, he wrote the music for Samuel Goldwyn's movie *Street Scene*. Newman worked constantly for the next four decades, receiving 45 Academy Award nominations and winning nine times. His first win was in 1938 for *Alexander's Ragtime Band*. His last was for *Camelot* in 1967. In the 1940s, comedian Henry Morgan featured a character on his radio program named Alfred Newman, which borrowed composer Newman's name. A satire magazine publisher liked the name and slightly changed the spelling to Alfred E. Neuman, which became the mascot for *Mad* magazine.

Jimmy Stewart

May 20, 1908–July 2, 1997

✵ 34 07 38 N 118 14 58 W

Wee Kirk Churchyard (space 2, lot 8, near the statue of a man holding an arrow)

Actor James Maitland Stewart is best known for his self-effacing everyman persona. He was nominated for Academy Awards five times, won the Best Actor Award for *The Philadelphia Story* in 1941, and received a Lifetime Achievement Award in 1985. Stewart's career never really faltered—from an uncredited role in the 1934 film *Art Trouble* to his 100th film, *An American Tail: Fievel Goes West* (1991), where he did the voice for the Sheriff Wylie Burp character. American Film Institute considers James Stewart the third Greatest American Male Screen Legend after Humphrey Bogart and Cary Grant. Stewart also had a distinguished military career, serving in World War II and then rising to the rank of Brigadier General in the United States Air Force Reserve.

Forest Lawn Memorial Park– Hollywood Hills

6300 Forest Lawn Drive

Los Angeles, California 90068

800-204-3131

⊛ 34 08 59 N 118 19 41 W

www.forestlawn.com/

Maps in office

When Hubert Eaton got ready to open another Forest Lawn Memorial Park, he scaled back the religious matter but ramped up the patriotic theme. The 450-acre Forest Lawn–Hollywood Hills is flanked by Griffith Park and Burbank's television and movie studios. Indeed, before Eaton acquired the property from the Providencia Land and Water Development Company, it was an oft-used movie location by the likes of Carl Laemmle, D. W. Griffith, and Cecil B. DeMille. The area was most notably used by Griffith for some of the scenes of his epic film *Birth of a Nation*. Most of the architecture at Forest Lawn–Hollywood Hills leans towards English and American Colonial Revival.

Forest Lawn Office
⊛ 34 08 59 N 118 19 37 W

The sparkling white office/mortuary/flower shop is roughly modeled after George

Washington's home, Mount Vernon, in Alexandria, Virginia. The original Mount Vernon was built in 1757 in the neoclassical Georgian style. The eastern façade of Mount Vernon, which faces the Potomac River and sports eight columns, was the inspiration for the Forest Lawn version.

Church of the Hills
✳ 34 08 57 N 118 19 29 W

The Church of the Hills, which seats 265, plays host to funerals, weddings, and christenings. It is modeled after the First Parish Church in Portland, Maine (establishment dating to 1674), where poet Henry Wadsworth Longfellow worshipped. The building that served as a model for

Church of the Hills

Forest Lawn's version was constructed in 1826. The First Parish Church has ascribed to the Unitarian faith since 1809. The Church of the Hills at Forest Lawn has a history room where a number of documents and artifacts pertaining to Henry Wadsworth Longfellow are on display.

Old North Church

Old North Church
✳ 34 08 43 N 118 19 03 W

Forest Lawn–Hollywood Hills sports an almost exact copy of Boston's Old North Church, which has been forever immortalized in the Henry Wadsworth Longfellow poem "Paul Revere's Ride," where Revere instructed three Patriots to signal the arrival of the British troops with lanterns atop the church's steeple to Charlestown Patriots across the Charles River. The patriots were instructed to use "One if by land, and two if by sea." The Forest Lawn version of Old North Church has a history room with various artifacts from America's Colonial period.

The Washington Memorial
✳ 34 08 39 N 118 19 02 W

Across from the Old North Church replica and the centerpiece to the Court of Liberty is a statue of America's first president, George Washington. The bronze and marble work is the creation of American sculptor Thomas Ball (1819–1911). The memorial was first exhibited at the World's Columbian Exposition of 1893 in Chicago and was later acquired by Forest Lawn. The portrait busts on the pedestal are four of Washington's generals: the Marquis de Lafayette, Benjamin Lincoln,

Nathanael Greene, and Henry Knox. Out of view are seated figures that, according to the description on the plaque, "represent the forces that shaped his life: oppression, revolution, victory, and the return to peace, symbolized by Cincinnatus, the citizen-soldier."

Birth of Liberty
✳ 34 08 35 N 118 19 02 W

The most patriotic of all buildings at Forest Lawn–Hollywood Hills is the Hall of Liberty, which contains a 1,200-seat auditorium, a museum, and a store. It is often used for meetings and graduations. On the backside of the Hall is

The Washington Memorial

a massive 162 x 28-foot mosaic panel titled *Birth of Liberty*, which consists of ten million pieces of Venetian glass. The mosaic depicts twenty-five scenes from early American history (1619–1787), including Betsy Ross presenting the flag to George Washington, Washington crossing the Delaware River on Christmas Eve, and Paul Revere's ride.

Birth of Liberty

Plaza of Mesoamerican Heritage

⚙ 34 08 33 N 118 18 57 W

Catering to the large Latino population in Los Angeles, Forest Lawn has recently added a Plaza of Mesoamerican Heritage (originally named the Plaza of Mexican Heritage), which features sculptures by Meliton Salas Rodriguez, of Guadalajara, Mexico. He used hand tools to work the native Mexican stone into representations of the Aztec, Huastec, Maya, Mixtec, Olmec, Teotihuacán, Toltec, Totonac, and Zapotec civilizations. Other sculptures are also in the area, including an Olmecan head and an Aztec sun calendar. The Museum of Mesoamerican History is open from 10 a.m. to 5 p.m.

Plaza of Mesoamerican Heritage

Notable Residents

Like its Glendale counterpart, Forest Lawn–Hollywood Hills is the final address of hundreds of notable Angelenos. It would be impossible to list them all. However, excellent resources can be found on the Internet starting with findagrave.com. A sampling follows.

Edie Adams

April 16, 1927–October 15, 2008

⚙ 34 09 00 N 118 19 19 W

Remembrance Lawn (two markers to the right of Ernie Kovacs)

Edie Adams (Elizabeth Edith Enke) was a Broadway, television, and film actress, as well as a singer and comedienne. Although she often portrayed empty-headed sexy blondes, she did it with a tongue-in-cheek comedic flair. She was married to Ernie Kovacs from 1954 until his death in 1962.

Gene Autry

September 29, 1907–October 2, 1998
✳ 34 08 54 N 118 19 34 W
Sheltering Hills (grave 1048, in front of one of the statues)

Orvon Gene Autry gained fame as The Singing Cowboy on the radio, in movies, and on television. He is well known for his rendition of "Rudolph the Red-Nosed Reindeer." A shrewd businessman, he owned the Flying A gasoline company and in 1983 bought the California Angels baseball team. The five stars on his grave marker represent his five stars on the Hollywood Walk of Fame (Recording, Movies, Television, Radio, and Live Theater).

Clyde Beatty

June 10, 1903–July 19, 1965
✳ 34 08 58 118 19 14 W
Court of Remembrance (crypt 2175)

As alluded to on his grave marker, Clyde Beatty was a lion tamer. At one time, his act included 40 lions and tigers. He also trained other animals and started his own circus, eventually merging with the Cole Brothers as the Clyde Beatty–Cole Bros. Circus.

Bette Davis

April 5, 1908–October 6, 1989

✿ 34 09 00 N 118 19 15 W

Court of Remembrance (large white tomb to the left of the entrance)

Hard-edged Bette Davis (Ruth Elizabeth Davis) was known for her willingness to play unsympathetic characters. Davis was acclaimed for her performances in contemporary crime melodramas, historical and period films, and occasional comedies. She was a heavy smoker, and her imposing tomb often has snubbed-out cigarettes left by fans. Her epitaph reads, "She did it the hard way."

Albert Romolo "Cubby" Broccoli

April 5, 1909–June 29, 1996

✿ 34 08 59 N 118 19 11 W

Court of Remembrance

Albert "Cubby" Broccoli is best known as the producer of a number of James Bond films. He and partner Harry Saltzman shepherded the Bond films from low-budget movies to big-budget extravaganzas. His heirs continue to produce Bond films.

Sandra Dee

April 23, 1942–February 20, 2005
✲ 34 08 58 N 118 19 10 W
Court of Remembrance, Sanctuary of Enduring Protection (wall crypt 3739)

Pretty, blond Sandra Dee (Alexandra Cymboliak Zuck) began her career as a model and progressed to film. She won a Golden Globe Award in 1959 for New Star of the Year/Actress. In the late 1950s and early 1960s, she played popular girl-next-door roles in Gidget and Tammy movies. She married Bobby Darin in 1960 at age 18. Like most ingénues, her star faded in her 30s and she fell into obscurity.

Andy Gibb

March 5, 1958–March 10, 1988
✲ 34 08 58 N 118 19 10 W
Court of Remembrance
(crypt 2534, outside and
facing the Serenity section)

Andrew Roy Gibb was a
late 1970s and 1980s singer,
pop icon, and musician. His
three older brothers—Barry,
Maurice, and Robin—were
the Bee Gees of disco fame.
Andy was much younger
and struck out on his own, finding almost immediate success, charting three #1 Billboard Hot 100 singles in a row. Alas, life in the fast lane took its toll, and Andy Gibb succumbed to a heart attack at the age of 30, no doubt induced by years of drug use.

Gabby Hayes

May 7, 1885–February 9, 1969
✲ 34 08 47 N 118 19 30 W
Hillside (lot 4972)

Gabby Hayes (George Francis Hayes) was the quintessential comedic character actor. Because of his graying beard, he always looked like an old loveable geezer. He appeared in two hundred movies and television programs from 1929 to 1958.

Buster Keaton

October 4, 1895–February 1, 1966

⚙ 34 08 40 N 118 19 03 W

George Washington Section, Court of Valor (lot 5512)

Joseph Frank Keaton was an award-winning comic, actor, and filmmaker, best known for his silent films. He excelled at physical comedy, which he executed with a stoic deadpan expression. In 1999, the American Film Institute ranked Buster Keaton the 21st greatest male actor of all time.

Ernie Kovacs

January 23, 1919–January 13, 1962

⚙ 34 09 00 N 118 19 19 W

Remembrance Lawn (two markers to the left of his wife, Edie Adams)

Ernest Edward Kovacs was a legendary television comedian from the Golden Age of Television. Since there was little idea of how television was supposed to be, there was much experimentation in television's early days, and Kovacs was one of the true innovators. His ad-libs, gags, and camera techniques inspired future television hosts like Johnny Carson and David Letterman. Kovacs' simple marker is inscribed with his signature and the epitaph, " 'Nothing in moderation' / We all loved him."

Dorothy Lamour

See page 167.

Walter Lantz

April 27, 1899–March 22, 1994

and

Gracie Lantz

November 7, 1903–March 17, 1992
✣ 34 09 00 N 118 19 12 W
Columbarium of Radiant Light

Walter Lantz was a cartoonist and animator best known for his creation of Woody Woodpecker. Mel Blanc was the first to voice Woody Woodpecker's manic laugh, but after Blanc sued Lantz for using Blanc's voice without permission, Lantz's wife Gracie took over and voiced the Woody character from 1950 until 1972.

Charles Laughton

July 1, 1899–December 15, 1962
✣ 34 08 58 N 118 19 10 W
Court of Remembrance (wall crypt C-310)

Charles Laughton was a critically acclaimed actor, director, producer, and screenwriter, whose acting career spanned from 1928 until 1962. In 1933, he won a Best Actor Oscar for his lead role in *The Private Life of Henry VIII*. Even though Laughton was gay, he was married for many years to actress Elsa Lanchester.

Stan Laurel

See page 138.

Liberace

May 16, 1919–February 4, 1987
✴ **34 08 59 N 118 19 14 W**
Court of Remembrance

Liberace (Wladziv Valentino) is one of a select group of performers known only by one name. Of Polish and Italian descent, he was a flamboyant entertainer and pianist, wowing audiences with his outrageous costumes. Many of his costumes and pianos reside at the Liberace Museum on Liberace Plaza in Las Vegas.

Nelson Family

✴ **34 08 45 N 118 19 25 W**
Revelation Section (Ozzie and Harriet, lot 3540; Ricky, lot 3538)

Three simple markers mark the graves of Ozzie, Harriet, and Ricky Nelson of television's *The Adventures of Ozzie and Harriet*. Ricky went on to become a pop star, dying tragically in an airplane accident.

Lou Rawls

December 1, 1933–January 6, 2006
✴ **34 08 58 N 118 19 10 W**
Courts of Remembrance (wall elevation 9A, wall crypt 3186)

Louis Allen Rawls was a soul music, jazz, and blues singer, best known for his smooth vocal style. Frank Sinatra once said that Rawls had "the classiest singing and silkiest chops in the singing game." Rawls sold more than 40 million records, acted in movies and television, and did voice-overs for cartoons.

John Ritter

September 17, 1948–September 11, 2003
※ 34 08 38 N 118 19 03 W
Court of Liberty (lot 1622, just outside the enclosure on the right)

Actor and comedian John Ritter is best known for playing Jack Tripper in the ABC sitcom *Three's Company* and for starring in *8 Simple Rules for Dating My Teenage Daughter*. His epitaph is a verse from the Beatles' song "The End": "And in the end, the love you take is equal to the love you make . . ."

Rod Steiger

April 14, 1925–July 9, 2002
$ 34 08 58 N 118 19 10 W
Court of Remembrance, Columbarium of Providence

Rod Steiger was an award-winning actor known for his intense performances in such films as *Waterloo* (1970), *On the Waterfront* (1954), *The Pawnbroker* (1964), *Doctor Zhivago* (1965), and *In the Heat of the Night* (1967), for which he won the Academy Award–Best Actor. One of his most memorable roles was as a mortician (Mr. Joyboy) in the 1965 movie *The Loved One*, which spoofed what proved to be Steiger's last address: Forest Lawn.

Dick Wilson (Mr. Whipple)

June 30, 1916–November 19, 2007
$ 34 08 49 N 118 19 25 W
Enduring Faith (lot 822, space 1)

Dick Wilson (Riccardo DiGuglielmo) was a British-born character actor who played the role of finicky grocery store manager Mr. Whipple, who scolded customers with "Please don't squeeze the Charmin" in over 500 toilet paper television commercials (1965–1989, 1999).

Hillside Memorial Park

6001 West Centinela Avenue

Culver City, California 90230

310-641-0707

✳ 33 58 45 N 118 23 26 W

www.hillsidememorial.org/Home.aspx

Maps in office

Closed Saturdays and Jewish holidays

On May 23, 1941, two brothers, Robert and Harry Groman, and Lazare F. Bernhard established a new Jewish burial ground in Los Angeles. The 40-acre property was incorporated as B'nai B'rith Memorial Park and was then changed to Hillside Memorial Park on March 24, 1942. In 1951, Hillside Memorial Park Mausoleum and Hillside Memorial Park Garden Crypts were incorporated. Aptly named, the cemetery scoots up a hill adjacent to the roaring San Diego Freeway. Over the years, the cemetery has filled out with over 60,000 interments, and now almost all the available land has been developed. However, much of the land consists of multitiered, multistoried community mausoleums with thousand of spaces still available. The most recent additions are the Court and Garden of the Matriarchs, completed in 2004, and the restricted access Garden of Solomon, completed in 2009. A scattering garden has also been added. Hillside Memorial Park is one of the most visitor-friendly cemeteries for celebrity hunters. They gladly give out lists of grave locations. (and the cemetery has lots of very clean bathrooms). In 1956, ownership and management of the cemetery was transferred to Temple Israel of Hollywood.

Kent Twitchell Mural
✳ 33 58 43 N 118 23 26 W

True to the Los Angeles larger-than-life ethos, Hillside commissioned noted muralist Kent Twitchell to create a mural depicting a bride and groom being blessed by a rabbi. The mural is one of a number of art installations at Hillside that depict the

Kent Twitchell Mural

stages of life. The mural is on a wall in the Acacia Gardens section. The name Kent Twitchell may not be known to many outside the art community, but his work is seen by tens of thousands of people every day, since many of his most popular murals can be viewed while motoring along L.A.'s many freeways.

Al Jolson Memorial

❀ 33 58 47 N 118 23 22 W

The highlight and most obvious feature of Hillside Memorial Park is the Al Jolson tomb. The monument, which cost about $75,000, was constructed in 1951. After completion, Jolson's body was disinterred from Beth Olam Cemetery in Hollywood (which wouldn't allow an appropriately large monument to be built) and reinterred at Hillside. The monument, which consists of a pavilion, waterfall, and sarcophagus, was somewhat ironically designed by Paul R. Williams, an African-American, since Jolson is best known for performing as a blackface. Williams was the first African-American Fellow of the American Institute of Architects. In 1939, he won an AIA award of merit for his design of the MCA building in Beverly Hills. Williams may be best known for his design of the flying-saucer-shaped terminal at Los Angeles International Airport. He had a number of celebrity clients, including Lon Chaney Sr., Frank Sinatra, Lucille Ball, Zsa Zsa Gabor, Barbara Stanwyck, and Anthony Quinn.

Al Jolson Memorial

Notable Residents

Al Jolson
❀ May 26, 1886–October 23, 1950

Al Johnson (Asa Yoelson) was born to Moses Reuben and Naomi Yoelson in Srednik, Lithuania. The family moved to the United States in 1891. Following the death of his mother in 1895, Asa and his brother became fascinated with show business and started singing together. By age 14, he

ran away from home to seek his fortune in New York. He had a tough time for a couple of years since he wasn't technically able to work until age 16. However, he had a strong voice and physical energy, and when he did finally get some bookings, he impressed audiences and agents. In 1904, he experimented with wearing blackface when he sang and got good reviews for his performance, so blackface became his trademark. He changed his name to Al and adopted a more Americanized spelling of Yoelson. Jolson's first hit record was "That Haunting Melody" in 1911. Other memorable songs were "Swanee" (1919), "California, Here I Come" (1924), and "My Mammy" (1927). Jolson is probably best known for his role in the *Jazz Singer* (1927), which was the pivotal film that ushered in talking movies. Jolson was not known for his modesty. He billed himself as "The World's Greatest Entertainer." He has been criticized for his now-politically-incorrect use of blackface. However, at the time it was simply part of a costume. Jolson fought hard to improve race relations. The *St. James Encyclopedia of Popular Culture* states: "Almost single-handedly, Jolson helped to introduce African-American musical innovations like jazz, ragtime, and the blues to white audiences . . . [and] paved the way for African-American performers like Louis Armstrong, Duke Ellington, Fats Waller, and Ethel Waters . . . to bridge the cultural gap between black and white America."

David Janssen

March 27, 1931–February 13, 1980
✳ **33 58 47 N 118 23 19 W**
Memorial Court Mausoleum (north wall, crypt 116)

David Janssen (David Harold Mayer) was born in Naponee, Nebraska, to Harold Edward Meyer and Berniece Graf. Following his parents' divorce in 1935, his mother took him to Los Angeles. She married Eugene Janssen in 1940 and nine-year-old David took his stepfather's name. A natural actor, David Janssen got his first film role at age 13. He is best known for his portrayal of Dr. Richard Kimball in the 1963–1967 ABC television series *The Fugitive*. The final episode of the series garnered the highest rating at the time of any television program. Janssen was a heavy drinker and smoker, and worked almost constantly, factors that no doubt contributed to his sudden death by heart attack two days into filming a television movie about Father Damien and the leper colony he tended to.

Max Factor Sr.

1877–August 30, 1938
✳ **33 58 46 N 118 23 16 W**
Courts of the Book, Isaiah (outer court, wall U, crypt 312)

Max Factor (Factorowitz/Faktorowicz) was born in what is now Lodz, Poland. While still a child, he apprenticed to a pharmacist/dentist, then opened up his own shop near Moscow, where he sold his own formulation of cosmetic creams in addition to wigs and fragrances. His creams got the attention of some Russian nobles, and he was appointed the official cosmetic expert to the royal family and the Imperial Russian Grand Opera. He married and had three children, and then immigrated to the United States through Ellis Island in 1904. The family arrived with only $400, but they quickly made a new start, showcasing their products under the Max Factor name at the 1904 Louisiana Purchase Exposition in St. Louis (the same fair where waffle-style ice cream cones were introduced and the hot dog and hamburger were first marketed to mass audiences). Factor saw an opportunity to sell his products to the newly emerging movie industry and moved the family to Los Angeles. His non-cracking, non-caking makeup known as flexible greasepaint was a big hit with movie stars, and his quality wigs, which he rented rather than sold, were a big hit with movie executives. Soon the name Max Factor became synonymous with movies and movie stars, so much so that the common slogan referred to Max Factor products as making any girl look like a movie star.

Max Factor Jr.

August 18, 1904–June 7, 1996
✹ 33 58 46 N 118 23 16 W
Courts of the Book, Isaiah (outer court, wall U, crypt 314)

Francis Factor changed his name to Max Factor Jr. after his father died in 1938. Both Max Factors were responsible for ushering in special makeup for full-color films. Max Factor was the only makeup used for the color film *Vogues of 1938*. It was Max Factor Jr. who turned Max Factor & Company into a household name. He took the cosmetics out of Hollywood into mainstream America. Max Factor Jr. is known as the father of waterproof mascara and long-lasting lipstick. In 1946, he invented special camouflage lipstick for the Marine Corps. In 1976, Max Factor merged with Norton Simon Industries. Today, Max Factor brand is owned by Proctor and Gamble.

Shelley Winters

August 18, 1920–January 14, 2006
✹ 33 58 49 N 118 23 14 W
Hillside Slope
(block 11, plot 358, grave 8)

Shelley Winters (Shirly

Schrift) was one of a very few full-figured actresses who were sexy, bawdy, outspoken, and talented. She was born Shirley Schrift in East St. Louis, Illinois, to Jewish parents. Although she didn't have movie star looks, she had a lot of gumption and found roles that suited her personality. Early in her career, she roomed with Marilyn Monroe. When Winters tired of blond bombshell roles, she reinvented herself into a dramatic actress, winning Best Supporting Actress Oscars for the *Diary of Anne Frank* (1959) and *A Patch of Blue* (1965). Although she continued acting until the year she died (she appeared in over 100 films), she also was successful at writing and producing. In her later years, she wrote a couple of tell-all biographies that ruffled more than a few feathers.

David Begelman

August 26, 1921–August 7, 1995

❀ 33 58 47 N 118 23 19 W

Memorial Court Mausoleum (bottom row)

David Begelman was born in New York City. After college, he got a job at the Music Corporation of America (MCA), where he worked for 11 years. He rose to the position of vice president and then left the company to cofound the talent agency Creative Management Associates (CMA). The agency represented a number of A-list celebrities, including Judy Garland, Marilyn Monroe, Woody Allen, Richard Burton, Gregory Peck, Henry Fonda, Carol Channing, and Rock Hudson. In 1973, Begelman left CMA to take over the lackluster Columbia Studios. He recruited some of his former clients and went on to produce some blockbuster movies such as *Tommy* (1975), *Shampoo* (1975) and *Close Encounters of the Third Kind* (1977). Unfortunately, Begelman had a habit of sticking his hand in the till, which led to investigations by the IRS, FBI, and L.A. Police Department. There was much finger-pointing and many lawsuits filed, all of which tainted Begelman's star. After things had settled down, he became CEO and president of MGM. Despite his lofty position, he couldn't match his earlier successes, and by the mid-1990s, he declared bankruptcy. Apparently the pressure got to him, and he shot himself in his room at L.A.'s Century Plaza Hotel.

Jerry Rubin

July 14, 1938–
November 28, 1994

❀ 33 58 55 N 118 23 21 W

Mount of Olives
(block 14, plot 466, grave 3)

Jerry Rubin is best remembered as one of the leading social activists in the 1960s. He was born and raised in Cincinnati, then moved to California where he attended the University of California–Berkeley in 1964. While at Berkeley, he became involved in left-wing causes and dropped out to spend more time protesting. Along with others, he founded the Yippies (Youth International Party) that was instrumental in the disruption of the 1968 Democratic Convention in Chicago. He and six others were arrested and tried in what became known as the Chicago Seven Trial. Thanks to the antics of the defendants and a somewhat befuddled Judge Julius Hoffman, the trial degenerated into a circus, and after a series of appeals, all the defendants were released. A few years later, Rubin embraced capitalism and became a Yuppie (Young Upwardly Mobile Professional). He was said to be an early investor in Apple Computers. After he made the move to Yuppiedom, he engaged in a number of debates with Abbie Hoffman, also a Yippie. The verbal sparring matches were billed as Yippie vs. Yuppie. However, Rubin still liked to buck the system, and on the night of November 14, 1994, he was hit by a car while jaywalking on Wilshire Boulevard. He died 14 days later. He would have found it ironic that when the picture of his grave marker was taken, it was embossed with lawnmower tire tracks.

Meyer H. "Mickey" Cohen

September 4, 1913–July 29, 1976

✸ **33 58 48 N 118 23 29 W**

Garden of Memories, Alcove of Love (wall A, crypt 217)

Mickey Cohen was born in Brooklyn, New York (note: birth year of crypt plaque is wrong), but he settled in Los Angeles with his mother, sister, and three brothers. With the exception of his brother Sam, who became an Orthodox Jew, all the family became involved with crime. Mickey was the most "successful" at his endeavors. By age 9, he was delivering bootleg alcohol; as a teenager, he boxed in illegal prizefights. He then moved to Chicago, where organized crime was a respected occupation, and became an enforcer with the "Chicago Outfit." Cohen spent a brief time in prison but found opportunities after his release to run various gambling games. Seeking greener pastures, he moved to Cleveland, and then to Los Angeles, where he was hired by Meyer Lansky to watch Bugsy Siegel. Cohen must have lapsed somewhat in his Bugsy-watching assignment, as Siegel was murdered in Beverly Hills on June 20, 1947. After Siegel's demise, Cohen took over control of the mob's Las Vegas operations. Cohen himself was fairly bulletproof. There were many attempts on his life, including bombing his Brentwood home. Cohen did serve two terms in prison for tax evasion, but he took it in stride, even becoming an advocate for prison reform. Cohen possessed an engaging personality and counted Frank Sinatra, Marilyn Monroe, Merv Griffin, Billy Graham, Richard Nixon, and William Randolph Hearst among his friends. On July 29, 1976, Meyer Mickey Cohen died quietly in his sleep.

Mark Goodson

January 14, 1915–December 18, 1992

⊛ 33 58 47 N 118 23 20 W

Garden of Abraham (sarcophagus B, front of the mausoleum)

Look closely at the shape of the emblem on the onyx-colored sarcophagus of Mark Goodson. It's in the shape of a specialized cathode ray
tube, better known as a tube-type television. Mark Goodson was born in
Sacramento, California, to Russian emigrant parents. An intelligent lad,
he attended the University of California–Berkeley, partially financing his
education through scholarships. He had dabbled in theater as a child and
got a job as a disc jockey in San Francisco after graduation from college
in 1937. By 1939, he was producing a quiz show on another radio station
in San Francisco; then in 1941, he moved to New York City, where he
teamed up with Bill Todman, and the duo started producing radio game
shows. That led to producing television game shows and other enterprises. The Goodson-Todman production company was responsible for
some of the most memorable television game shows, including *I've Got a
Secret*, *Beat the Clock*, *Family Feud*, *The Price is Right*, *To Tell the Truth*, and *What's
My Line*. Following Bill Todman's death in 1979, Goodson acquired Tod-
man's shares and renamed the company Mark Goodson Productions.

George A. Jessel

April 3, 1898–May 23, 1981

⊛ 33 58 47 N 118 23 19 W

Memorial Court Mausoleum (north wall, crypt 516)

George Jessel
was born in
the Bronx,
New York.
After his
father's death,
he helped sup-
port the family
by working a
variety of jobs
on Broadway

and in vaudeville. At age 10, his mother helped him form a group of ush-
ers to entertain theater patrons, and by age 11, he had teamed up with
Eddie Cantor in a kid sketch. When he grew older, he moved to leading-
man roles, and in 1925, he secured the lead in a Broadway production
of *The Jazz Singer*. When Warner Bros. decided to make *The Jazz Singer*
into a movie, they approached Jessel to be the lead, but Jessel's salary
demands were too high and the role went to Al Jolson. By all accounts,

Jessel's ego was even bigger than Jolson's. He had numerous affairs with actresses and at one point broke into his ex-wife's home, brandishing and firing a pistol. Despite his egotism, he continued to thrive, producing musicals for Fox and becoming a frequent master of ceremonies. In later life, he was known as the "Toastmaster General" for his frequent speaking engagements and for being one of the founding members of the California branch of the Friars Club. In 1969, he was awarded a Jean Hersholt Humanitarian Award at the Academy Awards ceremony for his charity work.

Irving Wallace

March 19, 1916–June 29, 1990
⊛ 33 58 46 N 118 23 16 W
Courts of the Book, Isaiah (outer court, wall V, crypt 136)

Irving Wallace was born in Kenosha, Wisconsin, to Bessie and Alex Wallace. His parents were Russian emigrants whose names were changed at Ellis Island from Wallenchinsky. Irving had a gift for writing and sold stories to magazines while still a teenager. He served in World War II and continued to write for magazines after the war but was lured to the more lucrative field of writing screenplays for Hollywood movies. He was one of the writers for *The West Point Story* (1950), *Split Second* (1953), and *The Big Circus* (1959). Feeling somewhat constrained as a screenwriter, he turned to writing books. His first blockbuster book was *The Chapman Report*, a 1961 novel based on the Kinsey Report, the first mainstream survey of the sexual proclivities of Americans. That book was made into a 1962 movie of the same name. Wallace was a prolific and successful writer, authoring or co-authoring 33 books, most notably *The Prize* (1962), *The Word* (1972), and the *People's Almanac* (1975), which he co-wrote with son, David Wallenchinsky. Irving Wallace's epitaph reads, "Life is not a daily dying, not a pointless end, but a soaring and blind gift snatched from eternity."

Hank Greenberg

January 1, 1911–
September 4, 1986
⊛ 33 58 46 N 118 23 16 W
Courts of the Book, Isaiah
(outer wall, wall V, crypt 340)

One would be hard-pressed to put together an all-Jewish all-star team. However, if you did, Henry "Hank" Greenberg would be one of them. He was born in New York City to an Orthodox

Jewish family. Although not terribly athletic as a child, he loved sports and practiced to sharpen his skills. He excelled in basketball at James Monroe High School and helped his team win the city championship. In 1929, he was recruited by the New York Yankees, but since Greenberg's position on first base was more than adequately filled by iron man Lou Gehrig, Greenberg elected to go to college for a year and then signed with the Detroit Tigers, where he became the youngest player in the majors at age 19. After one year in the majors, he went down to the minors to hone his skills and then returned to Detroit for the 1933 season. Like many baseball players whose careers began in the mid- to late 1930s, he lost much of his primetime playing time by serving in World War II. He lost part of the 1941 and 1945 seasons and all of the 1942, '43, and '44 seasons. He also missed most of the 1936 season with a broken wrist. Nevertheless, he compiled impressive statistics in the nine solid seasons he played, batting .313, being selected for five All-Star teams, leading the Tigers to two World Series, and being selected American League Most Valuable Player twice. His #5 has been retired by the Detroit Tigers. Hank Greenberg was inducted into the Baseball Hall of Fame in 1956, the first Jewish player to be bestowed that honor.

Dinah Shore

February 29, 1916–February 24, 1994
✺ **33 58 46 N 118 23 16 W**
Courts of the Book, Isaiah (outer wall, wall V, crypt 247)

Dinah Shore (Frances Rose Shore) was born to Russian emigrants Solomon and Anna Stein Shore in Winchester, Tennessee. When she was two years old, she contracted polio but, through the care of her parents, only developed a slight limp. The bout with polio left her shy and

a bit insecure, but with her parents' encouragement, she learned to sing, sometimes singing for customers at her father's department store. Shore went on to college after her mother unexpectedly died of a heart attack, but she continued singing and eventually caught the eye and ear of Eddie Cantor. With Cantor's tutelage, she overcame her shyness and developed a stage presence. Shore's first hit, *Yes My Darling Daughter* (1940), sold over a half million records in a few weeks. Shore got her own radio program, *Call to Music*, in 1943 and also started appearing in movies. In 1950, she reportedly received a million dollars from RCA to record 100 songs. Even though her singing star somewhat faded, she hit the ground running with television. She had actually performed on experimental television as early as 1937. Shore is most famously known for *The Dinah Shore Show* (1951–1956) and the *The Dinah Shore Chevy Show* (1956–1963), where she sang the jingle "See the USA in Your Chevrolet." Shore is also famous for being a golfer (she founded the LPGA Colgate Dinah Shore Tournament in 1972) and for her affair with Burt Reynolds, who was twenty years her junior.

Only half of Dinah Shore resides at Hillside Memorial Park. She was cremated and the other half of her ashes was interred at Forest Lawn–Cathedral City, near her home in Palm Springs.

Jack Benny
See page 160

Moe Howard
See page 144

Lorne Greene
See page 164

Dick Shawn
See page 157

Michael Landon
See page 165

Selma Diamond
See page 159

Milton Berle
See page 156

Other Notables

Ben Blue/Benjamin Bernstein
1901-1975 ✺ Comedian
Sanctuary of Meditation Mausoleum (first floor, crypt 314)

Neil Bogart
1943-1982 ✺ Record Executive (created disco craze)
Court of Patriarchs Mausoleum (ground floor family room)

Eddie Cantor/Edward Israel Iskowitz
1892-1964 ✺ Singer, Actor
Hall of Graciousness Mausoleum (crypt 207)

Nell Carter
1948-2003 ✺ Singer, Actress
Acacia Gardens (wall KK, crypt 7040)

Jeff Chandler/Ira Grossel
1918-1961 ✺ Actor
Hall of Graciousness Mausoleum (second floor, crypt 4015)

Percy Faith
1908-1976 ✺ Composer
Garden of Memories, Court of Honor (grave 407)

Arthur Freed/Arthur Grossman
1894-1973 ✺ Songwriter, Producer
Garden of Memories, Court of Honor (grave 418)

Ruth Handler
1916-2002 ✺ Inventor of the Barbie Doll
Canaan (wall H, crypt 299)

Sheldon Leonard/Sheldon Leonard Bershad
1907-1997 ✺ Actor, Producer, Writer, Director
Courts of the Book (outer lawn, block 6, plot 1000, grave 8)

Sol Lesser

1890–1980 ✡ Motion Picture Pioneer
Garden of Memories, Court of Devotion (wall A, crypt 224)

Ted Mann

1917–2001 ✡ Founder, Mann's Theaters
Acacia Gardens (estate 8, grave 1)

Hal March/Hal Mendelson

1920–1970 ✡ Actor, Game Show Host
Mount Sholom (block 4, plot 144, grave 6)

Frederick N. Mellinger

1913–1990 ✡ Founder, Frederick's of Hollywood
Courts of the Book (outer lawn, block 5, plot 600, grave 2)

Marvin Mirisch

1918–2002 ✡ Co-founder, Mirisch Co., an independent production company
Garden of Memories, Court of Devotion (wall A, crypt 322)

Stanley Mosk

1912–2001 ✡ California Supreme Court Judge
Hall of Graciousness Mausoleum (second floor, crypt 4019)

Julia Miller Phillips

1944–2002 ✡ Producer
Acacia Gardens (wall SS, niche 433)

Bernard J. Schwab

1908–2003 ✡ Co-founder, Schwab's Pharmacy, Sunset Boulevard
Courts of the Book, Isaiah (outer court, wall U, crypt 205)

Allan Sherman/Allen Copelon

1924–1973 ✡ Writer, Singer, Comic
(famous for the song "Hello Muddah, Hello Fadduh")
Sanctuary of Hope Mausoleum, Columbarium (niche 513)

Max Shulman

1919–1988 ✡ Writer
Eternal Rest Urn Garden (block 4, plot 31, grave 9)

Lew R. Wasserman

1913–2002 ✡ Chairman and Chief Executive, Music Corporation of America (MCA)
Canaan (estate 8A, grave 1)

Hollywood Forever Cemetery

6000 Santa Monica Boulevard

Los Angeles, California 90038

213-469-1181

✦ 34 05 26 N 118 19 12 W

www.hollywoodforever.com/Hollywood/

Maps available in flowershop

This 60-acre cemetery (originally 100 acres before pieces of it were sold off) in the heart of Tinseltown was founded in 1899 by Isaac Van Nuys under the auspices of the Hollywood Cemetery Association. In order to gather support of their neighbors, the developers of the cemetery promised a park-like atmosphere with winding roads, beautiful architecture and monuments, lush plantings, and, most importantly, a perpetual care endowment program to guarantee the maintenance of the cemetery. For the first two decades, Hollywood Memorial Park Cemetery continued to have its critics, many of whom decried the cemetery's for-profit business model, but when the movie industry formally planted itself in Hollywood and deceased stars started moving in, most criticism stopped. Indeed, like the stars' homes, Hollywood Memorial Park Cemetery became a major tourist attraction. For years, it was the burial spot of choice for the stars of the silver screen. Rudolph Valentino, Peter Lorre, Tyrone Power, and Douglas Fairbanks Sr. repose here. Carl Switzer, who won fame as Alfalfa of the *Our Gang/Little Rascals* comedies, has the *Our Gang* dog Pete (pronounced

Eros and Psyche

Petey) etched on his granite plaque. Mel Blanc, the man of a thousand voices, has his best-known phrase "That's All Folks" on his grave marker. Directors like Cecil B. DeMille and John Huston sleep with a host of other directors, producers, agents, stars, and starlets.

Despite the initial success of Hollywood Memorial Park, larger cemeteries like Forest Lawn started to siphon off much of its business a few decades after it opened. To bolster the cemetery's finances, a large undeveloped parcel of the property was sold to neighboring Paramount Studios. But, despite the cache of being buried in the nucleus of Hollywood, the cemetery had a hard time enticing customers to purchase their last piece of real estate.

In the mid-1940s, former stockbroker Jules Roth, who had just been released from San Quentin prison for illegal use and mismanagement of his clients' funds, bought the property. Unfortunately, over the years, many of Roth's other real estate investments (he seemed to have a knack for losing money when speculating in the oil and gold markets) suffered losses, and he started selling off pieces of the cemetery to buoy up his faltering real estate empire. The first major transaction was the sale of a large portion of the cemetery's frontage to a strip mall for close to nine million dollars; then he sold some of the statuary in the public mausoleums; next, he sold the bronze statuary in the main mausoleum, which was valued at one million dollars, for $250,000. It seems that everything that wasn't owned by one of the plot holders had a price tag on it. Even the cemetery's most memorable fixture, a risqué marble statue of *Eros and Psyche* was being offered at $250,000. Luckily, no buyer was found.

Roth even raided the cemetery's endowment care funds of millions of dollars. With little money for upkeep and maintenance available, the cemetery continued its downward slide. Grounds maintenance was neglected; what were once beautiful ponds became slimy fetid swamps; and construction projects were halted—frustrated workers didn't even bother to take down scaffolding. The only people who visited the cemetery were a few curiosity seekers and some neighborhood drug dealers who took advantage of the cemetery's lack of security to ply their trade. The 1994 Northridge earthquake damaged crypts, buildings, and roads, all of which were left unrepaired.

Finally, in early 1996, Roth's company—the Hollywood Cemetery Association—defaulted on a 2.7 million dollar loan, putting the cemetery's fate in the hands of the bank. Roth left the scene, eventually dying in early 1998. After months of legal wrangling, the bank put the cemetery on the block with a minimum price of $500,000. Alas, the only bid was for $275,000 from a Vallejo, California, mortuary owner. Not enough, said the bank, which then filed a motion with the bankruptcy court to simply abandon the forlorn property.

Enter a new player—Tyler Cassity, a 1992 graduate of Columbia University—armed with a degree in literature and, more importantly, with the cemetery business in his blood. Tyler and his brother Brent had recently sold twelve of the family's St. Louis and Springfield, Missouri, properties to Service Corporation International, a cemetery conglomerate. The terms of the agreement between SCI and Cassity were that Cassity agreed not to open up another cemetery in the St. Louis area.

When Tyler's father, Douglas Cassity, who owned a number of pre-need companies under the corporate name of Forever Enterprises, heard about the availability of the Hollywood Memorial Park property while watching the evening news, he jetted off to Los Angeles to have a look for himself. He toured the cemetery, attended the bankruptcy hearings, and attended some public hearings where plot holders were venting their anger and frustration. After a few calculations, he advised Tyler and Brent that the cemetery didn't look like a viable investment.

Eros and Psyche

But a few months later, Tyler and Brent were in Los Angeles on a business trip and couldn't resist having a look at Hollywood Memorial Park for themselves. Whether Tyler saw a good business opportunity or was simply starstruck is hard to say. But he plunked down a $75,000 check as a deposit toward a final price of $375,000. The bank turned over the cemetery to Cassity on April 10, 1998.

Cassity started revamping the cemetery almost immediately. He hired landscapers, bought books on cemetery design, moved in road graders, tore down walls, installed computerized memorials, and hired new sales staff. Within three months, the sales staff recouped the $375,000 sale price by selling plots and markers to the neighboring Armenian and Russian community. In the ensuing years, Hollywood Forever has spent millions on restoring and renovating the cemetery, adding new burial plots by eliminating some of the roads and building a new community mausoleum. Hollywood Forever has also tried some innovative programs such as turning the cemetery grounds into an outdoor movie theater on selected evenings, promoting tourism, and installing kiosks where visitors can see video tributes of people interred in the cemetery. The cemetery has also installed a number of cenotaphs (a monument to someone who is not actually there), including ones to Anne Frank, Hattie McDaniel (Mammy in *Gone with the Wind*), and blond bombshell Jayne Mansfield (her body was moved). There is even a grave marker for Def Records. In May 2000, Hollywood Forever Cemetery was entered into the National Register of Historic Places.

Like many other Los Angeles cemeteries, Hollywood Forever has dozens of notable residents, and we can only list a few. For a more comprehensive list, we suggest searching the Internet, starting with findagrave.com.

Eros and Psyche
⊛ 34 05 23 N 118 19 14 W

The *Eros and Psyche* marble statue welcomes visitors to Hollywood Forever Cemetery. The previous owner of the cemetery tried to sell the statue for $250,000 to bolster his failing real estate empire.

Stupas

The Los Angeles area has an ethni-
cally diverse population. The end
of the twentieth century saw an
influx of immigrants from Southeast Asia, where burial customs
tend towards cremation. Sensing a
need for nontraditional interment
options, Hollywood Forever has
installed a number of stupas, which
house cremains (cremated remains).

Notable Residents

Carl Bigsby
November 14, 1898–
May 3, 1959

and

Constance Bigsby
June 28, 1914–April 17, 2000
⊗ 34 05 19 N 188 19 09 W
Section 13

A scaled-down replica of
an Atlas Pioneer rocket
marks the graves of Carl
and Constance Bigsby.
The rocket represents
Bigsby's pioneering
achievements in the
publishing and graphic
arts fields. He had no
direct involvement in
America's space program.
Constance Bigsby was
a bit more modest:
the inscription on her
tombstone (on the right-hand side of the rocket) reads simply, "too bad,
we had fun."

Tyrone Power
May 5, 1914–November 15, 1958
⊗ 35 05 20 N 118 18 59 W
Section 8 (near the water)

The bench tomb of Tyrone Edmund Power Jr. contains a sculpted book.
Carved into the top of the bench are lines from *Hamlet*, including "Good
night sweet prince: / And flights of angels sing thee to thy rest!" Dark,
handsome Tyrone Power appeared in dozens of films, often in a swashbuckler role. Among his most noted were *Alexander's Ragtime Band* (1938),

The Mark of Zorro (1940), *The Black Swan* (1942), *The Black Rose* (1950) and *The Sun Also Rises* (1957). Power was a chain-smoker, which may have contributed to his death from a massive heart attack at age 44.

William Andrews Clark Jr.

March 29, 1877–June 14, 1934

✿ 34 05 20 N 118 19 00 W

Clark Mausoleum

The mausoleum of William A. Clark, founder of the Los Angeles Philharmonic, sits on an island in the middle of a pond. The elegant Classical Revival family mausoleum was built in 1920, well before his death in 1934. It was constructed by Georgia Marble Company of Georgia marble and was designated the most beautiful monument constructed between 1925 and 1928 by the Architectural Society of America.

Avetis Blikian

1926–1992

✳ 34 05 22 N 118 18 59 W

Garden of Legends,
Section 8

Increasingly, Eastern
Europeans are choosing
to be buried at Holly-
wood Forever Ceme-
tery. The tomb of Avetis
Blikian features a marble
statue of an imposing
seated figure of Blikian.
He was described by
cemetery personnel as a
"businessman."

Marion Davies

**January 3, 1897–
September 22, 1961**

✳ 34 05 20 N 118 18 59 W

Douras Mausoleum

Marion Davies, whose
real name was Marion Cecelia Douras, was a Ziegfeld Follies dancer.
Shortly after meeting publisher William Randolph Hearst, she became
his mistress. With Hearst's sponsorship, she was cast in a number of films
and proved to be a credible actress, appearing in films in the 1920s and
'30s. Also residing in the mausoleum are Patricia Van Cleve, acknowledged niece of Marion Davies, and her husband, Arthur Lake, most noted
for playing the role of Dagwood Bumstead in the *Blondie* movies.

Rudolph Valentino

May 6, 1895–August 23, 1926
✴ **34 05 18 N 118 18 59 W (mausoleum entrance)**
Cathedral Mausoleum (corridor A, crypt 1205)

Rudolph Valentino (Rodolfo Alfonzo Raffaelo Pierre Filibert Guglielmi di Valentina d'Antonguolla) was one of the Silver Screen's first male sex symbols. He acted in 38 films, including *The Four Horsemen of the Apocalypse* (1921) and most famously in *The Sheik* (1921). After dying as the result of a ruptured appendix, over 100,000 people (mostly grief-stricken young women) attended his funeral in New York. Riots broke out while they waited in line at the funeral home. His body was shipped to California for a second funeral before being interred in the Cathedral Mausoleum.

Mel Blanc

May 30, 1908–July 10, 1989
✴ **34 05 18 N 118 19 12 W**
Garden of Exodus (L-149)

Melvin Jerome Blank was known as "The Man of 1000 Voices." Although he appeared on the radio, in movies, and on television, he is best known for his vocalizations of Looney Tunes characters, including Porky Pig, Daffy Duck, Bugs Bunny, Yosemite Sam, Foghorn

Leghorn, Wile E. Coyote, and others. He requested that the ending of every Looney Tunes cartoon (voiced by Porky Pig) of "That's All Folks," be on his tombstone.

Cecil B. DeMille

August 12, 1881–January 21, 1959
✺ **34 05 23 N 118 19 00 W**
Section 8 (lot 50)

Cecil Blount DeMille was a pioneering producer and director. He directed dozens of movies from his first, *The Squaw Man*, in 1914 to *The Ten Commandments* in 1956. Also residing in the DeMille plot are his mother and father, wife, brother, and sister-in-law.

Peter Finch

December 28, 1912–January 14, 1977
✺ **34 05 18 N 118 18 59 W (mausoleum entrance)**
Cathedral Mausoleum (corridor A, crypt 1224, across from Rudolph Valentino)

Peter Finch was a well-regarded Australian actor who was born in London, England, but grew up in Sydney, Australia. He was the first actor to win an Academy Award posthumously, a Best Actor Oscar for his role as a crazed anchorman in the 1976 movie *Network*, where he instructs viewers to lean out their windows and scream, "I'm mad as hell and I'm not going to take it anymore."

Peter Lorre
June 26, 1904–March 23, 1964
✳ 34 05 18 N 118 18 59 W (mausoleum entrance)
Cathedral Mausoleum, Alcove of Reverence (corridor C, niche 5, tier 1)

Character actor Peter Lorre (Laszlo Loewenstein) has one of the most imitated voices and acting styles. He usually played villains, often with a sly comedic touch. He is probably best known for his roles in the *Maltese Falcon* (1941), *Casablanca* (1942), and as Mr. Moto in the 1930s. When he was at Bela Lugosi's funeral (Lugosi was laid out with his Dracula cape), he is said to have quipped to Vincent Price, "Do you think we should drive a stake through his heart?"

Def/Def Records
ca. 1983–August 27, 1993
✳ 34 05 23 N 118 18 57 W
(behind a cypress tree across from Avetis Blikian; see p. 64)

While he was a student at Long Island College in the early 1980s, Rick Rubin founded Def Jam Records, which he operated out of his dorm room. In 1983, he teamed up with Russell Simmons and released a number of hip-hop records. One of the first artists they signed was 16-year-old James Todd Smith, known to the hip-hop community as LL Cool J. Rubin and Simmons produced a number of hit records with various artists until 1988, when Rubin left the company to found Def American Recordings. Under this label, Rubin released records by a number of artists, including The Red Hot Chili Peppers and Mick Jagger.

By 1993, Rubin was tired of the violent stigma that was attached to the term Def and changed the name Def American Recordings to American Recordings. To formalize the passing of Def, Rubin purchased a plot and a tombstone inscribed with "DEF." On August 27, 1993, a New Orleans–style funeral at the cemetery with a eulogy by Reverend Al Sharpton (who Rubin had flown in from New York) put the name "Def"

to rest. Referring to the origin Def as a synonym for "excellent," Sharpton said it meant "more than excellent. Like, def-iantly excellent with a bang. Now the bang is out of def. It lost its exclusivity to the in-defiant crowd. It died of terminal acceptance."

Before Def was officially buried, some of the 2,000 or so mourners placed flowers, record albums, and personal mementos in the open casket. As the casket was lowered, guarded by Black Panthers with prop shotguns, The Amazing Kreskin (who usually doesn't do funerals) performed his mind-reading act on a grieving Tom Petty and Rosanna Arquette. After the ceremony, 500 or so of the bereaved retired to a bowling alley for an "after party."

Estelle Getty

July 25, 1923–July 22, 2008
✺ 34 05 19 N 118 19 15 W
Section 14 (row CC, grave 88)

Ms. Getty (Estelle Gettleman) is best known for her role as sassy Italian octogenarian Sophia Petrillo on the hit sitcom *The Golden Girls*.

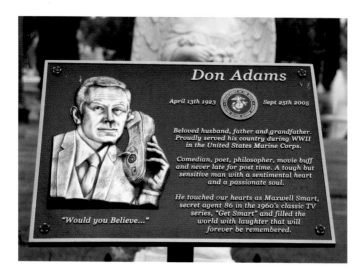

Don Adams

April 13, 1923–September 25, 2005
🜨 34 05 23 N 118 19 00 W
Section 8 (lot 57, grave 20)

Don Adams (Donald James Yarmy) is best known for his Emmy-winning role as agent Maxwell Smart in the 1960s television spy spoof *Get Smart*. He was also the voice of cartoon characters Tennessee Tuxedo and Inspector Gadget.

John Huston

August 5, 1906–August 28, 1987
🜨 34 05 21 N 118 19 02 W
Garden of Legends (formerly Section 8, lot 6, west side of lake)

John Huston directed a number of classic Hollywood movies from the 1920s through the 1980s. Among the most memorable were *The Treasure of the Sierra Madre* (1948), *The Asphalt Jungle* (1950), and *The African Queen* (1951). He won dual Oscars (best-adapted screenplay and director) for *The Treasure of Sierra Madre*. He was the father of actress Angelica Huston and the son of actor Walter Huston.

Hattie McDaniel

June 10, 1895–
October 26, 1952
🜨 34 05 19 N
118 19 01 W
Garden of Legends
(formerly Section 8,
south of lake)

Hattie McDaniel was the first African-American to win an Academy Award. She won best supporting actress for her role in the

Angelus Rosedale Cemetery

TO HONOR HER LAST WISH
HATTIE McDANIEL
1895 ∞ 1952
RENOWNED PERFORMER

ACADEMY AWARD
1939
GONE WITH THE WIND

"AUNT HATTIE, YOU ARE A CREDIT
TO YOUR CRAFT, YOUR RACE
AND TO YOUR FAMILY"
EDGAR GOFF

DEDICATION
OCTOBER 26, 1999

Cenotaph, Hollywood Forever Cemetery

1939 Civil War epic *Gone With the Wind*. Originally denied burial in the cemetery because of the segregationist policies at the time, a cenotaph was erected in her honor in 1999. Her body resides under a simple stone across from the entrance gates in Angelus Rosedale Cemetery (34 02 26 N 118 17 54 W) on 1831 West Washington Boulevard in Los Angeles.

Johnny Ramone
October 8, 1948-September 15, 2004
$ 34 05 19 N 118 19 01 W
Garden of Legends (formerly Section 8)

Johnny Ramone, born John Cummings, was a cofounder and guitarist of the punk rock band The Ramones. The band was inducted into the Rock and Roll Hall of Fame in 2002. After Ramone died of prostate cancer in 2004, he was cremated. It's unclear if some of his remains were interred next to his monument or if the monument is a cenotaph like Hattie McDaniel's a few paces away.

Darren McGavin
May 7, 1922–
February 25, 2006
✸ 34 05 22 N 118 19 02 W
Section 7 (lot 203, grave 14)

Despite having a critically acclaimed career in movies, television, and theater, Darren McGavin is best remembered in the oft-aired classic Christmas movie *A Christmas Story*, where he plays Ralphie's father.

Douglas Fairbanks Sr.
See page 178.

Carl Switzer (Alfalfa, *Our Gang* comedies)
See page 152.

Darla Hood (Darla, *Our Gang* comedies)
See page 153.

Inglewood Park Cemetery

720 East Florence Avenue

Inglewood, California 90301

310-412-6500

⊗ 33 58 17 N 118 20 33 W

www.inglewoodparkcemetery.org/

Maps in office

Inglewood Park Cemetery was established in 1905 by the Inglewood Park Cemetery Association in the Centinela Valley on the outskirts of Los Angeles. The cemetery's claim to fame is that it has the first community mausoleum in California. Built in 1914, the Inglewood Mausoleum is the first in a series of community mausoleums built over the decades. Aboveground entombment in a mausoleum has often been described as "the burial of the kings." Since a large and imposing freestanding structure was expensive to build, community mausoleums, with their multitiered crypts, provide an economical solution to those preferring a regal aboveground eternal home. The Mausoleum of the Golden West, Inglewood's most spectacular community mausoleum, is an Art Deco delight designed by Walter E. Erkes and constructed of reinforced concrete. The sleek mausoleum was begun in the early 1930s, at the height of the popularity of the Art Deco style. The final phase was completed in the early 1940s. When the Mausoleum of the Golden West approached capacity, the Manchester Garden Mausoleum was built in the 1970s. It has five chapels and over two dozen sanctuaries. In the late 1990s, construction of the Sunset Mission Mausoleum was begun. When all stages of construction are completed, over 30,000 spaces will be available.

Although its community mausoleums are the most visible feature of Inglewood Park Cemetery, the cemetery also features an impressive array of private mausoleums. These mausoleums are constructed in almost every architectural style from Egyptian Revival to Classical Revival to Modern Classicism. There is also an assortment of monuments, statues, and obelisks that will keep architectural sleuths busy for hours. Inglewood also has some specialty plots, including areas reserved for fallen members of the Benevolent and Protective Order of Elks (BPOE) and the Salvation Army.

While Inglewood Park Cemetery doesn't have the number of celebrities that other cemeteries have, there are still a number worth tracking down. Many of them are in the Mausoleum of the Golden West and the adjacent courts.

Salvation Army Plot

✦ 33 57 44 N 118 20 25 W

Many organizations purchased plots in cemeteries for the specific use of their members. Some, such as the Freemasons, even have their own cemeteries. For more information on the Salvation Army, see Secret Societies, Clubs and Organizations, pages 219–20.

Elks Plot

✦ 33 58 16 N 118 20 29 W

Many large cemeteries have an Elks plot. It is easy to spot since there is always a large statue of the majestic ruminant perched on a rock. For more information on the Elks, see Secret Societies, Clubs, and Organizations, pages 206–7

Notable Residents

Elks Plot

Ray Charles
September 23, 1930–June 10, 2004
✸ 33 58 21 N 118 20 23 W (mausoleum entrance)
Mausoleum of the Golden West, Eternal Love Corridor (crypt A-32)

Ray Charles Robinson was born in Albany, Georgia, the son of share-cropper Aretha Williams and handyman Bailey Robinson, who never married. Ray was totally blind by age 7 from causes that were never determined, although speculation suggests it was glaucoma or an infection. He was sent to the St. Augustine School for the Deaf and the Blind in St. Augustine, Florida, where he became adept at writing music and playing instru-

ments. While there, both parents died, leaving him an orphan. Ray started playing for various bands while still in school before moving to Seattle in 1947. He signed with Swingtime Records and recorded the song "Confession Blues" in 1949, which rose to number two on the R&B charts. Shortly afterward, he changed his name to Ray Charles to avoid confusion with the boxer Sugar Ray Robinson (who ironically is also buried in Inglewood).

Charles was a talented pianist as well as a saxophonist. One of his most significant achievements was breaking down musical barriers and stereotypes, playing everything from jazz and blues to country music. Ray Charles's twelve Grammy Awards, included the best R&B recording three consecutive years ("Hit the Road Jack," "I Can't Stop Loving You," and "Busted"). His version of the 1931 Hoagy Carmichael and Stuart Gorrell song "Georgia on My Mind" became Georgia's official state song in 1979, long after Ray Charles turned it into an American standard. His last Grammy was for "A Song for You" in 1993. *Rolling Stone* magazine ranked Charles number ten on their list of the 100 Greatest Artists of All Time and number two on their list of the 100 Greatest Singers of All Time.

Johnnie L. Cochran

October 2, 1937–March 29, 2005

⊛ 33 57 39 N 118 20 19 W
(mausoleum entrance)

Manchester Garden Mausoleum,
Chapel of Honor (crypt 1202)

Johnnie Cochran was born in
Shreveport, Louisiana, into a
family that stressed education
and equality. The family moved
to Los Angeles, where he
earned a bachelor's degree from UCLA in 1959. He enrolled at Loyola
Marymount School of Law, where he earned a law degree and then
passed the California Bar in 1963. He worked as a prosecutor for the
City of Los Angeles for two years before entering private practice,
working for prominent criminal defense lawyer Gerald Lenoir. In the
late 1960s and early '70s, he defended a number of clients, and though
he lost many of his cases, he gained valuable experience. In 1978, he
went to work in the public sector again, becoming the first African-
American assistant district attorney for the Los Angeles County District
Attorney's Office. He reinvented himself once again in 1983, opening
the Johnnie L. Cochran Jr. law firm, which eventually became Cochran,
Mitchell and Jenna. The firm and especially Cochran became known
as a celebrity law firm, with a client list that included Michael Jackson,
Black Panther Geronimo Pratt, singer Sean (P. Diddy) Combs, football
player Ron Settles, and actor Todd Bridges. Cochran is best known as
one of the members of the Dream Team that defended O. J. Simpson,
who was accused of murdering his ex-wife Nicole Brown Simpson
and Ron Goldman, eventually winning an acquittal for Simpson.
Another member of the Dream Team, Robert Kardashian (February
22, 1944–September 30, 2003), is also buried in Inglewood in the Park
Terrace Section (lot 628).

Betty Grable

December 18, 1916– July 2, 1973

⊛ 33 58 21 N 118 20 23 W (mausoleum entrance)

Mausoleum of the Golden West, Sanctuary of Dawn (crypt A78)

Elizabeth Ruth Grable was
born in St. Louis, Mis-
souri, the youngest of three
children born to John Conn
Grable and Lillian Rose
Hoffmann. Lillian enrolled
young Betty in dancing,
singing, and music classes.
In 1929, at age 12, Betty
was cast as a chorus girl
in the movie *Happy Days*,
even though she was legally
underage for that role. By the mid 1930s and into the early '40s, she was
landing small roles in films with Fred Astaire and Ginger Rogers, Don
Ameche, Robert Young, and George Montgomery. However, what really
rocketed her to stardom was a pinup photograph taken of her by studio
photographer Frank Powolny. It hung in tens of thousands of GI lockers
during World War II, making Betty Grable the most recognized celebrity

in the world. *Life* magazine has included the photograph as one of the 100 Photographs That Changed the World. She was noted for having the most beautiful legs in Hollywood. By the end of the 1940s, she was Hollywood's highest-paid actress. Over the years, she appeared in close to 100 movies and short subjects. After essentially retiring from movies in the mid-1950s, she transitioned to television programs and nightclub and stage shows, where live audiences loved her. Hugh Hefner once said that Betty Grable was his inspiration for *Playboy* magazine. A heavy smoker, Grable developed lung cancer, but because she didn't have health insurance, she had to force herself to keep working to pay the bills. After she died, her safe deposit box was opened, revealing a solitary note that purportedly said, "Sorry, there's nothing more."

Gypsy Rose Lee
January 8, 1911– April 26, 1970
✺ 33 58 02 N 118 20 21 W
Pinecrest Plot (lot 1087, grave 8, directly across from the Utopia Plot)

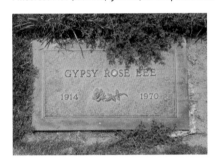

Gypsy Rose Lee was born Rose Louise Hovick to Rose and Jack Hovick in West Seattle, Washington (note: date on grave marker is wrong). The couple divorced a few years later, and Rose Hovick started training young Rose Louise and her sister June as a vaudeville act. Nowadays, the mother would be described as a stage door mother, pushing her children to perform and make money. June emerged as the talented one (she changed her name to Havoc and had a long successful career in movies and stage), while Rose Louise was nicknamed Plug because of her chubby ungainly appearance. Eventually, Rose Louise blossomed and changed her name to Gypsy Rose Lee. She found that she could make great money as a stripper, especially when she added comedy to her act. She essentially turned burlesque stripping into a respectable art form.

In 1937, Gypsy Rose Lee made her film debut in the movie *Ali Baba Goes to Town* under her real name, Louise Hovick. In 1941, she wrote the critically acclaimed *The G-String Murders*. Lee had three marriages, each ending in divorce, and numerous affairs, including one with Otto Preminger, the father of her only child, Erik Lee Preminger. She is best known for her 1957 tell-all autobiography, *Gypsy*, which was made into a long-running Broadway play in 1959. Decades later, *Gypsy* continues to be performed in various venues. In 1962, the play was made into the movie *Gypsy*, which starred Natalie Wood. In the 1960s, Gypsy Rose Lee made a number of cameo appearances on television and in movies. She succumbed to cancer in 1970.

T-Bone Walker
May 28, 1910–March 16, 1975
✺ 33 58 20 N 118 20 26 W (court entrance)
Capistrano Court (next to the Mausoleum of the Golden West, memorial panel 26)

T-Bone Walker (Aaron Thibeaux Walker) was an influential blues guitarist, singer, pianist, and songwriter. His most prolific period was in the late

1940s, but his career stretched until his death. He won a Grammy in 1971 for "Good Feelin'." Much of his legacy rests in his distinctive style, which influenced other musicians. He was known to play the guitar with his teeth while contorting his body in odd positions. Both Chuck Berry and Jimi Hendrix credit T-Bone Walker as having a strong influence on their performance and musical style.

LaWanda Page (Aunt Esther)
October 19, 1920–September 14, 2002
⊛ 33 58 20 N 118 20 25 W (court entrance)
Capistrano Court (next to the Mausoleum of the Golden West, memorial panel 43, row F-3)

LaWanda Page, born Alberta Peal, is best known for her role portraying the salty but church-going character Aunt Esther in the television series *Sanford and Son,* which ran from 1971 to 1977. Page started her career in small nightclubs, billing herself as "The Bronze Goddess of Fire" (she lit cigarettes with her fingertips), then drifted into stand-up comedy. She

appeared in a number of movies and television programs, but it was her Aunt Esther character that gave her the most success. Her catchphrase on *Sanford and Son* was "Watch it, sucka!" That phrase became the title of a best-selling comedy album.

William B. Thomas (Buckwheat, *Our Gang/Little Rascals*)
See page 154

Other Notables

Ella Fitzgerald
April 25, 1918–June 15, 1996
Sunset Memorial Garden Mausoleum, Sanctuary of the Bells
(second floor, crypt 1063)

Known as the First Lady of Jazz, Lady Ella, and the First Lady of Song, she was one of the most celebrated jazz singers of the twentieth century.

Richard Berry
April 11, 1935–January 23, 1997
Sunset Mission Mausoleum, Sanctuary of El Sereno (220 D)

Richard Berry was the proverbial One Hit Wonder. He wrote and recorded the song "Louie, Louie" in 1957, which was recorded by The Kingsmen in 1962. The lyrics, which were hopelessly garbled by The Kingsmen, were rumored to be pornographic. "Louie, Louie," which has achieved cult status, has been recorded over 1,000 times with an assortment of lyrics.

Cesar Romero
February 15, 1907– January 1, 1994
Mausoleum of the Golden West, Alcove of Music (niche 408)

Cuban-American actor Cesar Julio Romero, Jr. was often cast in films and television as the handsome Latin Lover. He worked constantly from his first film in 1933 until his 119th film in 1994. Despite all his cinematic success, he is best remembered as The Joker in the original *Batman* television series from 1966 to 1968.

Sugar Ray Robinson
May 3, 1921–April 12, 1989
Pinecrest Section (upright marker in the center of the section)

In 1997, *The Ring* magazine named Sugar Ray Robinson (Walker Smith Jr.) "pound for pound, the best boxer of all time." However, since he

boxed as a welterweight and a middleweight, he never quite achieved the status of a heavyweight. His statistics are impressive. As an amateur he won 85 flights, 69 of which were by a knockout. He turned pro in 1949 at the age of 19, and by 1951, he had amassed a record of 128 wins, one loss, and two no-decisions. He retired in 1952 but came out of retirement in 1955 and continued to box until 1958. He was inducted into the International Boxing Hall of Fame in 1990. He acquired the name Ray Robinson when he used an Amateur Athletic Union card owned by his friend Ray Robinson. "Sugar" came from his longtime manager, who described his boxing style as "sweet as sugar."

Edgar Bergen
February 16, 1903–September 30, 1978
Miramar Plot (lot 131, grave 2)

Edgar Bergen (Edgar John Bergren) taught himself ventriloquism from a pamphlet when he was 11, and by age 16, he was performing with a puppet named Charlie McCarthy. He performed in vaudeville but found his greatest success on radio, where ventriloquism was hardly necessary. On his radio program, he introduced two other characters, Mortimer Snerd and Effie Klinker. Soon he found his way into movies, and from 1930 until 1976, he appeared in forty-one films. In 1945, Edgar Bergen married Frances Westerman. Their daughter, actress Candice Bergen, was born in 1946.

Tom Bradley
December 29, 1917–September 29, 1998
Sunset Mission Mausoleum (vault 1086D, on the left after entering)

Thomas J. Bradley was a five-term mayor of Los Angeles, serving from 1973 to 1993. He was the first African-American mayor of Los Angeles and also had the longest tenure of any mayor of Los Angeles. Bradley ran for governor of California in 1982 and again in 1986, losing both times to Republican George Deukmejian. His wife, Ethel, created the Tom and Ethel Bradley Foundation in 2003. In 2006, the Ethel Bradley Early Education and Health Career Center opened in Watts. Ethel died on November 25, 2008.

Norman Spencer Chaplin/"Little Mouse"
July 7, 1919 d. July 10, 1919
Del Ivy Plot (lot 496, grave #3)

Charlie Chaplin married 16-year-old child star Mildred Harris on October 23, 1918. Nine months later, Mildred gave birth to Norman Spencer Chaplin. The child apparently had birth defects and died three days later. Supposedly, Chaplin's 1921 film, *The Kid*, was a tribute to Little Mouse.

Hoot Gibson
August 6, 1892–August 23, 1962
Magnolia Plot (lot 92, grave 6)

Edmund Richard Gibson was born in Nebraska, and the family moved to California when he was seven. He had learned to ride horses while still in Nebraska, and after moving to California, he worked with horses on a ranch. His name Hoot was derived from his nickname, "Hoot Owl." He found his way into cowboy movies in 1910, first as a stuntman and later as an actor. He appeared in 218 movies from *The Fightin' Terror* in 1920 to an uncredited role in *Ocean's Eleven* in 1960. He also produced and directed films in the 1920s and '30s.

Jim Jeffries
April 15, 1875–March 3, 1953
Sequoia Plot (lot 122, grave 7)

James Jackson Jeffries was a world-champion heavyweight boxer most noted for his strength and stamina. He stood 6 feet 3 inches tall and weighed 225 pounds. His signature punch, The Boilermaker, became his nickname. He defeated Bob Fitzsimmons on June 9, 1899, to win the Heavyweight Championship of the World. Jeffries defended his title a number of times and retired undefeated in 1905. In 1910, he was coaxed out of retirement to fight the current heavyweight champion, African-American Jack Johnson. Jeffries was billed as "The Great White Hope." Despite the heavily racist atmosphere surrounding the fight in Reno, Nevada, Johnson prevailed, earning a TKO in the fifteenth round. The fight was Jeffries' only career loss. In his later years, Jeffries became a fight promoter and trainer.

Big Mama Thornton
December 11, 1926–July 25, 1984
'M' Plot (lot 2486-B)

Big Mama (Willie Mae) Thornton was . . . well . . . big. In 1952, the 350-pound blues singer was the first person to record "Hound Dog." Although Elvis Presley is most famously known for the song, Big Mama Thornton's version charted #1 on the Billboard R&B list for seven weeks. Thornton also wrote and recorded "Ball n' Chain," which became a successful hit for Janis Joplin. Although various renditions of Thornton's songs are best known when performed by other artists, her talents were well respected within the music industry. She was inducted into Blues Foundation's Hall of Fame in 1984. Unfortunately, hard living, hard drinking, and a life on the road took its toll and she withered away to 95 pounds, eventually dying of heart and liver complications.

M. C. Trouble
July 30, 1970–June 4, 1991
⊛ 33 58 03 N 118 20 24 W
Pinecrest Section (upright marker in the center)

M. C. Trouble, born LaTasha Sheron Rogers, was the first female rap artist signed by Motown Records. Her first hit was "(I Wanna) Make You Mine" in 1990. Her promising career was cut tragically short when she died of heart failure following an epileptic seizure.

Holy Cross Cemetery

5835 West Slauson Avenue

Culver City, California 90230

310-836-5500

⊛ 33 59 20 N 118 23 12 W

www.archdiocese.la/

directories/cemeteries/

Maps in office

Prior to 1822, Catholics who wanted to be buried in a Catholic cemetery in Los Angeles were buried in the churchyards of Mission San Gabriel Arcángel (1771) or the Mission San Fernando Rey de España. (1797). In 1822, the first formal burial ground in the city of Los Angeles was established next to Our Lady Queen of Angels Church at 535 North Main Street. Two decades later, a new cemetery was established on a twelve-acre site on Buena Vista Street (now North Broadway) at the southwest corner of Bishop's Road. That cemetery was called Calvary Cemetery. It served the Catholic population until a much larger cemetery dubbed New Calvary was established in 1896 on Whittier Boulevard.

In 1922, Pope Pius XI divided the 90,000-square-mile Diocese of Monterey–Los Angeles and created the Diocese of Los Angeles–San Diego. Then in 1939, Holy Cross Cemetery in Culver City was founded and became the first cemetery created in the new diocese. Its landscape design with flat markers set in vast rolling lawns make Holy Cross the Catholic equivalent of the Forest Lawn cemeteries. The Archdiocese of Los Angeles Catholic Cemeteries Department is currently comprised of the Crypt Mausoleum of the Cathedral of Our Lady of the Angels and eleven active cemetery locations within the five pastoral regions. At 200 acres, Holy Cross is the largest cemetery.

Grotto
⊛ 33 59 26 N 118 23 15 W

No proper Catholic cemetery is without a grotto or a representation of one. The word "grotto" comes from the Italian *grotta*, vulgar Latin *grupta*,

Latin *crypta,* or vault or crypt. Grottos are essentially caves and thus date from man's earliest beginnings. They are often associated with protection, meditation, and contemplation. Grottos have always been popular with Catholics and have permanently cemented themselves into that religion, thanks in no small part to what may be the most famous grotto in the world, the Grotto of Lourdes in France. On 11 February 1858, Bernadette Soubirous, a 14-year-old peasant girl from Lourdes, told her mother that she had seen a "lady" in the cave of Massabielle. She described the lady as a young woman dressed in a flowing white robe with a blue sash around her waist. The sighting became the talk of the village and word spread far and wide about the apparition. The grotto was actually closed at one point by the French government to prevent the increasing hordes of the curious from going there. Eventually the government relented, and people were allowed to go and seek the apparition and sample what became known as the healing waters. In 1864, Lyonnais sculptor Joseph-Hugues Fabisch created a statue of Our Lady of Lourdes that was older and taller than young Bernadette's description, and more in keeping with common representations of the Virgin Mary. Thus, Catholic grottos always have a water element and a statue of a woman with a white robe and usually a blue sash, nestled in a niche.

Just like traditional real estate, which touts location, location, location, plots around the Holy Cross Grotto are the most desirable, and that's where the most celebrity graves are located.

Notable Residents

Rita Hayworth

October 17, 1918–May 14, 1987

✤ 33 59 26 N 118 23 14 W

Grotto (lot 196, grave 6)

One of most prominent
burial locations is occu-
pied by Rita Hayworth
(Margarita Haworth), who
is buried on the right side
of the grotto in front of

the statue of a kneeling angel. Margarita Haworth was born in Brooklyn,
New York, the daughter of Spanish dancer Eduardo Cansino and Ziegfeld
Follies dancer Volga Haworth. Young Rita took up dancing and performing,
and appeared with her parents in two 1926 musical shorts, *Anna Case with
the Dancing Cascinos* and *La Fiesta*. By age 14, she became her father's dance
partner, and she started getting small parts in films. In 1937, she attracted
the attention of Columbia Studios bigwig Harry Cohn, who suggested
she change her name to Rita Hayworth. That same year, 18-year-old Rita
married 50-year-old car salesman Edward Juston, who devoted himself to
advancing her career. By 1942, she was a full-fledged star. Unfortunately for
Judson, Rita had fallen in love with Victor Mature, her co-star in the 1942
film *My Gal Sal*. She didn't marry Mature, but she did divorce Juston and,
over the years, went through four more husbands, including Orson Welles
and Prince Aly Khan, with whom she had a daughter, Princess Yasmin Aga
Khan.

Hayworth parlayed her sultry looks and dancing skills successfully
in a number of films, costarring in *You'll Never get Rich* (1941) and *You
Were Never Lovelier* (1942) with Fred Astaire and in *Cover Girl* (1946) with
Gene Kelly. Hayworth continued to secure good roles throughout the
1940s and well into the 1950s. Film roles fell off during the 1960s, but
she did briefly revive her career in the early 1970s. Unfortunately, she
was having trouble remembering her lines, which was a precursor of
Alzheimer's disease. In her final years, she was tended to by her daughter
Yasmin, who became an active fundraiser, and proponent for Alzheimer's
research. Hayworth's modest marker is inscribed with the words "To
yesterday's companionship and tomorrow's reunion."

On the left side (facing the grotto) is the small St. Ann Section of
Holy Cross. This small
section is host to a
number of luminaries.

Sharon Tate

**January 24, 1943–
August 9, 1969**

✤ 33 59 25 N 118 23 16 W

St. Ann Section
(tier 152, grave 6)

Sharon Tate was a vic-
tim of one of the most
horrific murder sprees

in the history of Los Angeles. Just after midnight on August 9, 1969, four members of the Manson Family, a cult headed by Charles Manson, burst into the home of actress Sharon Tate and director Roman Polanski (Polanski was away at the time). The four cult members—Charles "Tex" Watson, Susan Atkins, Patricia Krenwinkel, and Linda Kasabian—brutally butchered Steven Parent, Abigail Folger, her lover Voytek Frykowski, hair stylist Jay Sebring, and actress Sharon Tate, who was eight months pregnant. Thus ended the fairytale life of Sharon Tate.

Sharon Tate was a natural beauty, winning her first beauty contest, Miss Tiny Tot, when she was six months old. She was born in Dallas, Texas, to Paul and Doris Tate. Paul Tate was an Army officer, which meant the family moved often. When the family was in Italy, Sharon attended the American High School and was cast as an extra when a movie company was filming a Paul Newman movie, *The Adventures of a Young Man*. Tate made friends with Richard Beymer, one of the film's cast, who told her to look him up when the family returned to the United States. Although Tate was not a great actress, her adequate acting skills and stunning looks secured her a number of roles. In 1967, she appeared in four films, most notably in *Valley of the Dolls*, where she plays an aspiring actress known only for her body. She met director Roman Polanski during the filming of *The Fearless Vampire Killers* (1967), and the couple married in 1968. Although Tate never received much acclaim for her roles, some critics predicted that she had a great career ahead as a comedienne because of her sharp wit. Tate's grave marker also contains the name of her unborn child, Paul Richard Polanski; her younger sister, Patricia Gay Tate (1957–2000); and her mother Doris Gwendolyn Tate (1924–1992), who campaigned tirelessly for victim's rights.

James "Jim" Jordan (Fibber McGee)
November 6, 1896–April 1, 1988
and
Marian Jordan (Molly McGee)
November 16, 1896–April 7, 1961
✳ 33 59 25 N 118 23 16 W
St. Ann Section (lot 153, grave 2)

Next to the Tates and sharing a space in the St. Ann Section are James and Marian Jordan, better known to vintage radio fans as Fibber McGee and Molly. James and Marian were married on August 31, 1918, and soon began a career in radio together. In 1927, they were doing radio programs at WENR radio in Chicago. In *Luke and Mirandy*, which was in the form of a farm report, Jim played a character who was given to tall tales. In 1931, Jim took his tall tales character to Chicago station WMAQ, and with help from writer Donald Quinn and Marian, he created a 15-minute daily situation comedy titled *Smackout*. The team's next creation, titled *Fibber McGee and Molly*, debuted in 1935 and ran with various permutations until 1959. The radio program was so popular that the average American probably knew the couple's fictional address of 79 Wistful Vista as well as they knew 1600 Pennsylvania Avenue. The situation of the situation comedy was that blowhard Fibber always had some scheme that never worked out and his long-suffering but patient wife, Molly, endured his foibles and loved him just the same. The program was kept lively with a parade of neighbors, some who became regulars and others who were popular radio stars who made cameo appearances. The program also had a number of running gags. The most memorable was the jam-packed closet that Molly warned Fibber not to open. Every time he opened it, the contents came crashing and tumbling out. This formula of recurring gags and guests and cameos by popular stars has become the template for today's situation comedies on television. *Fibber McGee and Molly* couldn't make the transition to television, but they did appear in four movies in the late 1930s and early '40s. In real life, Marian Jordan battled alcoholism and was frequently absent from the program as the years progressed. In later years, she developed cancer and eventually succumbed to it.

John Candy
October 31, 1950–March 4, 1994
❋ 33 59 36 N 118 23 03 W (mausoleum entrance)
Mausoleum (room 7, crypt B1)

John Franklin Candy's professional debut was on the Canadian Broadcasting Company program *Coming Up Rosie*. He was soon offered a position as a writer and performer in Chicago's legendary Second City Troupe and Second City TV. His SCTV work earned him two Emmys. Movies followed including appearances in *The Blues Brothers* and *Stripes* in 1981 and most notably *Planes, Trains and Automobiles* with Steve Martin in 1987. While making the film *Wagons East* in Mexico in 1994, he died of a massive heart attack. Candy's father died of a heart attack in 1955 when John was five years old.

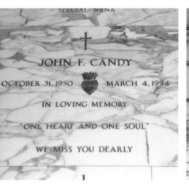

Fred MacMurray
August 30, 1908–November 5, 1991
❋ 33 59 36 N 118 23 03 W (mausoleum entrance)
Mausoleum (room 7, crypt D1)

Fred MacMurray is often touted as one of the most underrated and underappreciated actors of the twentieth century. He appeared in 88 feature films, starting with dramatic roles and then drifting into comedy. Despite his cinematic success in movies like *Double Indemnity* (1944), *The Caine Mutiny* (1954), and *The Apartment* (1960), MacMurray is best known as the paternal Steve Douglas in the long-running (1960–1972) television sitcom *My Three Sons*. He shares the crypt with his wife, actress June Haver (June 10, 1926–July 4, 2005).

Bela Lugosi

October 20, 1882–August 16, 1956
✺ 33 59 25 N 118 23 15 W
Grotto (L120, 1)

Bela Lugosi (Béla Ferenc Dezso Blaskó) was born in what is now Romania. He acted briefly in Europe before immigrating to the United States in 1921. He made his way to Hollywood and starred in a stage production of *Dracula* in 1929, which he reprised in the 1930 film version. His lanky

physique and heavy accent were perfect for the role, and despite acting in other films, he will be forever remembered as Count Dracula. Even when he didn't play the Dracula character, he found his most financially lucrative roles in horror films and comedy-horror films. Following his death of a heart attack, he was buried in his Dracula cape. During Lugosi's funeral, fellow actor Peter Lorre was said to have turned to Vincent Price and whispered, "Should we drive a stake through his heart?"

Lawrence Welk

March 11, 1903–May 17, 1992
✺ 33 59 38 N 118 22 55 W
Section Y (row 9, plot 110)

Lawrence Welk was born in Strasburg, North Dakota. Most of the Strasburg community were German-speaking immigrants, and young Lawrence developed a strong German accent. His father purchased a mail-order accordion for

Lawrence with the agreement that Lawrence would stay on the farm until he was 21, at which time Lawrence skedaddled, eventually forming his own band. Success followed, and he moved to Los Angeles in 1951, where he produced a local television show simply titled *The Lawrence Welk Show*. In 1955, ABC Television picked up the show. Including the show's 1951 local beginnings, *The Lawrence Welk Show* ran continuously until 1982. Family-oriented, it focused mostly on polkas, popular standards, and easy listening. He always started his songs with "an a-one, an a-two." The personalized license plate on his Model A Ford read "A1ANA2"

Jimmy Durante
See page 156.

ZaSu Pitts
See page 160.

Bing Crosby
See page 168-69.

Evergreen Cemetery

204 North Evergreen Avenue

Los Angeles, California 90033

323-268-6714

34 02 31 N 118 12 04 W

I f the rolling, perfectly manicured lawns, flawless stained-glass windows, and polished statuary of Forest Lawn Memorial Park can be likened to the sanitized and aseptic atmosphere of Disneyland, then Evergreen Cemetery—which is far from ever-green—is more like a carnival: a bit unkempt, rough around the edges, dangerous (or so say the signs alerting scallywags of police patrols), but full of character. In fact, the Pacific Coast Showmen's Association, an organization for carnival owners and employees, has a burial plot here.

Evergreen Cemetery holds title to being the oldest continuously operating cemetery in Los Angeles. Established on August 23, 1877, by a private company, Evergreen rapidly became the permanent address of many of L. A.'s movers and shakers. Look at some of the larger monuments, and you'll see names of many of streets, neighborhoods, and cities. Lankershim, Breed, and Van Nuys, and over 30,000 others call Evergreen home. In the years before most cemeteries were integrated, Evergreen became the burial ground of choice for the African-American population. Even after cemeteries were integrated, many members of the African-American community still preferred to designate Evergreen as their final destination. Eddie Anderson, who played Jack Benny's butler, Rochester, is buried here; so are Gilbert Lindsay, the first African-American to sit on the Los Angeles City Council; Negro League baseball star James Mackey; Bridget "Biddy" Mason, who established the first black-owned business in L. A., and Bobby Nunn, the original bass vocalist for the Coasters.

The most striking feature of Evergreen Cemetery is the towering monument dedicated to the 442nd Infantry, composed of second-generation Japanese American (Nisei) soldiers who served in World War II. The area around the monument has become a popular burial ground for Japanese Americans from all over the greater Los Angeles area. The cemetery also contains a burial ground for Grand Army of the Republic (GAR) members, who served on the Union side in the Civil War.

Evergreen has enough mausoleums, statuary, and varieties of tombs to give the grounds a diversity and texture that few Los Angeles cemeteries have. Each bend on its serpentine roads will yield a treasure trove of history, architecture, and even an authentic Chinese shrine built in 1888. You may even run into a celebrity or two.

Grand Army of the Republic Monument

✸ 34 02 21 N 118 11 58 W

Although California was not an active participant in the Civil War, a number of Civil War veterans moved to the Golden State afterwards. Thus, many of the older historic cemeteries have a GAR plot reserved for members of that society. The GAR was a self-extinguishing society since its members had to have participated in the Civil War. For more information on the GAR, see Secret Societies, Clubs, and Organizations on page 201.

Grand Army of the Republic Monument Lankershim-Van Nuys Obelisk

Isaac Newton Van Nuys

November 20, 1836–February 12, 1912

✸ 34 02 22 N 118 11 57 W

The Lankershims and Van Nuyses were early business pioneers in the Los Angeles area. An obelisk marks their burial plot.

Isaac Newton Van Nuys was born in West Sparta, New York, to Peter Van Nuys and Harriett Kerr. At age 30, Isaac moved to Napa, California, and then to Monticello, where he opened a store. He became involved in various businesses and real estate ventures, eventually settling in the Los Angeles area on 60,000 acres of ranch land in the San Fernando Valley that he owned with business partners. Van Nuys raised sheep, farmed grain, opened a mill, was a vice-president of the Farmers and Merchants

Bank, and served as a director on the Los Angeles Pressed Brick Company. One year before he died, lot sales began for the newly formed town of Van Nuys.

Susanna Hill Lankershim Van Nuys

December 12, 1846–May 1, 1923

Susanna Lankershim was the daughter of Isaac and Annis Lydia Moore Lankershim. Susanna married Isaac Van Nuys in 1880, and soon after, her father and her husband formed a number of business partnerships. Like Van Nuys, Lankershim had a town named after him. However, Lankershim, California, has been swallowed up by North Hollywood.

Isaac Lankershim

April 8, 1818–April 10, 1882

Annis Lydia Moore Lankershim

June 15, 1818–June 6, 1901

Perry Monument

34 02 24 N 118 11 55 W

A number of Perrys are buried in the area around the Perry Monument and Sarcophagus. Many of their names are carved into the granite open book that rests on the sarcophagus. The most famous of them is William G. Perry (1831–1906), who was a Los Angeles lumber baron and close friends with Los Angeles kingpin William Mulholland. Perry's Victorian-era home was moved to Heritage Square in Highland Park, just off the Pasadena Freeway.

Pacific Coast Showmen's Association and Ladies Auxiliary

34 02 21 N 118 11 41 W

A ferocious feline tops the Pacific Coast Showmen's Association plot. The PCSA was organized in 1924 as a benevolent association for circus and carnival people. The fat lady who purportedly was too large for a standard casket is said to have been buried casketless directly under the monument. Just across the lane is the plot for the Ladies Auxiliary Pacific Coast Showmen's Association, which was organized in 1930. It is somewhat rare to see a relatively small organization like the PCSA and the Ladies Auxiliary have a plot in a cemetery reserved exclusively for their members. Most large plots are owned by large organizations that have or had nationwide membership in the hundreds of thousands, like the Elks, Freemasons, Odd Fellows, and Knights of Pythias.

Frederick Arthur Breed

July 7, 1862–February 19, 1885
⊛ 34 02 22 N 118 11 55 W

This angel, towering atop the monument to Frederick Arthur Breed, is tallying up his all-too-brief stay on planet Earth. According to the script beneath Frederick Breed's name, he was "killed in a railroad accident at Blue Water Station N.M." Little is known about his demise in New Mexico or about his life. However, much is known about his father, Levi Newton Breed.

Levi Newton Breed was born in Manlius, New York, in 1832. Like many young men, he set off for the West in 1853 to seek adventure and fortune. Arriving in California with "four bits in his pocket," he went through a series of jobs, and with a bit of luck and some shrewd investments, he established a merchandise business and acquired over 1,000 acres of land near Susanville, California. A few years later, he moved to Los Angeles and served on the City Council from 1886 to 1889. He was the founder of Lincoln Park in East Los Angeles. A plaque on a memorial to him in Lincoln Park reads: "Founder of this park 'So long as there shall be a city of Los Angeles its people shall here enjoy priceless benefits of light air and beauty' a heritage from this man." Breed Street in East Los Angeles is named in his honor.

African-American Burial Ground
⊛ Sections A, L, and G

Even in forward-thinking Los Angeles, many cemeteries were segregated until the 1960s. Not so with Evergreen. Most of the northeast quadrant of the cemetery is dominated by the resting places of African-Americans. Much of the front of section A is composed of domino-like rows of tomb-stones of Japanese Americans. Behind them lie members of the African-American community. A bit of sleuthing will reveal a number of graves for ministers, athletes, entertainers, soldiers, and just plain folks. Particularly popular in this area are porcelain portraits of dignified men and women. Many of the tombstones are adorned with the emblems of secret societies: Colored Odd Fellows, Prince Hall Freemasons, Rebekahs, and members of

Eddie Lincoln "Rochester" Anderson

Tombstone in the African-American Burial Ground

the Eastern Star. Of special note are the following:

🌾 **Eddie Lincoln "Rochester" Anderson** (September 18, 1905–February 28, 1977), who played Jack Benny's personal assistant in the *Jack Benny Show.*

🌾 **Matthew "Stymie" Beard Jr.** (January 1, 1925–January 8, 1981), who was one of the *Little Rascals.*

🌾 **Gilbert W. Lindsay** (November 29, 1900–December 28 1990), who was a Los Angeles City councilman.

🌾 **Jesse Belvin** (December 15, 1932–February 6, 1960), who was a singer-songwriter, best known as the writer of "Earth Angel."

🌾 **Everett Brown** (January 1, 1902–October 25 1953), who appeared in twenty-eight films but is best known for his role as Big Sam in *Gone With the Wind.*

🌾 **Bridget "Biddy" Mason** (August 15, 1818–January 18, 1891), who founded L. A.'s first African-American congregation in 1872.

442nd Infantry World War II Memorial
✣ 34 02 32 N 118 12 01 W

The 442nd Infantry was the most decorated unit in United States history. It was composed almost entirely of second-generation Japanese-Americans (Nisei). After the start of U.S. involvement in World War II, the activities of almost all Japanese Americans were severely curtailed, and many of them were sent to internment camps. However, many Nisei, especially those from Hawaii, wanted to serve in the military, and special arrangements were made. The 442nd fought with distinction in Italy, southern France, and Germany. The plaque on the monument reads: "In Sacred Memory. This memorial is reverently placed here by the Japanese American Community, under the auspices of the Southern California Burial and Memorial Committee, in memory of American soldiers of Japanese ancestry who fought, suffered, and died in World War II that Liberty, Justice, and Equal Opportunity in the Pursuit of Happiness might come to all democratic and peace-loving people everywhere regardless of race, creed, color or national origin. Dedicated: May 30, 1949." The area around the monument has become a popular burial ground for all Japanese Americans.

Among those buried around the monument are the following:

❀ **Sadao Munemori** (August 17, 1922–April 5, 1945), who was the first Japanese-American to received the Congressional Medal of Honor.

❀ **Kiyoshi Muranaga** (February 16, 1922–June 26, 1944), who received the Distinguished Service Cross for his action in Italy; then, after his service record was reviewed, he was given a Congressional Medal of Honor posthumously in 2000 by President Bill Clinton.

❀ **Ted T. Tanouye** (November 14, 1919–September 6, 1944), who, like Kiyoshi Muranaga, had his Distinguished Service Cross posthumously upgraded to a Congressional Medal of Honor in a ceremony at the White House on June 21, 2000.

Mon

Mon (also *monsho*, *mondokoro*, and *kamon*) are the Japanese equivalent of family crests or heraldic symbols. Almost all Japanese families have a mon symbol. Although they are not used as often in modern society as they were in the past, they are often seen decorating Japanese crafts and grave markers. For a more detailed explanation of mon symbols, see pages 241–43.

Facing: 442nd Infantry
World War II Memorial

Westwood Village Memorial Park

1218 Glendon Avenue

Los Angeles, California 90024

310-474-1579

 34 03 30 N 118 26 32 W

A side from Oscar night at the Kodak Theater in Hollywood, one would be hard-pressed to find as many celebrities gathered together in close proximity as you'll find at Pierce Brothers Westwood Village Memorial Park and Mortuary. The two-and-a-half acre postage-stamp-sized cemetery is wedged between high-rise office buildings and is a stone's throw from UCLA, Beverley Hills, and trendy Rodeo Drive.

The petite burial ground was established when the sleepy nineteenth century rolled into the bustling twentieth. It existed rather anonymously, serving the needs of the local community until 1962 when retired baseball player Joe DiMaggio selected it as the final resting place for his ex-wife Marilyn Monroe. DiMaggio chose the cemetery for its obscurity, little aware that placing the platinum blonde in a crypt there would vault the cemetery out of obscurity and onto the public stage. Suddenly, Westwood Village Memorial Park became the cemetery of choice for celebrities, eclipsing the vast Forest Lawn cemeteries per square foot. The empty crypt next to Monroe's has been purchased and reserved for Hugh Hefner, the man who profiled her in all her glory in his fledgling magazine, *Playboy,* in its premier December 1953 issue.

Well over 1,000 A-list celebrities and lesser lights call the cemetery their permanent address. It has recently added an ample outdoor columbarium to house cremains (cremated remains), which will assure the cemetery's viability for years to come. Despite the cemetery's compact size, there is usually ample parking space, except on days when a funeral is taking place. If parking isn't available, there is a large parking garage next door. Individual graves are easy to locate. You won't need lot markers or GPS coordinates, although we have included a few lot locations. You'll usually see fellow cemetery tourists hovering over Natalie Wood's grave, placing a hand or a kiss on Marilyn's crypt, or having a private chuckle as they view Rodney Dangerfield's stone that proclaims "There goes the neighborhood." A thorough listing of all the celebrities would take its own voluminous tome. However, we've listed a few notables here, and you'll be pleasantly surprised when you see or stumble over some of your favorite stars.

Pierce Brothers Westwood Village Memorial Park and Mortuary is located just off Glendon Avenue. Look for the sign at 1218 Glendon Avenue and turn into what appears to be an alley. A hundred feet farther on, take a sharp right turn into the cemetery (going straight will land you in the parking garage for a local theater).

Ray Conniff
November 6, 1916–October 12, 2002
(near a small bench by the side of the road)

Ray Conniff was a very successful composer and musician. In a career that spanned 65 years, he produced 100 albums that sold over 70 million copies. Among his most recognized songs are "We Wish You a Merry Christmas" and "Somewhere My Love" ("Lara's Theme" from the movie *Dr. Zhivago*), for which he won a Grammy in 1966.

Bob Crane
July 13, 1928 – June 29, 1978
and
Sigrid Valdis
September 21, 1935 – October 14, 2007
(lawn area, across the road from the upright markers)

Although flat markers don't take up a lot of real estate, actor Robert Edward Crane and his wife Sigrid Valdis (Patricia Annette Olson) man-

aged to cram a lot into a small space. On their grave marker are three porcelain portraits, a partial listing of their media roles, their children, a poem, and a statement of their Humanist leanings (a Darwin symbol). Bob Crane is best remembered for his title role in the television sitcom *Hogan's Heroes,* which aired from 1965 to 1971. Sigrid was also a regular on the program, appearing in 43 episodes as Colonel Klink's secretary, Hilda. Crane and Valdis were married from 1970 until Crane's death in 1978.

Rodney Dangerfield

November 22, 1921–October 5, 2004
Garden Estate (one of the upright markers on the office side of the road)

Rodney Dangerfield (born Jacob Cohen; legal name Jack Roy) was an actor and comedian best known for his catchphrase, "I don't get no respect." A late bloomer, his career didn't really take off until the late 1970s and early '80s when he starred in the films *Caddyshack, Easy Money,* and *Back to School.* A self-effacing comic to the end, the epitaph on his gravestone reads, "There goes the neighborhood."

Dominique Dunne

November 23, 1959–November 4, 1982
(lawn section, near the office)

Dominique Dunne was the daughter of Ellen Griffin, a ranching heiress, and producer/ journalist/novelist Dominick Dunne. Dominique landed some small roles in 1980s television shows and then was cast in

a major role in the 1982 movie *Poltergeist.* After that, she moved in with John Thomas Sweeney in a relationship that quickly turned abusive. Dunne ended the relationship, but Sweeney confronted her in front of her home and strangled her. She died five days later. Sweeney was convicted of manslaughter and was released after four years.

Eva Gabor

February 11, 1919–July 4, 1995
(near Natalie Wood)

Eva Gabor was
a voluptuous
Hungarian-
born actress
best known as
Lisa Douglas,
the wife of
Eddie Albert's
character, Oli-
ver Wendell
Douglas, on
the television
sitcom *Green
Acres* (1965–
1971). Her
elder sisters,

Zsa Zsa Gabor and Magda Gabor, were also actresses and socialites. All
three siblings were well known for their abundance of marriages. Eva was
married five times, Magda six and Zsa Zsa nine.

Merv Griffin

July 6, 1925–August 12, 2007
Garden Estate (one of the upright markers on the office side of the road)

Merv Griffin began his career as a singer and actor in movies and on
Broadway, but found success when he hosted his own television show,
The Merv Griffin Show, which ran for 20 years. While hosting the show, he
also developed game shows. Among the most successful were the long-
running *Jeopardy!* and *Wheel of Fortune.* His epitaph, which is a reference to
the commercial breaks on the television programs he developed, reads, "I
will <u>not</u> be right back after this message."

Armand Hammer

May 21, 1898–December 10, 1990

The only family mausoleum in Westwood Village Memorial Park houses
the remains of tycoon and owner of Occidental Petroleum—Armand

Hammer—and other members of the Hammer family. A controversial and self-promoting figure, he claimed at various times in his long life that he was friends with Vladimir Lenin, Ronald Reagan, and Richard Nixon. Numerous magazines and newspapers reported on his exploits, and five biographies have been penned about his life.

Don Knotts
See page 162–63

Jack Lemmon
February 8, 1925–June 27, 2001
Garden Estate (one of the upright markers on the office side of the road)

John Uhler "Jack" Lemmon III is known principally for his comedic roles, but he won critical acclaim for his dramatic roles as well. Lemmon starred in over 60 films, including *Some Like It Hot, The Apartment, Days of Wine and Roses, Irma La Douce, The Odd Couple, Glengarry Glen Ross, The China Syndrome,* and *JFK.* He won Academy Awards in 1955 for Best Supporting Actor in *Mister Roberts* and in 1973 for Best Actor in *Save the Tiger.* He was nominated for 22 Golden Globe Awards and won six. One word—"in"—appears on his tombstone as an epitaph.

Dean Martin
June 7, 1917–December 25, 1995
Sanctuary of Love (left side)

Dean Martin (Dino Paul Crocetti) was a legendary actor and singer. Some of his hit singles included "Memories Are Made of This," "That's Amore," "Everybody Loves Somebody," "Volare" and "Ain't That A Kick in the Head?" He had a successful movie career and may be best known for his movies with Jerry Lewis, where Martin played the straight man. Shortly after Martin and Lewis broke up, Martin and others formed the legendary Rat Pack.

Walter Matthau

October 1, 1920–
July 1, 2000
Garden Estate (one of
the upright markers
on the office side of
the road near Jack
Lemmon)

There is a
persistent and
oft-repeated
false rumor that
Walter Matthau's
real name was
Matuschans-
kayasky. However, he was an award-winning actor, garnering Tonys,
Golden Globes, and an Academy Award for Best Supporting Actor for
the 1966 movie *The Fortune Cookie*. Matthau is best known for his role as
Oscar Madison in *The Odd Couple* and for the 10 movies he did with Jack
Lemmon. Spending eternity with Walter Matthau is his wife, actress
Carol Matthau (1924–2003).

Marilyn Monroe

See page 170–72.

Carroll O'Connor

August 2, 1924–June 21, 2001
Garden Estate (one of the upright markers on the office side of the road)

Carroll O'Connor had a long career as an actor, but he found fame as
Archie Bunker, the main character in the 1970s CBS television sitcoms *All
in the Family* (1971–1979) and *Archie Bunker's Place* (1979–1983). O'Connor
later starred in the 1980s NBC television crime drama *In the Heat of the
Night*, where he played the role of Police Chief Bill Gillespie from 1988
to 1994. Sharing the plot is a space reserved for his wife, Nancy, whom
he married in 1951, and for the couple's son, Hugh, who committed
suicide in 1995 after a long battle with drug addiction.

Dorothy Stratten

28 February 1960–14 August 1980
(across from the office, near the road)

Dorothy Ruth Hoogstraten's life was the stuff of a classic Hollywood tragedy. Indeed, variations of her story have been depicted in a number of films, most notably the 1981 television film *Death of a Centerfold: The Dorothy Stratten Story.* She was a Canadian model who rose to prominence after she was the August 1979 *Playboy* magazine centerfold and then the 1980 Playmate of the Year. Movie roles soon followed, and the relationship with her jealous husband, Paul Snider, rapidly deteriorated. Stratten began having an affair with director Peter Bogdanovich, which essentially sent Snider over the edge. Snider lured Stratten into his home to talk about a divorce, killed her with a shotgun, and committed suicide by turning the gun on himself. Her epitaph bitterly speaks of her tragic death: "If people bring so much courage to this world the world has to kill them to break them. So of course it kills them. . . . It kills the very good and the very gentle and the very brave impartially. If you are none of these you can be sure that it will kill you too but there will be no special hurry.—We love you, D. R."

Mel Tormé

September 13, 1925–June 5, 1999
(section B, lot 114, first road left, near the wall)

Melvin Howard Tormé was nicknamed The Velvet Fog. He was known as one of the great jazz singers, a jazz composer and arranger, a drummer, an actor in radio, film, and television, and the author of five books. He co-wrote "The Christmas Song," commonly known as "Chestnuts Roasting on an Open Fire," with Bob Wells.

Billy Wilder (Samuel Wilder)

June 22, 1906–March 27, 2002

Garden Estate (one of the upright markers on the office side of the road)

Billy (Samuel) Wilder was a film-maker, screenwriter, and producer. The American Film Institute ranked four of Wilder's films among their top 100 American films of the twentieth century: *Sunset Boulevard* (#12), *Some Like It Hot* (#14), *Double Indemnity* (#38) and *The Apartment* (#93). Wilder won seven Academy Awards: Best Screenplay and Best Director for *The Lost Weekend* (1946), Best Original Screenplay for *Sunset Boulevard* (1951), Best Original Screenplay, Best Director, and Best Picture for *The Apartment* (1961), and the Irving G. Thalberg Memorial Award for Life-time Achievement (1988). Wilder's epitaph reads, "I'm a writer, but then nobody's perfect," a takeoff from the last line in *Some Like It Hot*.

Natalie Wood

July 20, 1938–November 29, 1981

(section D, #60)

Next to Marilyn Monroe, the second most-visited grave in the cemetery is Natalie Wood's. It is always adorned with coins to denote that someone was there. Natalie Wood (Natasha Nikolaevna Zakharenko)

burst into stardom opposite James Dean in *Rebel Without a Cause* (1955). Although she was known for her beauty, she was a talented and respected actress, garnering a number of Oscar and Golden Globe nominations. She won a Golden Globe for Most Promising Newcomer–Female in 1957 and a Golden Globe for the 1979 television remake of *From Here to Eternity*. She was married twice to actor Robert Wagner.

Darryl F. Zanuck
September 5, 1902–December 22, 1979
(on the lawn near Natalie Wood)

Darryl Francis Zanuck's daughter wanted to make sure the facts of her father's life were accurately noted, so she wrote a lengthy bio on his grave marker, which also sports the 20th Century Fox Film Corporation logo. It reads,

Darryl Francis Zanuck, Born—Wahoo, Nebraska, September 5, 1902; passed on—Palm Springs, California, December 22, 1979. Co-founder, president and producer of 20th Century Fox Studio. Doctor of Humanities, University of Nebraska. Mason 50 years receiving the highest degree. In his lifetime received such a host of degrees, diplomas and awards from all over the world, that it is impossible to state them all. Private World War I overseas, 14 years old. World War II Colonel. Active duty overseas, U.S. Signal Corp, Algeria. Listed below are a few of the service ribbons and decorations he was proudly authorized to wear: Victory Medal (WW I); Medal of French Legion of Honor with Rouge Rosette (WWI); Asiatic Pacific Campaign Ribbons and European-Africa-Middle Eastern Campaign Ribbons. A man who used his imaginative creative genius to deliver inspiration through his celebrated motion pictures. He imparted a lifetime message of decency, love, patriotism, justice, equality and hope throughout the nation and the world. Beloved husband, father, grandfather and great-grandfather. I love you daddy—you will never be forgotten—Darrylin.

Valhalla
Memorial Park

10621 Victory Boulevard

North Hollywood, California 91601

818-763-9121

 34 11 12 N 118 21 41 W

Maps available in office

Valhalla Memorial Park was founded on 63 acres in the sleepy little town of North Hollywood in 1923 by two Los Angeles financiers, John R. Osborne and C. C. Fitzpatrick. In mythology, Valhalla is the palace of Odin, the Norse god of fallen heroes. The memorial park design of spacious lawns and flat markers was first developed by Forest Lawn Memorial Park, which is just a few miles away. Osborne and Fitzpatrick were great salesmen, so much so that they sold some of the same burial plots up to sixteen times. The pair were convicted of fraud, fined $12,000 each, and sentenced to 10 years in prison, serving only half the time. The State of California took over stewardship of the cemetery until 1950, when the Pierce Brothers purchased it and added it to their chain of cemeteries. In 1958, Texas financier Joseph L. Allbritton purchased the cemetery and immediately sold off 20 acres that had not yet been developed. The cemetery was sold again in 1991 to Service Corporation International, but the Pierce Brothers sign remains.

The entrance to Valhalla was originally through a magnificent rotunda on Hollywood Way, but after the noisy United Airport (now the Bob Hope Burbank-Glendale-Pasadena Airport), with runways only a few steps away, was opened in 1930, a new entrance was created at the corner of Victory and Cahuenga. The cemetery has only a few celebrities, but the rotunda is well worth a visit.

The Portal of the Folded Wings

Shortly after Valhalla was founded, the cemetery commissioned architect Kenneth MacDonald Jr. and sculptor Federico Giorgi to create the Valhalla Memorial Rotunda. MacDonald designed the building in the Churrigueresque style, an architectural type imported from Spain and first seen in the United States at the Panama-California Exposition in San Diego (1915–1916). The rotunda cost $140,000 (about $1.7 Million in 2009 dollars). It was dedicated on March 1, 1925, and almost immediately became a tourist attraction. The rotunda and area around it were hosts to a variety of concerts, radio broadcasts, and public events throughout the 1920s and '30s. Because of the rotunda's proximity to the Burbank airport and Lockheed Aircraft, cemetery employee and aviation enthusiast James Gillette developed a plan to convert the rotunda into a shrine to aviators. His idea reached fruition on December 17, 1953, when the Rotunda was rededicated as The Portal of the Folded Wings—Shrine to Aviation.

The structure, which was already showing signs of age, suffered substantial damage during the 1994 Northridge earthquake. A restoration project restored the shrine to its former glory. It was rededicated for a second time on May 27, 1996, although the full restoration wasn't completed until 2001. From 1996 until 2001, there was a museum next to the portal, but it has closed because of the financial woes of Service Corporation International (SCI). The Portal of the Folded Wings was placed on the National Register of Historic Places on March 18, 1998. A recent addition to the portal is a large-scale model of a Space Shuttle, honoring the crew of the *Challenger* (which exploded shortly after takeoff on January 28, 1986) and the crew of the *Columbia* (which crashed on reentry on February 1, 2003). Individuals interred in The Portal of the Folded Wings are:

※ **Bertrand Blanchard Acosta** (1895–1954), who was a copilot with explorer Admiral Richard Byrd in 1927.

※ **Walter Richard Brookins** (1889–1953), who flew for the Wright brothers.

※ **Mark M. Campbell** (1897–1963), who was a stunt pilot and aircraft designer.

※ **John F. B. Carruthers** (1889 –1960), who was chaplain of the Portal of the Folded Wings and air historian.

※ **Warren Samuel Eaton** (1891–1966), a colonel and early pilot who built airplanes for Lincoln Beachy.

※ **Winfield Bertrum Kinner** (1882–1957), aka Bert Kinner, who built Kinner airplanes (Amelia Earhart flew a Kinner).

❋ **Augustus Roy Knabenshue** (1876–1960), balloon and dirigible pilot who flew in the Dominguez Air Meet in 1910.

❋ **Elizabeth Lippincott McQueen** (1878–1958), who was one of L.A.'s first women pilots.

❋ **John Bevins Moisant** (1868–1910), who won the Statue of Liberty Race in 1910; he was first to carry a passenger across the English Channel.

❋ **Matilde Moisant** (1878–1964), who was the second licensed female pilot in the United States in 1911.

❋ **Hilder Florentina Smith** (1890–1977), who was an aerial acrobat and parachute jumper; she was married to James Floyd Smith.

❋ **James Floyd Smith** (1884–1956), who was a test pilot and instructor for Glenn Martin and a manufacturer of parachutes.

❋ **Carl B. Squier** (1893–1967), a WWI aviator who was a barnstormer, test pilot, and salesman.

❋ **Charles E. Taylor** (1868–1956), a machinist for the Wright brothers who helped design and build the first engine for the Wright Flyer flown at Kitty Hawk.

Gorgeous George

March 21, 1915–December 26, 1963
⊗ **34 11 25 N 118 21 37 W**
Block J (section 9370, lot 4)

George Raymond Wagner was born in Butte, Nebraska. At age 7, his family moved to Houston, Texas, where young George went to school and worked odd jobs to help the family. He found that he was particularly adept at wrestling, and after dropping out of high school, he earned money by wrestling in carnivals. He was discovered by professional wrestling promoter Morris Siegel and won the Northwest Middleweight crown in 1938 followed by the Pacific Coast Light Heavyweight championship the same year. Wagner wasn't particularly big or athletic by modern-day standards, but his 5 foot 9 inch, 215-pound fireplug frame made him hard to take down. However, what really made Wagner special was the persona he developed.

Professional wrestling in the 1930s consisted mostly of a couple of sweaty men trying to tackle and pin each other, a far cry from the twenty-first-century theatrics viewers of cable television are used to. George Warner decide to spice up his appearance by dying his hair platinum and letting it grow long, by arriving in the ring wearing a colorful robe, and by behaving in an effeminate manner. The ensemble caused one announcer to remark "Here comes Gorgeous George," and the name stuck. Gorgeous George played the villain and would cheat whenever possible, which of course riled up the fans. As the years ticked on, he continually refined his act. He sprayed the ring with "Chanel #10" as a disinfectant. "Why be half-safe," he'd say. He also had his own theme music. Gorgeous George even got married in the ring. The stunt was so successful that he and his wife, Betty Hanson, performed the ceremony over and over at different venues.

When television became more mainstream, Gorgeous George was one of the first to take advantage of the medium. It's been said that wrestling programs featuring Gorgeous George were some of the first television programs to make money since they cost next to nothing to produce. Others say that Gorgeous George sold as many television sets as Milton Berle. Even when he was defeated, he turned it into theatrics. On two occasions, he said that if he lost he'd cut off his hair in the ring. He lost. He did. And the fans loved it. Boxer Muhammad Ali and singer James Brown acknowledged that much of their antics were based on tips they got from Gorgeous George. Even Bob Dylan was affected by Gorgeous George. In *The Chronicles: Volume One*, Dylan mentions meeting him: "He winked and seemed to mouth the phrase, 'You're making it come alive.'" I never forgot it. It was all the recognition and encouragement I would need for years."

Bea Benaderet

April 4, 1906–October 13, 1968
❋ **34 11 17 N 118 21 46 W**
Mausoleum of Hope (row C, crypt 34)

Bea Benaderet was born in New York City and raised in San Francisco. She had an infectious voice and landed a number of parts on radio, including appearances on *Fibber McGee and Molly*, *The Jack Benny Program*, *The Great Gildersleeve*, and *Amos 'n Andy*. Her first longtime job was voicing Granny in Tweety Bird cartoons. With the arrival of television, her most regular role was Blanche Morton on the *Burns and Allen* program. Benaderet was considered for the role of Granny in the *Beverly Hillbillies*, but after losing that role to Irene Ryan, she was cast as a spinster neighbor. Soon Benaderet found her most memorable role, Kate Bradley, the owner of the Shady Rest Hotel in *Petticoat Junction*. During the *Petticoat Junction*'s run, Benaderet also was the voice of Betty Rubble in the *Flintstones*, a role she started in 1960. Benaderet fell ill with cancer during the 1967 *Petticoat Junction* season and died of lung cancer the next year. Her husband's last name, Twombley, is the dominant name on the grave marker.

Joe DeRita (the Last Stooge of the Three Stooges)
See page 150.

Nels Nelson (a Munchkin in the *Wizard of Oz*)
See page 142.

Mountain View Cemetery

2400 North Fair Oaks Avenue

Altadena, California 91001

626-794-7133

⊛ 34 11 13 N 118 09 02 W

Maps in office

Mountain View Cemetery is one of the oldest continuously operated cemeteries in the Los Angeles area. Although the various Forest Lawn cemeteries may be the most recognizable burial grounds in Los Angeles, Mountain View just may be one of the most often viewed cemeteries by people who do not live in Los Angeles. Why? Because of its relatively secluded location and its mix of tombstone styles, the cemetery often plays host to film crews who use the cemetery to film dozens of movies, television programs, and commercials every year.

Mountain View was founded in 1882 by prominent Pasadenean Levi W. Giddings and his son, Joshua Reed Giddings. They carved out the land needed for the cemetery (currently about 50 acres) from part of the family's vast property just north of the Pasadena city limits. A significant amount of the impetus for the Giddings to establish the cemetery was the impending sale of property along the Arroyo Seco owned by family friend Colonel Jabez Banbury. The Arroyo Seco land had a small cemetery that contained the remains of Giddings' daughter Laura. In order to assure a permanent resting place for Laura, Mountain View Cemetery was established. The first permanent residents of what was originally named the Pasadena Cemetery were the remains of family members that, like Laura Giddings, were moved from private burials grounds on some of the larger local properties such as the Wrigley estate. The first burial in the cemetery was Mrs. Sophronia Johnson, who was interred on February 6, 1883. Later that year, Colonel Banbury's son Charles, Laura Giddings, and others were removed from the Arroyo Seco property and reinterred. By the end of 1883, Mountain View cemetery had 24 residents.

In 1905, Pasadena passed a law prohibiting burials within the city limits. The removal of remains from the large estates plus the anti-burial law provided an influx of customers for the cemetery and a guaranteed steady stream of clients for

the future. Like many nineteenth-century cemeteries, Mountain View was modeled on the garden cemetery aesthetic, which employs winding roads, lush plantings, and immaculate landscaping to create a pastoral environment meant to soften the impact of death and to encourage visits by the public. Over a century after its founding, Mountain View Cemetery is still owned by descendents of the Giddings family. During the year, the cemetery hosts a number of public events and tours. Among the most popular is the annual Walk Through History program, which occurs in early November.

Across the street on Marengo Avenue is the Mountain View Mausoleum. The Pasadena Mausoleum, which was originally entered from Raymond Avenue, was acquired by Mountain View, and an access road from Mountain View was added. All three burial grounds are grouped under the Mountain View Cemetery name.

Pasadena Mausoleum
✠ 34 11 02 N 118 08 58 W

The Pasadena Mausoleum is a magnificent example of Greek Revival architecture. Its gleaming corridors and stunning stained-glass windows are worth a look while visiting George "Superman" Reeves. This mausoleum is a great example of why cemeteries are America's most unspoiled resource of historic architecture.

Septimus J. Hanna

July 29, 1845–July 23, 1921

✸ 34 11 06 N 118 08 57 W

Plot 1698

The gravestone of Septimus J. Hanna and his wife, Camilla Hanna, has one of the more detailed epitaphs one will ever see. Septimus was one of 10 children born into a very devout Methodist family in Spring Mills, Pennsylvania. At age 18, he enlisted in the Union Army during the waning months of the Civil War. His innate leadership qualities propelled him to the rank of captain despite his young age. After the war, he enrolled in law school and was admitted to the Illinois bar in 1866. His excelling ways continued, and in 1869 at the young age of 23, he was appointed a judge of the county court in Council Bluffs, Iowa. He also met Camilla Turley, who would become his wife. In the next 15 years, he held a number of legal positions, and although not all of them were as judges, he always hung onto the title of Judge.

In 1885, when he was a registrar with the United States Land Office in Leadville, Colorado, he and Camilla were introduced to the new religion—Christian Science, "discovered" by Mary Baker Eddy in 1879—and became converts. Septimus's leadership and take-charge qualities soon had Mary Baker Eddy appointing him as editor of *The Christian Science Journal* (one of many Christian Science publications; the best known being the daily newspaper *The Christian Science Monitor*). Judge Hanna and Camilla soon took over stewardship of *The Christian Science Journal* while also serving a number of other posts within the church, eventually rising to the presidency of the Massachusetts Metaphysical College after Mary Baker Eddy's death in 1910. He held that post until his death in 1921 despite moving to Pasadena in 1911.

Eldridge Cleaver

August 31, 1935–May 1, 1998

✸ 34 11 04 N 118 08 43 W

Valley View Section (look for 4590 painted on the curb about halfway towards an upright gravestone marked Laugharn)

Leroy Eldridge Cleaver had a tormented soul. He was born in Wabbaseka, Arkansas, but grew up in the poverty-stricken Watts section of Los Angeles. He was involved in petty crime as a teenager, then graduated to felonies, and by age 22 became a long-term guest of the State of California after his conviction of assault with the intent to commit murder. While in prison, he penned *Soul on Ice* (published in 1968), one of the more influential tomes championed by the radical elements of the 1960s. Even before *Soul on Ice* was published, he rose to the position of Minister of Information of the radical Black Panther Party. The Panthers' ethos of violence ran contrary to the teachings of Dr. Martin Luther King, who advocated change through nonviolent means. By late 1968, Cleaver was on the run, jumping bail and fleeing first to Algeria and then to France after he was charged with attempted murder following a confrontation with Oakland, California, police.

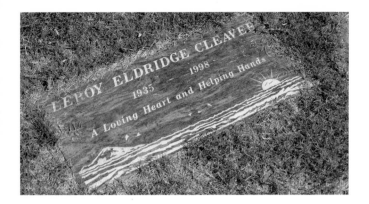

According to his follow-up book, *Soul on Fire* (1975), while in Algeria he was supported by a stipend from the government of North Vietnam. Part of his stipend was spent on training and housing other revolutionaries, many of whom were convicted criminals. He returned to the United States in 1975 after he was able to get his attempted murder charge reduced to a simple assault charge. In the years that followed, he underwent a series of religious conversions, becoming a "born again" Christian, a follower of Reverend Sun Myung Moon, and eventually was baptized into The Church of Jesus Christ of Latter-day Saints (Mormons). Still, his soul was tormented, and in the 1980s, he developed a serious crack cocaine addiction. In the last few years of his life, he kicked the cocaine addiction, became involved in promoting nutrition to conquer addiction, and became a popular talk-radio host in the Miami, Florida, area. He finally succumbed to complications from prostate cancer and died in Pomona, California, at age 62.

George Reeves

January 5, 1914–June 16, 1959

⊛ 34 11 02 N 118 08 58 W (mausoleum entrance)

Pasadena Mausoleum. To find his location, turn left after entering mausoleum. His niche is on the right side, a few feet past a large mirror (which will startle you!) on the left.

The original Superman was only vulnerable to Kryptonite—and his own hand. George Reeves (George Keefer Brewer/George Bessolo) was born in Iowa to Don Brewer and Helen Lescher (birthdate of January 6 on the urn plaque is wrong). Lesher was four months pregnant when the couple married and the couple separated soon after George was born. Helen moved to California where she met and married Frank Bessolo. Young George grew up thinking Frank Bessolo was his biological father (George's biological father never attempted to contact him). When George was a teenager and away visiting relatives, George's mother divorced Frank Bessolo and told George that Frank had committed suicide; thus, secrecy, alienation, and rejection became dominant themes in his life.

George found solace by acting and singing in high school and continued his pursuits while attending Pasadena City College. His acting ability and good looks quickly led to prominent roles at the Pasadena Playhouse and then a minor role as one of Vivien Leigh's promising paramours in *Gone with the Wind*. His screen name in this film is credited as George Reeves.

Reeves had a relatively successful run as a Hollywood star; then in

1951, he starred in the movie *Superman and the Mole Men*. The movie was intended as a pilot for a proposed television program and, owing to the success of the movie, the television series was launched. *The Adventures of Superman* was an immediate hit, and George Reeves became one of the most recognized television stars. The series, which was filmed in color but aired in black and white, lasted until 1957. After the demise of the series, Reeves found it difficult to find interesting roles because of his typecasting as Superman. Stories abound of his unhappiness of never being known for anything other than his role as a superhero, his wild parties, and his longtime affair with a married woman who was the wife of an MGM executive with mob ties. In 1959, the producers of *The Adventures of Superman* decided to go ahead with plans for another season of the series with Reeves reprising his role. He was reportedly happy with the new contract and was looking forward to steady work. Then, on the night of June 15, 1959, he shot himself with a single gunshot wound to the head. Or did he?

The Los Angeles coroner ruled George Reeves' death a suicide, and full-page headlines the next day screamed "TV's Superman Kills Self." There are three versions of what happened that night. The widely accepted suicide version says that George Reeves was despondent and inebriated, and simply killed himself because he was depressed about his career. The second version says that he was accidentally shot by his supposed fiancé, Leonore Lemmon, in an argument. The third (and most widely touted theory) is that Reeves was killed by a hit man hired by Reeves' longtime mistress, Toni Mannix, after he broke up with her. Conspiracy theorists point to the facts that there was no identifiable powder stippling, which would have occurred if Reeves held a gun to his head, that a shell casing was found *under* Reeves' body, and that Toni Mannix confessed to the crime on her deathbed (although she suffered from Alzheimer's disease). Unfortunately, all of the principals have died, and Reeves was cremated, making it unlikely that any new evidence can be uncovered.

Other notables at Mountain View are Civil War Congressional Medal of Honor recipient Milton Lorenzi Haney; sculptor George Baker; novelist Earl Derr Biggers, who created the fictional character Charlie Chan; scientist Richard Phillip Feynman; television and film actress Maudie Merrie Prickett; and seismologist Charles Richter, who coinvented (with Beno Gutenberg) the quintessential earthquake measuring device that bears his name—the Richter magnitude scale. The office staff at the cemetery will happily mark the locations of these famous Californians on a map.

Home of Peace
Memorial Park

4334 Whittier Boulevard

Los Angeles, CA 90023

323-261-6135

⊛ **34 01 25 N 118 10 31 W**

www.homeofpeacememorialpark.com

Closed Saturday

Community Mausoleum
⊛ 34 01 18 N 118 10 31 W

In 1854, the Hebrew Benevolent Society of Los Angeles was formed with the primary purpose of establishing a burial ground for the area's growing Jewish population. A three-acre site near what is now Dodger Stadium was chosen. The cemetery was officially established in 1855, with the first burial occurring in 1858. The care and maintenance of the burial ground was performed by a women's group—the Home of Peace Society. From 1858 until 1902, the Hebrew Benefit Society Burial Ground (known as the Jewish Cemetery) was the only official Jewish cemetery. When the cemetery neared capacity, the Congregation B'nai B'rith looked for a new site and found a 35-acre parcel in East Los Angeles. The remains of the 360 people at the Hebrew Benefit Society Burial Ground were disinterred and moved to the new Home of Peace cemetery. The Home of Peace was the Jewish cemetery of choice in the Los Angeles area until the establishment of Hillside Memorial Park in Culver City in 1941. The reason most folks visit the Home of Peace is to pay their respects to the most beloved of the Three Stooges, Curly Howard (see Reprised in Repose on page 146).

The Home of Peace is well maintained, and its magnificent mausoleum alone makes the cemetery worthy of a visit. Permanent residents of the mausoleum include MGM (Metro-Goldwyn-Mayer) mogul Louis B. Mayer (summer 1884–October 29, 1957), motion picture pioneer and founder of Universal Studios Carl Laemmle (January 17, 1867–September 24, 1939), and Shemp Howard (Samuel Horwitz), one of the Three Stooges (see Reprised in Repose on page 148).

Rabbi Edgar Fogel Magnin
July 1, 1890–July 17, 1984
⊛ 34 01 19 N 118 10 32 W

This granite mausoleum houses the earthly remains of Rabbi Magnin, sometimes called the "Rabbi to the Stars." Edgar Fogel Magnin was born in San Francisco and was a member of the family that founded the Magnin department stores (I. Magnin and Joseph Magnin Co.). Edgar attended the Hebrew Union College in Cincinnati and was ordained in 1914. He became the rabbi of the Congregation B'nai B'rith in 1915, now known as the Wilshire Boulevard Temple, a position he held for 69 years. He actively pursued motion picture and television celebrities and executives, and performed many Hollywood marriages and funerals. He also participated in the inaugural ceremonies of Presidents Richard M. Nixon and Ronald Reagan. Rabbi Magnin was a member of more than 20 local and national organizations, hosted a radio program, gave frequent lectures, and was a liaison between Jewish and Christian communities. During his tenure, his congregation grew from a few hundred to close to 3,000 families. His fundraising abilities were in large part responsible for the construction of the Wilshire Boulevard Temple, which opened in 1929. The temple, which is now designated a historic landmark, has a 100-foot-diameter dome and magnificent murals commissioned by the Warner Brothers. In 1980, the site of the temple was named Edgar F. Magnin Square.

The Warner Brothers' Mausoleums
✳ 34 01 19 N 118 10 31 W

The mausoleum on the left contains the remains of a number of members of the famed Warner Bros. family, most notably the brothers' parents Benjamin Warner (1857–1935) and Pearl Leah Warner (1857–1934) and their son, Samuel Warner (August 10, 1885–October 5, 1927), one of the founders of Warner Bros. (Sam, Harry, Albert, and Jack). Benjamin and Pearl were emigrants from Krasnosielc, Poland, moving first to Baltimore in 1883, then to Ontario, Canada, and then to Youngstown, Ohio. The family changed its name from Eichelbaum to Warner. All of the Warner boys had an entrepreneurial spirit and opened diverse businesses such as a bicycle repair shop, a bowling alley, and a grocery store.

In 1903, the brothers jointly purchased a movie projector and a print of the 10-minute-long film *The Great Train Robbery*. Using the profits from ticket sales, the brothers purchased a movie theater the following year. During the next few years, the brothers singly or as a group made their own films and became involved in film distribution. They moved to Los Angeles in 1918; then in 1923, they officially joined forces and established Warner Bros. Pictures, with Harry as president, Sam and Jack as vice-presidents, and Albert as treasurer.

As with all siblings, certain rivalries and tensions erupted through the years, but collectively the Warner brothers were responsible for many motion picture triumphs and innovations, and the company continues to thrive to this day. Perhaps Warner Bros.' most memorable achievement was the *The Jazz Singer* (1927), where spoken dialogue was used for the first time as part of the action of the film. Although the film was not the first movie with sound, it is widely credited with introducing "talkies."

The most famous occupant of the smaller Warner mausoleum, which is sandwiched between a couple of evergreen trees, is eldest son Harry Warner (December 12, 1881–July 25, 1958). Sharing space in the mausoleum is motion picture director Charles Vidor (July 27, 1900–June 4, 1959), who was married to Dorothy Warner, the daughter of Harry Warner.

Jack Warner
August 2, 1892–September 9, 1978
and
Ann Boyar Warner
December 18, 1907–March 8, 1990
✴ 34 01 20 N 118 10 33 W

Jack Warner and his wife Ann Boyar Warner are buried in the "A" section of the cemetery. Their gravesite consists of a small garden, a fountain, and an underground vault.

Ethelle Rubin
1859-1951
and
William Rubin
1859-1934
✴ 34 01 22 N 118 10 33 W

Certainly the most interesting and creative monument at Home of Peace is the stone tableau marking the graves of William and Ethelle Rubin. The homey ensemble, crafted in granite, consists of two overstuffed chairs and a fireplace.

Within the fireplace are flaming logs topped with two intertwined hearts, presumably symbolizing the enduring and passionate love between Ethelle and William. On the side of the monument is a bronze tablet titled "The Unfinished Fireside," with a detailed explanation of the significance of the dates: 1875, "Romantic Spring of Life"; 1900, "Children and Budding Blossoms"; 1925, "Mellowed with Golden Harmony"; and 1951, "Under God's Sheltering Wings." Above the fireplace is the verse "Good night / our dear ones all / until we meet again."

Los Angeles Pet Memorial Park

5068 Old Scandia Lane

Calabasas, California 91302

818-591-7037

✳ 34 09 23 N 118 39 07 W

www.lapetcemetery.com

One of the most beautifully maintained and sited cemeteries in the Los Angeles area is tucked into a hillside just off the Ventura Freeway in the town of Calabasas. The most interesting aspect of the cemetery is that not a single person is buried there—it is the domain of pets, not people. The Los Angeles Pet Memorial Park is operated by the not-for-profit perpetual care organization S.O.P.H.I.E. Inc. (Save Our Pets' History In Eternity).

The cemetery, which currently encompasses 10 acres, was founded in 1928 by veterinarian Dr. Eugene Jones and Rollins Jones. The Jones family operated the cemetery until 1978, when they donated it to the Los Angeles branch of the SPCA. In order to maintain the cemetery, the SPCA sold off some of the land, which was later developed into light industry and warehousing. Then in the early 1980s, when it looked like the SPCA would have to sell more (or perhaps all) of the land to developers, a group of pet owners got together to figure out a way to save the cemetery.

Members of the group, dubbed S.O.P.H.I.E., journeyed to the state capital in Sacramento and successfully lobbied the state legislature to enact the first-ever law to protect pet cemeteries. Members of the organization continued with their fundraising efforts, closed escrow on September 12, 1986, and formally dedicated the Los Angeles Pet Memorial Park as an endowment care cemetery.

Owing to its Los Angeles location, the cemetery has its own special feel, much of it flavored by the graves of pets owned by celebrities and pets who were celebrities themselves. Cemetery sleuths will find cherished personal pets and pets associated with stars of the silver screen, modern-day movies, and television. There are also graves of pets with special stories like that of "Room 8," a curious cat who is buried beneath one of the few upright markers.

Room 8
✳ 34 09 28 N 118 39 10 W

Forget the swallows returning to Capistrano or the buzzards to Hinckley, Ohio. For the children of the Elysian Heights Elementary School near Dodger Stadium in Los Angeles, the yearly cyclical return was signaled by a grey-and-white alley cat that acquired the moniker of Room 8. The story goes that at the start of the school year in 1952, a cat showed up in room 8 of the school. Nothing particularly unusual in that except the next year he also showed up in room 8 at the beginning of the school year, and the year after that, and the year after that. Soon people took notice of this curious behavior (the cat always disappeared every summer), and local television crews and newspapers started staking out the school, awaiting Room 8's arrival. Apparently relishing the attention, the perennial and oh-so-photogenic feline posed for pictures, appeared in a television documentary *Big Cats, Little Cats*, and even appeared on T-shirts. A story in the children's magazine *My Weekly Reader* yielded 10,000 fan

Kabar, owned by Rudolph Valentino

Bunky, owned by Jean Acker Valentino (Rudolph Valentino's first wife)

letters. Eventually, Room 8 was adopted by a local family, the Nakanos, but still he made the habit of appearing at the start of the school year and disappearing in the summer. When Room 8 died in 1968, after spending 16 school years at Elysian Heights Elementary School, he was interred in the cemetery, complete with a red granite marker and porcelain portrait of the predictable pet. Also part of his gravestone is a 40-line poem detailing his extraordinary life.

Room 8 isn't the only celebrity spending eternity at the cemetery. Among others are Lionel Barrymore's cat Pukie (origin of the unfortunate name, unknown), Lauren Bacall's dog Droopy (1941–1945) (the bronze marker refers to Betty Bacall, which was Lauren's birth name), Rudolph Valentino's dog Kabar, and one of the many dogs who portrayed Pete (commonly pronounced Petey) of the *Our Gang/Little Rascals* comedies. The Los Angeles Pet Memorial Park has been a particularly popular last destination for celebrity horses. Among the equines with the most screen credits and longevity was Smoke, owned by Victor Daniels (aka Chief Thunder Cloud). The palomino was credited in nine films, although he appeared in many more. He was mostly seen in the company of cowboy star Dick Foran, one of the original singing cowboys. Chief Thunder Cloud, who was the original Tonto in the silent film versions of *The Lone Ranger*, used his horse Sunny to portray Tonto's horse, Good Scout (later changed to Scout). Sunny/Good Scout (1925–1952) was laid to rest on a bed of straw next to Smoke. Next to Smoke is the most famous celebrity horse in the cemetery, Hopalong Cassidy's Topper.

Droopy, owned by Lauren (Betty) Bacall

Pete, from *Our Gang/Little Rascals*

Pukie, owned by Lionel Barrymore

Scout

Smoke

Topper

✳ 34 09 26 N 118 39 09 W

Topper was an Arabian white stallion with black ears.
He appeared in 66 movie westerns, including many of
the Hopalong Cassidy westerns from 1935 to 1948,
before moving to television for *The Hopalong Cassidy
Show* from 1949 to 1951. Topper and William Boyd
(Hopalong Cassidy) made numerous public appearances in parades throughout the 1950s.

Tawny

✳ 34 09 28 N 118 39 10 W

Some of the pets at the cemetery are a bit unusual
(as pets anyway). A case in point is Tawny the Lion
(1918–1940), who, according to his marker, was a
gentle king of the jungle who had "malice toward
none." Tawny had his own pet, a tomcat who is
buried with him. The imposing granite stone placed by the duo's owner
reads: "Beloved, always faithful companions of Mary McMellan who
reared them together with loving kindness."

Meatball
✳ 34 09 29 N 118 39 07 W

The cemetery staff is understandably a bit reluctant to reveal the locations of pets of current celebrities because of privacy concerns, but a little walking around will reveal some, including Adam Sandler's dog Meatball, whose memorial brick marker simply reads "Meatball, My First Son."

The Mausoleum
✳ 34 09 29 N 118 39 07 W

The cemetery, of course, is not just about celebrities. Its 40,000-plus interments are mostly just beloved family pets. In keeping with current trends, many of the interments are cremations, and the mausoleum, which was built in 1929, has been recently renovated and expanded to include more niches.

By the end of the twentieth century, the mausoleum had fallen into

The Mausoleum, interior

Showroom

The Mausoleum

Slumber/Viewing Room

disuse and disrepair. Then in 2003, through a fundraising campaign by S.O.P.H.I.E., sufficient donations, much of which was a large bequest by S.O.P.H.I.E. member Margaret S. Carey, allowed for the complete renovation of the mausoleum. The stucco exterior was stripped down to the bricks, then instead of re-stuccoing the surface, the cemetery opted to retain the rustic look of the exposed bricks. There, 453 (12 x12 x 8-inch) red-granite-surfaced niches were added and elegant stained glass windows were installed. The niches sell for $750 to $1,000, depending on location and lettering. Next to the mausoleum is "The Waiting Garden," which has a memorial brick path and Spanish-style tile fountain. Memorial bricks sell for $50 each.

Office and Showroom
34 09 24 N 118 39 04 W

The cemetery office and showroom is well stocked with a variety of caskets, urns, grave markers, books, and other pet-related items. Also located in the building is a slumber room, where pet owners and friends can view their pet and say their final goodbyes.

Thanks to the well-managed endowment fund, the Los Angeles Pet Memorial Park is assured a sunny future. The staff estimates that the cemetery won't reach capacity until 2030 or beyond.

Haunted Mansion— Disneyland

West Ball Road and
   South Disneyland Drive
Anaheim, CA 92802
714-781-7290
   33 48 35 N 117 55 08 W
   (Disneyland)
   33 48 42 N 117 55 19 W
   (Haunted Mansion)
www.disneyland.com

Although Disneyland is in Orange County, it is strongly associated with Los Angeles. Even the "Happiest Place on Earth" has cemeteries. They are found on the grounds of the Haunted Mansion, which is located in Disneyland's New Orleans Square, a paean to the American city most associated with cemeteries. Not counting the tombstones inside the Haunted Mansion, the grounds of the Haunted Mansion sport three tidy cemeteries.

While waiting in line to get in the mansion, guests are treated to a view of New Orleans–style cemetery wall crypts with humorous inscriptions like I. L. Beback, M. T. Tomb, U. R. Gone, I. Truly Departed, and others. Farther down the line and directly in front of the Haunted Mansion is a pet cemetery that was installed in 1993. A number of upright grave markers includes one for a frog, a cat (surrounded by smaller tombstones of five birds), a pig, a skunk, a bat, a snake, a dog, and Fifi the Dog's tombstone,

which is a cross made of bones. Around the side of the Haunted Mansion is the original pet cemetery that was built in the early 1980s.

New Orleans–style Aboveground Crypts

The original pet cemetery, installed in the early 1980s, is located in a seldom-seen area along the side of the Haunted Mansion.

Facing: The pet cemetery in front of the Haunted Mansion was installed in 1993.

Beloved Lilac
"Long on Curiosity . . .
Short on Common Scents 1847."

Buddy
"Our Friend Until the End."

Fi Fi, with a cross made of bones

Old Flybait
"He Croaked August, 9, 1869."

A cat with five birds, who presumably expired before the cat did.

Rosie
"She was a poor little pig, but she bought the farm 1849."

Miss Kitty (from the original pet cemetery)
"After losing eight lives you still had no fear. You caught a snake in your ninth and that's why you're here."

Freddie the Bat, 1847
"We'll miss you."

Reprised in Repose

Nowadays, it seems Tinseltown's stars don't like to share top billing, and even when they do, it is rarely for more than a film or two. However, during the golden ages of film and television, comedic and dramatic duos and ensembles were commonplace. Laurel and Hardy started in silent films and easily transitioned to talkies. Bob Hope, Bing Crosby, and Dorothy Lamour journeyed the world via Hollywood sets in a number of "Road" pictures. Bogie and Bacall steamed their way through noir dramas throughout the 1940s. Martin and Lewis ruled the comedies of the 1950s. And Lucy and Desi dominated the small screen with no small help from Fred and Ethel.

Movies were also populated with a number of large ensemble casts, some assembled for one film, such as the *The Wizard of Oz*, and others for a series of productions, like the *Our Gang/Little Rascals* shorts. Perhaps the greatest ensemble of all time was the wonderfully wacky 1963 film *It's a Mad, Mad, Mad, Mad World*. Essentially every working comedian and some who were extracted from retirement appeared in the three-hour-plus epic madcap extravaganza.

Few of these performers are buried near each other. Notable exceptions are Jack Lemmon and Walter Matthau, who are buried almost shoulder to shoulder in tidy Westwood Village Memorial Park Cemetery. Most are buried hundreds, if not thousands, of miles apart. Here we bring these stars and some lesser lights together again to share the page if not the stage.

The tomb of Douglas Fairbanks Sr. and Jr.
Hollywood Forever Cemetery

STAN LAUREL
1890 – 1965
A MASTER OF COMEDY
HIS GENIUS IN THE ART OF
HUMOR BROUGHT GLADNESS
TO THE WORLD HE LOVED.

Stan Laurel and Oliver Hardy

From the mid-1920s through the late 1940s, Hollywood's most famous comedic duo was Stan Laurel and Oliver Hardy. The first film that the pair appeared together in was in 1920 or 1921 (records are sketchy), a short titled *The Lucky Dog.* They worked in films separately for the Hal Roach Studio for a few years and then appeared in 1927 as Laurel and Hardy for the first time in the 23-minute silent short *Slipping Wives.* Their most notable films were *Sons of the Desert* (1933), *Way Out West* (1937), and *Block-Heads* (1938). They won an Academy Award in 1932 for their 30-minute short *The Music Box*, where they make multiple attempts to negotiate a ridiculously long set of stairs to deliver a piano.

Laurel and Hardy left the Roach Studios in the 1940s and made a number of "B" comedies (so-called because they were poorly funded compared to "A" films and appeared at the bottom of a twin-bill). After World War II, they mostly worked on their stage act and made their last film together, *Atoll K*, in 1950–51. All told, they appeared together in 40 short sound films, 32 short silent films, and 23 feature films. They also appeared in cameo rolls in 11 films.

Stan Laurel
June 16, 1890–February 23, 1965
✸ 34 08 39 N 118 19 03 W
Forest Lawn Memorial Park–Hollywood Hills,
George Washington Section (2nd Terrace, 910)

Stan Laurel was born Arthur Stanley Jefferson in Ulverston, England. His father (also named Arthur) was involved in the entertainment industry as an actor, director, playwright, and general entrepreneur in the theater. He encouraged his son to work in entertainment on the business rather than the acting side. But young Arthur caught the acting bug and worked his way up the ladder, eventually becoming an understudy to Charlie Chaplin. He immigrated to America in 1912 and performed in vaudeville and some small film roles. In 1918, he changed his stage name to Stan Laurel, supposedly at the suggestion of Mae Dahlberg, his vaudeville partner (and common-law wife). She thought Arthur Jefferson was too long. Mae returned to her native Australia in 1925. Laurel would

eventually marry five times, twice to the same woman.

Laurel had small roles in a number of dramatic films, but he hit his stride when he appeared in comedies as a rather inept and befuddled character. When he started appearing with Oliver Hardy, it was a marriage made in Hollywood heaven. There is no record of any significant strife in their relationship (it certainly lasted longer than any of Laurel's marriages), and when Oliver Hardy died in 1956, Stan Laurel was too grief-stricken to attend Hardy's funeral, telling friends that "Babe would understand." For the remaining eight years of his life, he continued working as a writer and not as a performer. He even turned down a role in Stanley Kramer's epic comedy film *It's a Mad, Mad, Mad, Mad World* in 1963 (see page 155). Stan Laurel was given a special Academy Award in 1960 for his contributions to film comedy. In his last years, he busied himself answering fan mail and receiving visitors (his telephone number was listed in the Santa Monica phone book). He died of a heart attack on February 23, 1965, in Santa Monica. His wife Ida, who died in 1966, is memorialized on a plaque directly below his.

Oliver Hardy

January 18, 1892–August 7, 1957
✸ **34 11 22 N 118 21 39 W**
Valhalla Memorial Park, North Hollywood
Garden of Hope (lot 48)

Oliver Hardy was born Norvell Hardy in Harlem, Georgia. He changed his name to Oliver Norvell Hardy in 1910 to honor his father, Oliver, who had died before young Norvell's second birthday. Off-screen his friends called him Babe, supposedly a reference to a friendly barber who would pat Hardy's face with talcum powder and say, "nice-a-baby." Hardy had a natural predilection towards entertainment, working as a projectionist and manager at a movie theater in Milledgeville, Georgia, while he was still a teenager. As he watched the films he was projecting, he decided he could do as good a job or better than the actors. He was a natural talent and soon found himself singing and acting, playing mostly "heavies," due in no small part to his six-foot one-inch, 250-pound-plus frame. Hardy was prolific, appearing in over 250 silent shorts. He moved to Hollywood in 1917 and later that year appeared with a young actor named Stan Laurel in a film titled *The Lucky Dog*. Hardy appeared separately from Laurel in a number of films and then teamed up with Laurel for good in 1927.

Hardy married three times—two short marriages and a long union with script girl Virginia Jones, whom he married in 1937 and who was with him until his death. Although Laurel didn't appear in any films without Hardy after their debut in 1927, Hardy took two small cameo roles. His friend John Wayne asked him to take a small role in *The Fighting Kentuckian* in 1949, and he appeared in *Riding High* with Bing Crosby in 1950. Both roles were encouraged by Laurel, who was battling diabetes. Hardy eventually grew tired of his portly profile, which peaked around 350 pounds. After a heart attack in 1954, he seriously began to take his doctor's advice to lose weight. He went on a crash diet, losing 150 pounds in only a few months. Despite his good intentions, the rapid weight loss was devastating to his health. Friends could barely recognize him; then in August 1956, he had a massive stroke that he never fully recovered from. He suffered two more strokes in the first few days of August 1957, lapsed into a coma, and died on August 7. There are two plaques memorializing Hardy: one is on the wall in the Garden of Hope and a smaller one is a few feet in front of the wall plaque.

The Wizard of Oz

In 1900, writer L. Frank Baum, with the assistance of illustrator W. W. Denslow, penned what has been called the greatest American children's novel, *The Wonderful Wizard of Oz*. Noted scholars and politicos with more than a little creative imagination have found all sorts of veiled references to turn-of-the-century politics. The yellow brick road represented the gold standard. Dorothy's silver slippers (they were changed to ruby for the movie) represented the silver standard. The Tin Man was the dehumanized industrial worker. Politician William Jennings Bryan was the Cowardly Lion, and on and on. Baum said this was all nonsense; he was only "writing entertainment . . . to please the children of today."

In 1903, Baum adapted the book into a Broadway musical, and then film adaptations were made in 1908, 1910, 1914, and 1925. The most memorable rendering of the original book was the 1939 film *The Wizard* of Oz, directed primarily by Victor Fleming. In 1938, MGM bought the rights to the book and began adapting the plot to appeal to a more modern-day audience. Buddy Ebsen (later Jed Clampett on the *Beverly Hillbillies*) was originally cast as the Tin Man but was replaced by Jack Haley after Ebsen became ill from inhaling the aluminum dust used for his makeup. Ray Bolger was cast as the Scarecrow, Bert Lahr signed up to portray the Cowardly Lion, and young Judy Garland was cast as Dorothy. In 2003, the American Film Institute designated the serpent-colored Wicked Witch of the West, portrayed by Margaret Hamilton, as the fourth-greatest movie villain of all time, bested only by Darth Vader, Norman Bates, and Hannibal Lecter.

The movie was a critical if not a financial success, but a reissue of it in 1949 and subsequent airings of it on television starting in 1956 have assured it a firm place as a classic American film.

L. Frank Baum
May 15, 1856–May 5, 1919
✸ 34 07 21 N 118 15 00 W
Forest Lawn Memorial Park–Glendale
Section G (the original cemetery, next to the road)

While Lyman Frank Baum may be best known today as the writer of *The Wonderful Wizard of Oz*, he was a prolific writer, penning 13 sequels to it, 9 other fantasy novels, and numerous other works, including over 72 short stories and 200 poems. Baum was born into a wealthy East Coast family. He was described as a sickly child and, rather than participating in the usual rough-and-tumble boyhood, took to daydreaming and writing. While he was still a teenager, his father bought him a small printing press, and young Frank began publishing journals and directories. He later became involved in theater and in the breeding of fancy poultry, a popular pastime of the well-to-do.

When it came time for Baum to strike out on his own, he moved to South Dakota and opened a general store and then a newspaper, both of which ultimately failed. In 1891, he and his wife, Maud, and their four sons moved to Chicago, where he took a job with the *Evening Post*. In 1897, he wrote a book titled *Mother Goose in Prose*, which was illustrated by Maxfield Parrish; then in 1899, he published *Father Goose, His Story*, with illustrations by W. W. Denslow, which became the best-selling children's book that year. Buoyed by the book's success, Denslow and Baum partnered again in 1900 to publish *The Wonderful Wizard of Oz*. When asked how he came up with the name Oz, Baum said he was looking at a file cabinet that was labeled O–Z. Following the financial success of *The Wonderful Wizard of Oz*, Baum spent the next 20 years riding the roller-coaster of success, failure, and multiple publishers and illustrators, but he always returned to his Oz books. Despite having financial problems at the end of his life (he wisely transferred his assets to his wife), he had a relatively happy life. His quest in life can be best summed up by a quote from the Tin Man: "I shall take the heart . . . for brains do not make one happy, and happiness is the best thing in the world."

Terry the Dog (Toto)
1935–1944
(somewhere underneath) Ventura Freeway, San Fernando Valley

The role of Toto was portrayed by Terry, a female Cairn terrier owned by famous pet wrangler Carl Spitz, a German emigrant who became well known in Hollywood for his ability to train animals with hand signals.

Terry was actually left at the kennel by her owners because of their failed attempts at housetraining her. A true working dog (she earned $125 a week, more than many of the human actors), Terry appeared in a

dozen movies, including *Ready for Love* (1934), *Fury* (1936) with Spencer Tracy, and *Twin Beds* (1942), where she starred with Margaret Hamilton, who also played the Wicked Witch of the West in *The Wizard of Oz*. Terry made numerous public appearances in the role of Toto (her name was eventually changed to Toto). When Terry/Toto died in 1944, she was buried in back of the kennel. The property was later acquired by Cal Trans and was demolished to make way for the Ventura Freeway (U.S. 101).

Carl Spitz (August 26, 1894–September 15, 1976) founded the Hollywood Dog Training School in 1927. Though usually uncredited, he trained dogs that appeared with Shirley Temple in *Bright Eyes* (1934), *The Call of the Wild* (1935), *Robinson Crusoe of Clipper Island* (1936), and *War Dogs* (1942). He worked well into his old age, hiring on as a dog trainer for the 1973 film *The Daring Dobermans*.

Nels P. Nelson (Munchkin)

November 24, 1918–1994

✲ 34 11 26 N 118 21 22 W

Valhalla Memorial Park, North Hollywood

Block IJ (Evergreen) (L-10640, space 3)

Nels P. Nelson was one of over 100 dwarfs who appeared in *The Wizard of Oz*. Although he was uncredited in the film, he capitalized on his Munchkin-ness by appearing as himself in *We're off to See the Munchkins* (1993) and *I Married a Munchkin* (1994). *The Wizard of Oz* was his first documented film role,

and throughout the ensuing decades, he appeared in a number of movies and television programs: as a Finnish camp cook in *Ski Patrol* (1940), as a midget policeman in a *Twilight Zone* episode (1960), and as a character named Audie in a *Bonanza* episode (1963).

The task of assembling the Munchkins fell upon the shoulders of one Baron Leopold Van Singer, who toured Europe with a vaudeville show of midgets. In 1938, MGM contracted with Singer to provide 124 little people for the production. Singer located about 120 little people throughout America, and they began arriving at the MGM studios in Culver City via bus and train. Eventually a few more Munchkin wannabes who lived in Hollywood showed up on the set, and about a dozen children were also signed on. Singer was also responsible for feeding and housing the Munchkins. The dozen or so children who filled out the Munchkin quota were not allowed to mingle with the Munchkins and were not allowed to attend the premier, lest the public become aware that Munchkinland was inhabited by a few faux-Munchkins. As of 2009, there were fewer than 10 of the original 124 Munchkins still living.

There are a number of members of the cast and crew of *The Wizard of Oz* buried in the Los Angeles area. The star of the film, Judy Garland (1922–1969), is buried in Hartsdale, New York.

Jack Haley (The Tin Man)
August 10, 1898–June 6, 1979
Holy Cross Cemetery, Culver City

Clara Blandick (Auntie Em)
June 4, 1881–April 15, 1962
Forest Lawn Memorial Park-Glendale

Pat Walshe
(Nikko, the head winged monkey)
July 26, 1900–December 11, 1991
Westwood Village Memorial Park, Los Angeles

Charley Grapewin (Uncle Henry)
December 20, 1869–February 2, 1956
Forest Lawn Memorial Park-Glendale

Mitchell Lewis
(Captain of the Winkie Guard)
1880–1956
Forest Lawn Memorial Park-Glendale

Billy Rhodes (Munchkin Barrister)
February 1, 1895–July 24, 1967
Holy Cross Cemetery, Culver City

Ray Bolger (The Scarecrow)
January 10, 1904–January 15, 1987
Holy Cross Cemetery, Culver City

The Three Stooges

Although their stage name is the Three Stooges, there were actually six actors who played their roles—or even seven if one counts an actor who was recruited to replace Larry after Larry's death in 1975. Three has long been regarded as a very powerful number, and despite the common saying that three is a crowd, trios have worked well for musketeers, wise men, pigs, bears, tenors, fates, and furies. The original Stooges got their start in 1925 as a vaudeville act called Ted Healy and His Stooges, also known as Ted Healy and His Southern Gentlemen, Ted Healy and His Three Lost Souls, and Ted Healy and His Racketeers. By 1930, the slapstick troupe—featuring Moe Howard, Shemp Howard,

Larry Fine, and Fred Sanborn—gelled in the film *Soup to Nuts* as Ted Healy and His Stooges. Fred Sanborn left the troupe after the film to pursue other interests. By 1932, Shemp was fed up with Healy's abrasiveness and increasing alcoholic behavior, and left the act. Shemp went on to work in a number of Vitaphone comedies.

Shemp's departure left a noticeable void, and Moe suggested that his brother Jerry would make an excellent replacement. Although Jerry's wavy red hair and handlebar mustache made for a visually interesting presence, Healy didn't see the look as being particularly funny. According to the story, Jerry Howard left the room, came back a few minutes later with a shaved head, and the Curly character was born. The characters, including Healy, appeared together and separately in feature films and shorts, making their last film as Ted Healy and His Stooges in 1934. Healy died in 1937 in what is widely regarded as mysterious circumstances, most likely as the result of injuries sustained in a brawl. Later that year, Moe, Larry, and Curly officially became The Three Stooges.

The Three Stooges churned out 190 shorts and five features for Columbia Pictures in the next 23 years for reportedly $7,500 per film divided among the three. Offstage, child-like Curly was the most rambunctious of the trio, eating, drinking, and carousing to excess (some say because of the insecurity he developed over his shaved head). He suffered a debilitating stroke in early 1947, no doubt as a result of his excessive lifestyle. Shemp was recruited to reprise his role and reluctantly agreed to fill in until Curly regained his health. Alas, Jerry Curly Howard never fully recovered, although he did appear briefly in the 1947 film *Hold That Lion* (the only time Moe, Larry, Curly, and Shemp appeared in a film together); Curly died in 1952.

Shemp appeared in 73 Three Stooges shorts and one feature film before he was felled by a heart attack in 1955. Joe Besser was recruited to replace the Shemp character and appeared in 16 shorts. In late December 1957, Columbia Pictures declined to renew the Three Stooges' contract, and Larry, Moe, and Joe were out on the street. Well . . . not exactly. Thanks to syndication by Screen Gems, the Stooges became all the rage for adolescent and preadolescent boys all over America.

Larry and Moe formulated plans to reinvent the Stooges and recruited Joe DeRita to resurrect the role of Curly, now christened "Curly-Joe." The newly formed trio teamed up to do a number of feature films from 1959 to 1965, 41 short comedy skits, and 156 cartoons where they voiced their characters and appeared in a live-action sequence that preceded the animated feature. Their most memorable appearance was a cameo in the 1963 Stanley Kramer film *It's a Mad, Mad, Mad, Mad World*, where they reprised their scene as firemen in the 1932 film *Soup to Nuts*. After Larry Fine died in 1975, Moe recruited Emil Sitka to replace Larry, technically making Emil the last Stooge. Moe died a short time after recruiting Sitka, and although Sitka did appear in a few publicity stills, he never appeared as a Stooge on film.

Moe Howard
June 19, 1897–May 4, 1975
✳ 33 58 48 N 118 23 29 W
Hillside Memorial Park, Culver City; Alcove of Love (farthest section)

Moses Harry Horwitz, who acquired the nickname Moe at an early age, was born in Brooklyn, New York, the fourth of five sons born to Solomon Horwitz and Jennie Gorovitz. He did well in school, gobbling up Horatio Alger books, but developed an early affinity towards acting and often skipped school to watch theater shows. He dropped out of high

school after attending for only two months and got a no-pay job running errands at Vitagraph Studios in Brooklyn. Thanks to his Horatio Alger–inspired assertiveness, he was soon getting bit parts in films. Like most aspiring actors, he held a number of jobs but always continued acting. His break came in 1921 when Ted Healy (aka Charles Earnest Lee Nash) hired Moe as part of his vaudeville show. Healy hired Shemp Howard soon after, followed by Larry Fine in 1925. In 1925, Moe Howard married Helen Schonberger, a union that lasted one month shy of fifty years.

Although the Stooges did not receive royalties for most of their films, Howard invested his money wisely and served as business manager after the Stooges parted ways with Ted Healy. Moe Howard's favorite Stooge comedy was *You Nazty Spy!* a not-so-subtle lampoon of Adolf Hitler, which came out a few months before Charlie Chaplin's *The Great Dictator.* Moe was always looking for ways to keep the Stooges working even when their stars had diminished. Well into the 1960s, the trio made numerous public appearances and cameos on film and television. In 1969 at age 72, Moe proposed a forerunner of today's reality shows by pitching the idea of camera crews following Moe, Larry, and Curly Joe as they toured the country. At age 77, while making plans for another Three Stooges production, he succumbed to lung cancer.

Larry Fine

October 5, 1902–January 24, 1975
✳ **34 07 20 N 118 14 04 W (mausoleum entrance)**
Forest Lawn Memorial Park-Glendale;
Freedom Mausoleum, Sanctuary of Liberation

Larry Fine (Louis Feinberg) was born in Philadelphia, Pennsylvania, to Joseph Feinberg and Fanny Lieberman, who owned a watch repair and jewelry shop. At a young age, Larry was burned with acid that his father used to test gold for purity, and Larry took up the violin and boxing to strengthen the damaged muscles. His pugilistic toughness would serve him well later when he needed to absorb Moe's assaults and the other very physical Stooge comedy. Fine was enjoying modest success as a violinist in vaudeville when he was recruited by Ted Healy. The story goes that during the interview, Larry's hair, which he had dampened, dried oddly, and Healy told him to keep the wacky hairstyle.

In many, but not all, of the Stooges comedies, the Larry character was a middleman or buffer, trying in vain to temper the antics and battering that occurred between Curly and Moe. In real life, Larry was the most socially effervescent of the trio. He and his wife, Mabel, loved to throw parties and spend money as fast as it came in. For the first few years of the couple's marriage, they lived in hotels, first in Atlantic City and later in Hollywood. They finally purchased a house in the Los Feliz district in 1940. After the Three Stooges' relationship with Columbia Pictures was terminated in late 1957, Fine hovered on the brink of bankruptcy, but with the infusion of funds generated by the Stooges' newfound popularity, soon Larry Fine was solvent again. His wife, Mabel, died of a sudden heart attack in 1967, and then he suffered a stroke in 1970 just as the Stooges were planning their reality show *Kook's Tour*. Larry never fully recovered from the stroke and was confined to a wheelchair during his remaining years, which he spent at the Motion Picture Country House retirement community in Woodland Hills.

Curly Howard

October 22, 1903–January 18, 1952
✳ 34 01 15 N 118 10 36 W
Home of Peace Memorial Park, East Los Angeles
Western Jewish Institute Section (row 5, grave 1)

Curly Howard (Jerome Lester Horwitz) was the fifth of five sons born to Solomon Horwitz and Jennie Gorovitz in Brooklyn, New York. Thanks to his position as the youngest child, he acquired the nickname Babe, a name that stuck with him for the rest of his life. According to Moe, the name Curly came from his curly red locks, which he sported prior to shaving his head. He looked up to and admired his older brothers, particularly Moe who, after 12-year-old Jerome accidentally shot himself in the leg while cleaning a rifle, rushed him to the hospital, thereby saving his life. The wound resulted in a slight limp that the Curly character greatly exaggerated.

After following Shemp and Moe around and watching their performances, particularly those as Ted Healy's Stooges, Curly decided the

showbiz life was for him. It seems he had a natural ability for physical comedy, and when Shemp decided to leave Ted Healy's act for greener pastures, Curly was a natural replacement. While it is arguable which of the Stooges is the most famous, there is little doubt that the most mimicked Stooge is Curly. His vocalistic antics—including "woo, woo, woo," "n'gahh," "ruff, ruff," and, most famously, "n'yuk, n'yuk, n'yuk"—have been ritually employed by young males for generations. Indeed, visitors to his grave have spelled out "n'yuk, n'yuk, n'yuk" in pebbles on his gravestone. Curly had a gift for spontaneity, and sometimes a director would just let the cameras roll and see what happened, changing the script to accommodate his antics.

In his personal life, Curly was rather private and shy, that is, until he had a few drinks on board. The drinks led to overindulgence in food, cigars, spending, and then women. It's been said that his biggest indulgences were dogs (he picked up numerous strays) and women (four marriages by the time he died at age 48). His indulgences eventually caught up with him, and with prodding by Moe, Curly checked into a hospital in January 1945, where he was diagnosed with extreme high blood pressure, obesity, and a retinal hemorrhage. He suffered a series of small strokes followed by a massive one in May 1946 and another massive stroke in 1949, which left him partially paralyzed and confined to a wheelchair. His physical and mental health continued to decline until he died of a cerebral hemorrhage at Baldy View Sanitarium in San Gabriel, California.

Shemp Howard
March 4, 1895–November 22, 1955
✳ **34 01 18 N 118 10 31 W (mausoleum entrance)**
Home of Peace Memorial Park, East Los Angeles
(alcove in back left-hand side of the mausoleum)

Shemp Howard (Samuel Horwitz) was born in Brooklyn, New York, the third of five sons born to Solomon Horwitz and Jennie Gorovitz. His nickname, Shemp, was the result of his mother's pronunciation of "Sam" in her thick Jewish Lithuanian accent. Not possessed with anything close to movie star looks, he nonetheless entered show business at an early age, and by the 1920s, he was hired from time to time as part of Ted Healy's boisterous vaudeville act. During one of the performances where Shemp was watching in the audience, Moe, who was in the performance, spotted

him and yelled at him. Shemp yelled back, and the back-and-forth banter between the performers and people in the audience (stooges) became part of the new act, Ted Healy and His Stooges.

After a series of disagreements with Healy, Shemp left to pursue his own acting career. From the early 1930s until he rejoined the Stooges following Curly's stroke in 1946, he appeared in feature films and worked with a number of comics, including Ben Blue, Jack Haley, W. C Fields, and Abbott and Costello. He also appeared in dramatic films as comic relief, including the Charlie Chan and Thin Man murder mysteries. When Curly could no longer work, Shemp reluctantly signed on with The Three Stooges, specifying he would only fill in until Curly came back. Shemp knew that without him or Curly, The Three Stooges couldn't go on, and Moe and Larry would be out of work. Shemp suffered a mild stroke in 1952, but it didn't hamper his performances; then on November 22, 1955, while lighting a cigar in a taxi after a boxing match, he slumped over and died from a massive heart attack.

Joe Besser
August 12, 1907–March 1, 1988
Forest Lawn Memorial Park–Glendale
Dedication Plot (L-4404, space 2A)

Joe Besser was born in St. Louis, Missouri, the ninth child of Jewish immigrants Morris and Fanny Besser. At age 12, he was hired as a "stooge," but as a plant in the audience as part of Howard Thurston's magic act. Throughout the 1930s and '40s, he appeared in a number of Abbot and Costello films as well as Olsen and Johnson Broadway reviews. His character was usually a disagreeable sissy who flew into temper tantrums. He was under contact with Columbia Pictures when Shemp Howard, also under contract at Columbia, died of a sudden heart attack. Although Moe Howard suggested that he and Larry continue on as The Two Stooges, Columbia studio chief Harry Cohn prevailed and hired Joe Besser to replace Shemp.

Rather than adopt the physical comedy of Shemp and Curly, Besser successfully negotiated to keep his submissive whiny character, a move that did not prove popular with most Stooge fans. Joe's time with the Stooges was brief (spring 1956 to the end of 1957, when the Stooges' contract was terminated after the death of Harry Cohn); but, much to Besser's displeasure, his role of Joe eclipsed all of his previous work. He recounted his Stooge identity in his 1984 book titled *Not Just a Stooge* (reissued following his death as *Once a Stooge, Always a Stooge*). Moe asked Besser to join The Three Stooges on a tour in 1958, but he declined, citing the ill health of his wife, who suffered a heart attack in late 1957. That opened the door for the last Stooge, Curly-Joe DeRita.

Curly-Joe DeRita

July 12, 1909–July 3, 1993
❋ **34 11 15 N 118 21 39 W**
Valhalla Memorial Park, North Hollywood
Block D (section 338, lot 19)

Curly-Joe DeRita (Joseph Wardell) was born in Philadelphia, Pennsylvania. His father was a stage technician and his mother was a dancer. After taking his mother's maiden name, DeRita, in the 1920s, he joined the bawdy burlesque circuit. He carved out a career in the 1930s and '40s in burlesque and later performed in USO shows in England and France. Three Stooges director Jules White tried to recruit DeRita after it was clear Curly would not be able to return. DeRita's resemblance to Curly would allow for a relatively easy transition. However, DeRita didn't want to change his on-screen act to be more like Curly and talks broke off.

Then a few years later, after the fifth Stooge, Joe Besser, declined to go on the road with Larry and Moe, DeRita was asked again and was allowed to bring more of his character into the act. DeRita's Curly-Joe was more assertive than the original Curly and considerably more assertive than the Joe Besser character. Curly-Joe, Moe, and Larry did star in some memorable feature films, including *Have Rocket, Will Travel* and *Snow White and the Three Stooges* plus an animated series. Unfortunately, DeRita's burlesque background, Larry and Moe's inability to perform some of their trademark physical antics, and the PTA's (most productions were aimed at children) directive to tone down the violence didn't make for a happy union. After Larry died in January 1975 followed by Moe in May, DeRita attempted to reinvent The Three Stooges with actors Mousie Gardner and Frank Mitchell, but the project never got off the ground, and DeRita retired. He died from complications from diabetes. His epitaph reads, "The Last Stooge."

Our Gang/The Little Rascals

Before there were Mouseketeers, South Park denizens, or a Peanut Gallery, there was the ragtag tribe of children known as *Our Gang* and, later, *The Little Rascals*. Unlike the groomed and polished kids that populate today's children-centric television programs and movies, the kids that inhabited *Our Gang*'s neighborhood were a little rough on the edges. *Our Gang* was conceived in 1922 by comedy producer Hal Roach. His vision was to portray a child's-eye view of the world, largely uninhabited by adults. Roach's free-range children were a mix of boys and girls and even blacks and whites. When adults appeared in the films, they had secondary roles and were quickly disposed of so the kids could continue with their adventures. The children were portrayed in very stereotypical roles. There was the fat kid, a snobbish rich kid, a pretty blond girl, and a mischievous freckled boy. The four black actors were portrayed in what was known as the Hollywood pickaninny style, which today is understandably far from politically correct. Because the films were geared toward children, when the series was packaged for television, many of the episodes were heavily edited for "insensitivity, racism, bad taste, negative stereotypes of women, negative treatment of women and negative stereotypes of Jewish Americans and Asian Americans." Despite the stereotypes, the *Our Gang* casting was groundbreaking, with blacks and whites sharing equal billing. Many publicity stills show blacks and whites together.

The first series of *Our Gang* comedies were silent films. Primary director Robert F. McGowan employed a rather loose directorial style, simply giving the kids a synopsis of the story and then giving direction with a megaphone while the cameras rolled. That approach had to change slightly with the advent of talkies, but the young actors didn't need a lot of rehearsal and studying since most of the films ran only about 10 minutes. Since *Our Gang*'s cast members were a fairly narrow age range, the cast was constantly changing as cast members grew too old to portray children. From *Our Gang*'s first film, *One Terrible Day*, released on September 10, 1922, until *Dancing Romeo* debuted on April 29, 1944, there were 220 *Our Gang* shorts and one feature film, *General Spanky*. A total of 42 children appeared in the films. In 1951, the *Our Gang* shorts were rereleased under the *Little Rascals* name.

The most famous and long-lived *Our Gang* cast member was George (Spanky) McFarland, who joined the cast as a 3-year-old in 1931 and stayed on for another 11 years. McFarland was one of only two *Our Gang* members to receive a star on the Hollywood Walk of Fame; the other was Jackie Cooper. Spanky died of a heart attack on June 30, 1993, and was cremated.

Joe Cobb (The Fat Kid)

November 7, 1916–May 21, 2002

34 07 37 N 118 14 52 W

Forest Lawn Memorial Park–Glendale; Wee Kirk Churchyard (lot 1070, space 3)

Joe Cobb was discovered when he was visiting the Hal Roach Studios in Culver City. His first film was a small role in a 1922 Snub Pollard short titled *A Tough Winter*. Cobb's spherical proportions soon landed him the role of "The Fat Kid" in *Our Gang*. His first role was in *The Big Show*, the 9th *Our Gang* short, which was released in February 1923. He appeared in 86 *Our Gang* shorts until he was let go in 1929 when his weight increased to 120 pounds (after all, he was The Fat Kid). His successor was Norman

"Chubby" Chaney. Cobb continued to act, appearing now and then in *Our Gang* comedies and other films until the early 1940s. Around that time, he got a job as an assembler for North American Aviation. He made an appearance in a 1986 documentary *Classic Comedy Teams*, which had a segment featuring *Our Gang*. He died of natural causes in Santa Ana at age 85.

Carl Switzer (Alfalfa)

August 7, 1927–January 21, 1959
❀ 34 05 20 N 118 19 10 W
Hollywood Forever Cemetery, Los Angeles
Garden of Memory (formerly Section 6) (grave 6, lot 26)

Carl Switzer was born in Paris, Illinois, to Gladys Shanks and her husband G. Frederick Switzer. Both Carl and his older brother, Harold, had a gift for music and acting, and were known to give performances around town. In 1934, the family took a trip to California and toured the Hal Roach Studios. While having lunch at the Our Gang Café, which was open to the public, Carl and Harold gave an impromptu performance that was witnessed by Hal Roach, who liked what he saw and signed

both boys for the *Our Gang* comedies. Their first film was the 1935 short *Beginners Luck*, with Carl playing Alfalfa and Harold playing Deadpan or Slim (the studio had given him two names). Harold was confined to playing small roles, but the Alfalfa character soon rose to the top, replacing Scotty Beckett as Spanky's sidekick. Alfalfa was one of the most recognizable *Our Gang* characters, thanks to his unruly cowlick. Ironically, the recognizability of the Alfalfa character made it difficult for Switzer to get meaningful roles after his departure from *Our Gang*.

When the Alfalfa character was discontinued in 1940, Switzer continued to appear in supporting roles in a number of movies, but he found most of his success when reprising his Alfalfa character. In the early 1950s, he moved to Kansas, where he met and married the daughter of a wealthy owner of grain elevators. The marriage was brief, but according to film critic Leonard Maltin, it produced a son, Lance. Switzer drifted back to California and continued to get small film roles; he also had a business breeding dogs and guiding hunting expeditions. The circumstances of his death have long been controversial. What is known for sure is that he and his friend Jack Piott went to the home of Moses "Bud" Stiltz to collect a small debt. An argument ensued, weapons were brandished (Switzer had a knife; Stiltz had a gun), and Switzer died of a gunshot wound to the groin. There have been at least three versions of the events that led to the gunshot that killed Switzer. Officially, Switzer's death was ruled as justifiable homicide/self-defense. Switzer's gravestone sports an image of *Our Gang* regular Pete the Dog, minus the ring around his eye, which was painted on.

Darla Hood

November 8, 1931–June 13, 1979

✳ 34 05 20 N 118 19 16 W (mausoleum entrance)

Hollywood Forever Cemetery, Los Angeles

Abbey of the Psalms, Sanctuary of Light

It's a bit hard to pin the label of "sex symbol" on a girl whose age is measured in single digits, but if *Our Gang* had one during the mid- to late 1930s, Darla Hood was it. After all, one of her most memorable scenes was when she was 6 years old and sang *I'm in the Mood for Love* in the January 1936 20-minute short *The Pinch Singer*.

Darla Jean Hood was born in Leedey, Oklahoma, to James Hood and Elizabeth Davner. Perceiving her talent at a young age, her mother took her to Oklahoma City for singing and dancing lessons, then to New York City to meet with Joe Rivkin, a casting director for Hal Roach Studios. Rivkin was sold on Darla's talent and sent her to Culver City for a screen test, where she was promptly hired. Her first on-screen role was in the Laurel and Hardy film *The Bohemian Girl*, shot in 1935 and released in 1936. She shot her first *Our Gang* comedy, *Our Gang Follies of 1936*, after *The Bohemian Girl*, but the *Follies* debuted in November 1935. Darla was most often cast as the love interest of Alfalfa, Butch, or Waldo.

After she retired from *Our Gang*, she attended Fairfax High School in Los Angeles, where she organized a singing group with four boys, called the Enchanters. Following high school, she became a regular on a number of television programs, most often on the *Ken Murray Show*. In 1957, she had a hit record titled *I Just Want to Be Free*. Throughout the 1960s and '70s, she continued to work in the entertainment industry, appearing in nightclub acts, guest starring on television shows, often doing recreations of her *Our Gang* character, and finding work doing voiceovers for commercials. In 1979, she was preparing an *Our Gang* reunion the following year and entered the hospital for what was reportedly a minor procedure, contracted hepatitis, and never recovered, dying at age 47.

William "Billie" Thomas (Buckwheat)

March 12, 1931–October 10, 1980
✳ 33 57 49 N 118 20 13 W
Inglewood Park Cemetery, Inglewood
Acacia Slope Plot (lot 773, grave D)

The Buckwheat character has been one of the most controversial characters in the *Our Gang* comedies. Much of the original footage was cut out of the *Our Gang* shorts when it was rereleased as *The Little Rascals* because of the racial stereotyping. However, Thomas vigorously defended his work in the series, noting that Buckwheat and the rest of the black *Our Gang* kids were treated as equals with the white kids. In later life, Thomas became a film technician. He may have left acting but his role as Buckwheat lived on when it was lampooned by Eddie Murphy on *Saturday Night Live*. Later, a man named Bill English claimed to be Buckwheat on a segment of the ABC television newsmagazine *20/20*. English claimed he had been unfairly treated because of his race. The ruse was discovered when George McFarland (Spanky) contacted the network. The *20/20* producer resigned, and William Thomas's son sued ABC.

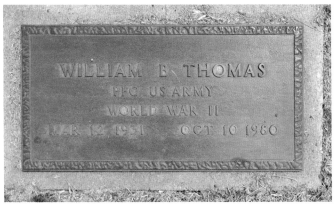

Buckwheat

There are a number of other Rascals buried in the Los Angeles area. Their names, characters and locations follow:

Mathew Beard Jr. (Stymie)
January 1, 1925–January 8, 1981
Evergreen Cemetery, East Los Angeles

Scotty Beckett (Scotty)
October 4, 1929–May 10, 1968
San Fernando Mission Cemetery, Mission Hills

June Marlowe (Miss Crabtree)
November 6, 1903–March 10, 1984
Our Lady of the Angels Cathedral, Los Angeles

Wally Albright (Wally)
September 3, 1925–August 7, 1999
Forest Lawn Memorial Park-Glendale

Pete (pronounced Petey) the Dog
Los Angeles Pet Memorial Park, Calabasas (page 125)

It's a Mad, Mad, Mad, Mad World

Without a doubt, the most incredible comedic ensemble was the cast of characters assembled for Stanley Kramer's zany 1963 extravaganza *It's a Mad, Mad, Mad Mad World*. Virtually every working comedian (71 in all) was enlisted to fill roles from major characters to cameos. The story starts with an automobile driven by "Smiler" Grogan (Jimmy Durante) careening down a mountain road, then spectacularly launching itself off a cliff when Smiler misses a turn. A crowd of other drivers who witnessed the crash gathers at the site and locates Smiler. He tells them about a cache of money he has buried "under the big W" in the town of Santa Rosita. Just before he expires, he kicks a rusty bucket that tumbles down the hill. Then the race is on to find the money. The witnesses eventually break into different groups, and most of the rest of the film centers on their mishaps as they make their way to Santa Rosita to find the Big W.

The original road show version of *It's a Mad, Mad, Mad, Mad World* ran over three hours, including the overture, intermission, and credits. Over the years, there have been a number of versions of the film, some longer, some shorter, and some with extra features. According to Kramer's widow, Karen Sharpe Kramer, the original cut was more that five hours long. *It's a Mad, Mad, Mad, Mad World* was filmed in a process called Ultra Panavision. In the late 1950s and early 1960s, movie studios scrambled to find ways of attracting customers who were being lured away from theaters by television. One of the most common forms of bait was a number of wide-screen formats such as Cinerama, Ultra Panavision, and Super Panavision 70, plus other gimmicks like 3-D and Smell-O-Vision that tiny television sets couldn't offer.

Jimmy Durante ("Smiler" Grogan)

February 10, 1893–January 29, 1980
🜨 33 59 26 N 118 23 15 W
Holy Cross Cemetery, Culver City
Section F (T96, space 6)

James F. "Jimmy" Durante is best known for his large nose (the Great Schnozzola) and his gravely voice. Born in Brooklyn, he dropped out of school in the eighth grade, partly due to being poked fun at because of his big nose and ears. Although he would later become a comedian, because of the abuse he endured as a child, he vowed never to make fun of anyone and instead made fun of himself. That promise served him well. He got his start in a band, then started performing on radio programs, and eventually started acting in films. By the time he appeared in *It's a Mad, Mad, Mad, Mad World*, he had appeared in 48 movies. Most people remember him as a television star and for his particular style of singing, which was more like talking. His renditions of *As Time Goes By* and *Make Someone Happy* were featured in the 1993 Tom Hanks and Meg Ryan movie *Sleepless in Seattle*.

Milton Berle (J. Russell Finch)

July 12, 1908–March 27, 2002
🜨 33 58 43 N 118 23 21 W
Hillside Memorial Park, Culver City
Acacia Gardens (wall MM, crypt 3054)

Milton Berle, born Mendel Berlinger, is one of the few performers who did well in vaudeville, radio, movies (sound and silent), television, and nightclubs, and in comedic and dramatic roles. He is best remembered as being one of the first bona fide television phenomenons. At the time, he was alternately called "Mr. Television" or "Uncle Miltie." In 1948, along with three other rotating hosts of radio's NBC's *Texaco Star Theater*, Berle was asked to reprise that role on television. By the fall of 1948, he became the sole host. Berle's wild on-screen antics on Tuesday nights drew a huge audience (up to an 80 percent share). He was so popular that, reportedly, some restaurants closed during the hour that the *Texaco*

Star Theater aired (many people watched the program through store windows). Berle's performances are also partially credited with doubling the sales of television sets from 1948 to 1949.

When not appearing on television, he played to packed showrooms in Las Vegas and also found time to take large and small movie roles. He was also one of the founders of the Friars Club of Beverly Hills, and it was there that he was able to sprinkle his comedic routines with a bit more salty language, language he rarely used even in his Las Vegas acts. His character in *It's a Mad, Mad, Mad, Mad World* is a pill-popping, henpecked (by his mother-in-law) neurotic.

Dick Shawn (Sylvester Marcus)

December 1, 1923–April 17, 1987
✴ **33 58 47 N 118 23 20 W (mausoleum entrance)**
Hillside Memorial Park, Culver City
Mausoleum, Memorial Court (north wall, crypt 734)

Dick Shawn, born Richard Schulefand in Buffalo, New York, is probably best known for his portrayal of Sylvester Marcus, a hipster/beach bum/momma's boy in *It's a Mad, Mad, Mad, Mad World*. Shawn appeared in over 50 movies and television episodes from the 1950s to his death in 1987. He was known as an unpredictable wild man who pushed the boundaries of comedy. When he did his standup comedy show, he would sometimes emerge from a pile of bricks that was placed on the stage. At a Friar's Club roast, he once fake-vomited (using pea soup) on himself and other speakers on the stage. He died in the same style he entertained—dramatically. When doing a standup bit on surviving a nuclear war, he suddenly collapsed onstage. The audience waited some time, thinking he would get up. Even when someone started performing CPR followed by the arrival of an ambulance, many still thought it was part of his act. His epitaph reads, "The greatest entertainer, father & friend in the whole wide world."

Spencer Tracy (Captain C. G. Culpeper)
April 5, 1900–June 10, 1967
✷ **34 07 21 N 118 14 06 W**
Forest Lawn Memorial Park-Glendale
Garden of Everlasting Peace

There are few actors, past and present, quite like Spencer Tracy. Born into an Irish American family in Milwaukee, Wisconsin, young Spencer displayed an early talent for acting, securing leading roles in college plays. In the early 1920s, he was accepted to the American Academy for the Dramatic Arts in New York City. He acted in Broadway plays and performed stock on the road. In 1930, director John Ford saw one of Tracy's performances and signed him to play opposite Humphrey Bogart in the 1930 film *Up the River.* Tracy moved his family to Hollywood, and he began acting in films at a frantic pace, churning out 25 films in five years. Tracy won a Best Actor Academy Award for his performance in *Captains Courageous* (1937), duplicating his feat in 1938 for *Boys Town.* Although Tracy never won another best actor award, he was nominated seven more times, the last one posthumously for his performance in *Guess Who's Coming to Dinner?*

Tracy is also famously remembered for his 26-year affair with Katherine Hepburn. The on-and-off affair started in 1941 when they were filming *Woman of the Year.* The American Film Institute has ranked Spencer Tracy as the ninth greatest film star of all time. He gave a masterful performance in *It's a Mad, Mad, Mad, Mad World* despite suffering from the ravages of alcoholism and diabetes. In the early 1960s, Tracy also gave two of his best performances in *Inherit the Wind* and *Judgment at Nuremburg,* both under the direction of *It's a Mad, Mad, Mad, Mad World* director Stanley Kramer.

Joe E. Brown (union official)

July 28, 1892 (memorial reads 1891)–July 6, 1973
✻ 34 07 19 N 118 14 51 W
Forest Lawn Memorial Park-Glendale
Sunrise Slope (prominent statue and bench)

Joseph Evans Brown was born in Holgate (near Toledo), Ohio. Naturally athletic, by age 10, and with his parents' approval, he became a member of a traveling circus act, the Five Marvelous Ashtons. As time went on, he incorporated comedy into his act. He returned to Toledo in 1902 and played for amateur and semipro baseball teams. However, show business beckoned, and he soon won a role in the Broadway play *Jim Jam Jems*, which yielded him offers to make movies. His athleticism, comic wit, and likable screen presence made him an instant star, and by the 1930s, his name was appearing above the movie's title on theater marquees. During World War II, he was a frequent USO performer, a role that was

somewhat driven by the death of his son, Captain Don E. Brown, whose plane crashed near Palm Springs.

Joe E. Brown is best known for his cavernous mouth, which he used to great comedic affect, and for his role as Jack Lemmon's suitor in the romantic comedy farce *Some Like it Hot*. In the last scene of the movie when Lemmon reveals that he is actually a man, Brown nonchalantly comments, "Well, nobody's perfect." His monument at Forest Lawn–Glendale was originally constructed for his son. A small bronze medallion at the center of the exedra-like monument reads "The Joe E. Browns/we laugh to win."

Selma Diamond (voice of Ginger Culpeper)

August 5, 1920–May 13, 1985
✻ 33 58 47 N 118 23 20 W
(mausoleum entrance)
Hillside Memorial Park,
Culver City
Courts of the Book, Jacob
(inner court,
wall I, crypt 4004)

Selma Diamond was
known as much for

her raspy voice and writing as she was for her on-screen presence. She was born in Montreal but grew up in Brooklyn, which no doubt influenced her aural elucidations. She wrote for *The Adventures of Ozzie and Harriet, Duffy's Tavern,* and *The Big Show* on the radio before moving to television, where she was one of the original writers for Sid Caesar and Imogene Coca's *Your Show of Shows.* Selma Diamond was, by all accounts, the same on-screen as off. Thus, she was perfect as Selma Hacker, a caustic, chain-smoking, raspy-voiced court matron on the television series *Night Court.*

ZaSu Pitts (switchboard operator)
January 3, 1894–June 7, 1963
⚙ **33 59 25 N 118 23 17 W**
Holy Cross Cemetery, Culver City
St. Ann Section (lot 195, grave 1)

ZaSu Pitts' highly unusual name (pronounced Zay-sue) was the result of a compromise between two relatives, Eliza and Susan, who wanted Nellie Pitts to name her child after them. Not possessed with movie star good looks, young ZaSu nevertheless made a name for herself, appearing in the 1917 film *Little Princess* with Mary Pickford, then as a leading actress in Erich von Stroheim's epic masterpiece *Greed* in 1924. Von Stroheim labeled her as "the greatest dramatic actress." From her first film to *It's a Mad, Mad, Mad, Mad World,* she appeared in over 200 movies. Her greatest success occurred in the 1930s when she played roles that allowed her to transition easily between drama and comedy. In the 1950s, she played a number of comedic sidekicks, most memorably as a shipboard beautician on *The Gale Storm Show,* later retitled *Oh, Susanna.* She was married to John E. Woodall from 1933 until her death in 1963.

Jack Benny (uncredited in movie)
February 14, 1894–December 26, 1974
⚙ **33 58 47 N 118 23 20 W (mausoleum entrance)**
Hillside Memorial Park, Culver City
Mausoleum, Hall of Graciousness (sarcophagus F)

Although Jack Benny, born Benjamin Kubelsky, had an uncredited cameo role as someone driving a Maxwell automobile down the road in the desert in *It's a Mad, Mad, Mad, Mad World*, his star loomed large in Hollywood. Born in Chicago, Benjamin Kubelsky grew up in neighboring Waukegan, Illinois. He was the son of Jewish emigrants from Lithuania. His parents encouraged him to play the violin, a skill he would later craft into his act as a screechy violin player. Luckily he was also a talented violin player and at age 17 was earning $7.50 a week playing at a local vaudeville club. In 1911, he wound up playing at the same vaudeville theater as the Marx Brothers (then called the Marks Brothers) and struck up a friendship with the Marx Brothers' mother, Minnie Palmer, and Zeppo Marx. In the next few years, Benjamin Kubelsky changed his name to Jack Benny, served in World War I (spending most of his time entertaining the troops), and met and married Sadye (Sadie) Marks, who would later change her name to Mary Livingstone. Benny's big break came when he signed on to do the weekly *Canada Dry* [Ginger Ale] *Program*, which eventually became *The Jack Benny Program*, and ran from 1932 to 1948 on NBC radio and then from 1949 to 1955 on CBS radio. The television version of the program ran on CBS from the fall of 1950 until 1965.

Benny's carefully crafted persona was a vain, worrisome skinflint who was forever 39 years old. He was a master of the comedic pause, striking a pose with his hand under his chin and eyes cast upward. His most famous skit involved a man who attempts to rob him. The man says, "Your money or your life!" After a long pause and more egging by the robber, Benny says, "I'm thinking it over." In reality, Jack Benny's real persona was exactly opposite his on-screen character. He was generous, humble, and a surprisingly good musician. This unaffected genuineness made it possible for him to get major personalities on his program such as Humphrey Bogart, Marilyn Monroe, and Walt Disney. He was also one of the few Hollywood types who actively tried to break down racial barriers. Although the Rochester character, played by Eddie Anderson, was a servant, Benny gave him high billing on the program, and Rochester often one-upped the Benny character by pointing out his stinginess and vanity. When Benny died of pancreatic cancer at age 80, Bob Hope

DON KNOTTS
1924 — 2006

delivered his eulogy. As a final tribute, the Jack Benny Middle School in Waukegan, Illinois, adopted the motto "Home of the 39er's." Spending eternity with Benny is his wife of 47 years, Mary Livingstone, who died on June 30, 1983.

Don Knotts (nervous motorist)
July 21, 1924–February 24, 2006
✳ 34 03 30 N 118 26 29 W
Westwood Village Memorial Park, Los Angeles
(near the road in front of the Hammer Mausoleum)

This modest grave marker belongs to a man who always played rather modest characters but with a special comedic flair. Don Knotts rose to prominence as a nervous man in the "Man in the Street" segments on *The Steve Allen Show* and later as Deputy Barney Fife in the long-running *Andy Griffith Show*, a role that earned him five Emmys. In the 1980s, he played landlord Ralph Furley on the television sitcom *Three's Company*. Knotts also appeared in 28 movies, most notably as the lead role in the 1964 live action/animated film *The Incredible Mr. Limpet*.

There are many others who played starring or cameo roles in *It's a Mad, Mad, Mad, Mad World,* spending eternity in the Los Angeles area. Some with more prominent roles follow:

Edie Adams (Monica Crump)
April 16, 1927–October 15, 2008
Forest Lawn Memorial Park–Hollywood Hills, Los Angeles
(also see page 38)

Phil Silvers/Fischl Silver (Otto Meyer)
May 11,1911–November 1, 1985
Mount Sinai Memorial Park, Los Angeles

William Demarest (Aloysius, the Santa Rosita Police Chief)
February 27, 1892–December 27, 1983
Forest Lawn Memorial Park–Glendale

Jim Backus (drunken airplane owner Tyler Fitzgerald)
February 25, 1913–July 3, 1989
Westwood Village Memorial Park, Los Angeles

Buster Keaton (Jimmy the Crook)
October 4, 1895–February 1, 1966
Forest Lawn Memorial Park–Hollywood Hills, Los Angeles
(see page 42)

The Three Stooges
(see page 143-50)

Bonanza

The television program *Bonanza*, which aired on NBC from 1959 to 1973, was the second longest-running television western (*Gunsmoke* ran for 20 seasons). *Bonanza* got its name from a silver ore discovery in Virginia City, Nevada's Comstock Lode called "The Big Bonanza." The original main characters were Ben Cartwright (Lorne Greene) and his three sons: Adam (Pernell Roberts), Little Joe (Michael Landon), and Hoss (Dan Blocker). Each of the sons had a different look and personality, which was explained by Ben Cartwright having had three wives, each of whom died tragically. The three characters' identities and uniqueness was further enhanced by having them wear the same clothing every episode. This also allowed for easy retakes. Their costumes ranged from Adam's all-black tough-guy look to Hoss's white-shirt/ten-gallon hat jovial look.

Of the three men who played Ben Cartwright's sons, Pernell Roberts was the most accomplished actor. As a young actor in 1955, he won a Drama Desk award for his role in an Off-Broadway production of *Macbeth*. Roberts was also the first Bonanza casualty, leaving early in 1965 after complaining about repetitious and uninspired scripts. Next to go was 300-pound Dan Blocker, who died unexpectedly in 1972 of a blood clot after surgery. The show's producers scrambled to find another likeable character to replace Hoss, but the ratings, which were already slipping, continued to plummet, and *Bonanza* expired in January 1973.

Lorne Greene (Ben Cartwright)

February 12, 1915–September 11, 1987

✷ 33 58 47 N 118 23 20 W (mausoleum entrance)

Hillside Memorial Park, Culver City

Courts of the Book, Outer Lawn (block 5, plot 800, grave 8)

Lorne Greene (Lyon Chiam Green) was born in Ottawa, Canada, to Russian-Jewish immigrants. During college, he took a liking to broadcasting on the campus radio station. His baritone voice soon won him a job with the Canadian Broadcasting Corporation (CBC), and not long afterwards, the CBC began touting him as "The Voice of Canada." Since many of his CBC broadcasts were reports from war-torn Europe, he acquired another nickname, "The Voice of Doom." Greene also narrated documentaries and garnered a few roles as supporting characters in films. His first American television role was as Ben Cartwright, the patriarch of the vast Ponderosa on *Bonanza*. During his tenure at *Bonanza* he also recorded a #1 single, a ballad titled *Ringo*. After the demise of *Bonanza*, he reprised his wise father role in the cult series *Battlestar Galactica* (1978–1979) and *Galactica 1980*. His father-figure persona continued as a fire department chief in the short-lived series *Code Red* (1981). A worker to the end, shortly before his death he signed a contract for a *Bonanza* revival.

Michael Landon
(Joseph "Little Joe" Cartwright)

October 31, 1936–July 1, 1991
⊗ **33 58 47 N 118 23 20 W (mausoleum entrance)**
Hillside Memorial Park, Culver City
Mausoleum, Memorial Court, Family Room

Michael Landon (Eugene Maurice Orowitz) was born into a show business family. His father, Eli Orowitz, was a Jewish American theater manager and actor, and his mother was an Irish American Catholic dancer and comedienne. Unfortunately, it was a troubled childhood, peppered with his mother's suicide attempts. However, he persevered and challenged himself with athletics and acting. After changing his name to Landon, which he reportedly picked after browsing through a phone book, he secured a number of acting roles in the mid- to late 1950s, most memorably in the title role of the 1957 teen exploitation film *I Was a Teenage Werewolf*. His rebellious teenage character was a perfect fit for feisty Little Joe in *Bonanza*. When *Bonanza* ended its 14-year-run in 1973, Michael Landon didn't take any time to rest on his laurels. In 1974, he began a nine-year-run starring as Charles Ingalls in the television version of the Laura Ingalls Wilder book *Little House on the Prairie*. Then in 1984, he took the role of Jonathan Smith in the series *Highway to Heaven*, which ran until 1989. Not long after *Highway to Heaven* ended, Landon wrote, produced, directed, and starred in a television movie titled *Us*, which was a pilot for another television series. However, Landon was diagnosed with pancreatic cancer in April 1991 and decided to go public with his illness rather than hide it. He made a number of public appearances as he battled the disease and died less than three months after the initial diagnosis. He is buried a few paces away from his *Bonanza* co-star Lorne Greene.

Dan Blocker (Eric "Hoss" Cartwright)
December 10, 1928–May 13, 1972
Woodmen Cemetery, De Kalb, Texas

Victor Sen Yung (Hop Sing)
October 18, 1915–November 9, 1980
Greenlawn Memorial Park, Colma, California

The "Road" Movies

From 1940 to 1962, Bob Hope, Bing Crosby, and Dorothy Lamour made a series of "Road" movies. The formulaic films were a mixture of comedy, musical interludes, and gentle romance. Starring roles in the first film, *Road to Singapore*, were originally offered to Fred MacMurray and Jack Oakie, and when they declined, to George Burns and Gracie Allen. Allen declined, saying the film was just too silly even for her. Eventually Paramount snagged Hope and Crosby, then signed Dorothy Lamour, who had already done a number of popular films with a South Seas theme. The film was an immediate success, and through the years, seven other Road movies were made, including the *Road to Zanzibar* (1941), *Road to Morocco* (1942), *Road to Utopia* (1946), *Road to Rio* (1947), *Road to Bali* (1952), and *Road to Hong Kong* (1962). An eighth film, *Road to The Fountain of Youth*, was planned for 1977, but Crosby died of a heart attack before formal production began.

All of the films were very loosely scripted, with Hope and Crosby frequently ad-libbing their lines. One of the most unusual cinematic devices employed was the frequent breaking of what is known as the "fourth wall" (traditional theaters have three walls and an invisible fourth wall between the actors and the audience), when Hope speaks directly into the camera and makes comments to the audience. Most of the films were either made by or released by Paramount, and there are a number of jokes and gags that refer to other Paramount actors.

Dorothy Lamour

December 10, 1914–September 22, 1996

✳ 34 08 48 N 118 19 20 W

Forest Lawn Memorial Park–Hollywood Hills, Los Angeles

Enduring Faith (lot 387, space 2)

Dorothy Lamour was born Mary Leta Dorothy Slaton in New Orleans, Louisiana. Her mother married and divorced twice, and Lamour dropped out of high school so she could get a job and earn money. At age 17, she won a Miss New Orleans beauty contest. She and her mother moved to Chicago, where she was discovered employed as an elevator operator. The next couple of years were a whirlwind of radio, singing, and nightclub appearances in Chicago and New York before winding up in Hollywood in 1936. At that time, she was appearing under the last name of Lambour, her mother's second husband. She later changed it to Lamour because of the similarity of it to the French word for love, *l'amour.*

Owing to her exotic looks, she found starring roles in Hollywood almost immediately. In the 1936 Paramount film *The Jungle Princess,* she wore a sexy sarong as Ulah, capitalizing on the popularity of Tarzan films. The role and the sarong catapulted her to stardom, sex symbol, and pretty Polynesian pinup girl. In other films, she was variously cast as Aloma, Lalah, Lona, Luana, Lucia, Lulu, Manuela, Mima, Moana, Marama, Tama, and Tura. Through it all, she maintained a good sense of humor and rather than resenting her role as a sex symbol, she used it to further her career, in particular to raise millions of dollars in war bonds during World War II. From the 1960s until her death at age 81, she continued to act and sing on television, in nightclubs acts and in plays. In 1980, she wrote her road-movie-referenced autobiography, *My Side of the Road.*

Bob Hope

May 29, 1903–July 27, 2003

✳ 34 16 27 N 118 27 43 W

San Fernando Mission Cemetery

15151 San Fernando Mission Boulevard, Mission Hills, California

Bob Hope (Leslie Townes Hope) was born in London, England, the fifth of seven sons of a stonemason and a cleaning woman (and sometime light opera singer). The family immigrated to the United States in 1908 through Ellis Island, then settled in Cleveland, Ohio. Hope worked a variety of jobs and also tried his hand at comedy and dancing. In 1925, silent film comedian Fatty Arbuckle saw him and signed him to Hurley's Jolly Follies. Hope finally settled on comedy, and by 1930, he made it to Hollywood, where he failed his first screen test for Pathé. Nevertheless, he persevered and sustained himself with roles in educational films. His big break came in Paramount's *Big Broadcast of 1938*, where he and

Shirley Ross sang what would become his signature song, "Thanks for the Memory." Hope became one of Paramount's biggest stars in the 1940s and '50s, appearing in over 46 films from 1938 to 1960, including seven "Road" films.

Hope is perhaps better known for his numerous television specials, his longtime support of the military via his USO performances, and his love of golf. In 1960, he founded the Bob Hope Desert Classic, which is held in Palm Springs. In 1995, Hope played in a foursome that included three United States presidents: Bill Clinton, George H. W. Bush, and Gerald R. Ford. Hope has been bestowed a panoply of awards and honors, including the Presidential Medal of Freedom, Honorary Knight Commander of the British Empire, Kennedy Center Honor, Jean Hersholt Humanitarian Award (via the Academy Awards), the Silver Buffalo Award (Boy Scouts of America), and an Honorary Veteran of the United States Armed Forces, bestowed on him by the United States Congress. When Hope celebrated his 100th birthday on May 29, 2003, he joined a rarefied group of people in the entertainment industry that achieved the century mark. Others in the rather exclusive club include George Burns, Adolph Zukor, Irving Berlin, Señor Wences, and Hal Roach.

Harry Lillis "Bing" Crosby

May 3, 1903–October 14, 1977 (birth year on gravestone is wrong)
✳ **33 59 25 N 118 23 15 W**
Holy Cross Cemetery, Culver City
Grotto (L-119, space 1)

Harry Lillis Crosby was born in Tacoma, Washington, the fourth of seven children (five boys and two girls) of Harry Lincoln Crosby and Catherine Helen Harrigan. The family moved to Spokane, Washington, in 1906, and it was there that Harry acquired his nickname Bing. The story goes that the Sunday *Spokesman-Review* newspaper had a regular supplement called The Bingville Bugle that Harry loved to read. The Bingville Bugle was a parody of a hillbilly newspaper. A neighbor, who shared Harry's love of the supplement, started calling Harry "Bingo from Bingsville," and the name simply stuck. In 1917, while working at a local theater, Bing was able to see some well-known entertainers but was absolutely enthralled when he saw Al Jolson perform. Crosby caught the entertainment bug but followed a traditional course for the next couple of years, eventually enrolling at a local college to become a lawyer. While there, he ordered a set of mail-order drums and practiced until he got a spot with a local band. He also discovered he had a knack for singing and soon dropped out of college.

By 1926, he and two friends, Al Rinker and Harry Barris, secured a music contract after catching the eye of one of the most noted bandleaders of the time, Paul Whiteman. Whiteman dubbed the group The Rhythm Boys, and by 1928, The Rhythm Boys and Whiteman's band had a number-one single, *Ol' Man River*. It was clear that the best singer was Crosby, and 10 of the top 50 songs for 1931 featured Bing in either a group or a solo. Crosby's biggest hit was *White Christmas*, which he recorded in 1942. *White Christmas* has sold over 100 million copies, making it the best-selling song of all time.

Crosby was not content to be just a singer. Banking on his star power, he easily negotiated contracts for movies. His first movie appearance was in *The King of Jazz* in 1930. His last was in *That's Entertainment* in 1974. In between, he appeared in or sang in over 72 other movies. Along the way, he sang four Academy Award–winning songs and won a Best Actor Academy Award for *Going My Way* in 1944. Although ranking for most popular star is hard to tabulate accurately, with over one billion in ticket sales Crosby ranks just behind Clark Gable and John Wayne.

Like many celebrities, Crosby's personal life was a bit untidy. He married twice. His first wife, Dixie Lee (1911–1952), died of ovarian cancer compounded by alcoholism. In fact, the 1947 film *Smash-Up: The Story of a Woman*, starring Susan Hayward, is said to have been based on the Crosby-Lee relationship. Two of the four children from that union committed suicide. In 1957 at age 54, he married 24-year-old Katherine Grant. That union produced three children. After Bing's death, his eldest son, Gary, penned a vitriolic biography of Bing Crosby titled *Going My Own Way*, which described Crosby as abusive and remote. Many of the claims in the book have been rebuked by other family members, but still, permanent damage has been done to Crosby's warm and fuzzy family image. Perhaps the best-known aspect of his non-entertainment life was as a golfer. Crosby was a two-handicap player who made a hole-in-one at the 16th hole in Cypress Point. It's been said that he did more than Bobby Jones or Arnold Palmer to popularize the game of golf in America.

Marilyn Monroe
and Joe DiMaggio

Marilyn Monroe and Joe DiMaggio's marriage may have lasted a mere 274 days, but their relationship is the stuff of a Hollywood legend. The story goes that the New York Yankee baseball legend saw a picture of Marilyn with two Chicago White Sox players that was part of a publicity shoot in 1951 and, being a somewhat shy and reserved man, waited until 1952 to ask her out on a date. She was reportedly reluctant to go out with a jock but was soon enthralled with Joltin' Joe, and they eloped on January 14, 1954. The couple went off to Japan to

honeymoon, but after a few days, Monroe was convinced she should go to Korea to entertain the servicemen stationed there. Monroe craved the spotlight, while DiMaggio shunned it. Their relationship went steadily downhill until Monroe filed for divorce for mental cruelty. Although the couple couldn't live together, they continued to love each other. In 1961, when Monroe was locked up in a sanitarium, it was DiMaggio who secured her release; then, according to DiMaggio biographer Maury Allen, on August 1, 1962, DiMaggio asked Monroe to remarry him. Monroe died 4 days later. It was Joe who claimed her body and arranged for her funeral, choosing a small, sleepy cemetery in Westwood for her burial. Thanks to Monroe, Westwood Village Memorial Park has become one of the most popular celebrity burial grounds. For years DiMaggio had a dozen red roses placed on her crypt three times a week.

Marilyn Monroe

June 1, 1926–August 5, 1962

⊛ 34 03 31 N 118 26 26 W

Westwood Village Memorial Park, Los Angeles

Corridor of Memories (crypt 24)

Marilyn Monroe, born Norma Jeane Mortenson but baptized Norma Jeane Baker, was the third child of Gladys Pearl Monroe. Norma Jeane's father was Edward Mortensen. Monroe and Mortensen separated before Norma Jeane was born, but the couple didn't formally divorce until October 15, 1928. Due to her mother's instability, young Norma Jeane was shuttled between a number of foster homes, family friends, and orphanages in Southern California. Her mother would appear periodically, always with the message that Norma Jeane would grow up to be a movie star. In 1942, Gladys Monroe convinced Norma Jeane to marry James Dougherty to avoid being transferred to another orphanage. The marriage lasted until 1946. She had already worked as a part-time model, and now it was time to pursue the big time. Twentieth Century Fox executive Ben Lyon suggested she change her name to Marilyn because Norma Jeane reminded him of actress Marilyn Miller. Then Marilyn took her mother's maiden name, Monroe. The new name, along with straightening her hair and dyeing her brunette locks a golden blond, completed the transformation.

Dubbed by studio execs as the new Jean Harlow, Monroe signed a six-month contract with Columbia Pictures in 1948. Her first roles weren't critically successful, but audiences loved her. A nude photograph of her appeared in the premier issue of *Playboy* magazine in December 1953. To avoid a scandal, she simply admitted she did the photo for money to pay rent. If anything, the photo and another image that graced the cover boosted her career. Her breakthrough film was 1953's *Gentlemen Prefer Blonds*, followed by her critically acclaimed performance in *The Seven Year Itch*, and later *Some Like it Hot*. Marilyn Monroe was often described as fragile, insecure, chronically late, and troublesome on the movie sets. It all came to a head during the filming of John Huston's *The Misfits* in Nevada, with Clark Gable, Montgomery Clift, and Thelma Ritter. Monroe was often late or didn't show up at all. At one point, she was rushed to a hospital in Los Angeles. The months after *The Misfits* finished filming were a whirlwind of misguided adventures, including singing "Happy Birthday" to President Kennedy, a series of nude photographs by photographer Bert Stern, and an increasing dependence on sedatives and sleeping pills. Marilyn was found dead on the morning of August 5, 1962. Her death was ruled a probable suicide, but over the years, there has been much controversy. Theories range from an accidental overdose to murder. We'll probably never know for sure. Marilyn Monroe's crypt is one of the most visited graves in Los Angeles.

The crypt directly to the left of Marilyn Monroe's was purchased by Hugh Hefner in 1992. The crypt directly above Monroe's was purchased from Joe DiMaggio by Richard Freddie Poncher. When Poncher died in 1986, his wife Elsie abided by his wishes and, after the funeral, had the funeral director inter him face down. In August, 2009, in order to raise money to pay off her mortgage, Elsie auctioned off the crypt on eBay. A man from Japan bid $4,602,100, but backed out of the deal after the close of the auction.

Joe DiMaggio

November 25, 1914–March 8, 1999
❀ 37 40 16 N 122 26 44 W
Holy Cross Cemetery, Colma, California
Section I (row 11, area 6/7)

Giuseppe Paolo DiMaggio was the eighth of nine children born to Sicilian emigrants Giuseppe and Rosalie DiMaggio. Soon after Joe's birth, the family moved to San Francisco, where his father made a living as a fisherman. The DiMaggio boys grew up playing sandlot baseball in the heavily Italian North Beach area of San Francisco. Three of the boys, Joe, Dom, and Vince, displayed a real talent for the game and one by one were snapped up by local recruiters to play for minor league teams. In Joe's first game for the San Francisco Seals, he hit a home run in his first at-bat. The next year, he hit safely in 61 consecutive games; the following year, despite nursing a torn ligament, he batted .398. He made his debut as a New York Yankee in 1936, batting ahead of the legendary Lou Gehrig. During DiMaggio's 13-year career with the Yankees, the team won an astounding 10 pennants and 9 World Series. His most memorable feat and a record that most sport commentators say will never be broken was in the 1941 season, when he hit safely in 56 consecutive games. After going hitless in his 57th game, he got hits in the next 16 consecutive games. His on-field performance earned him the titles "Joltin' Joe" and "The Yankee Clipper."

Alas, DiMaggio's public persona of the all All-American boy was far from the truth. He has been described as "cold, tightfisted, uncaring and self-absorbed," caring little about anything except baseball and Joe DiMaggio—and Marilyn Monroe. Although his relationship with Monroe was tortured, she continued to impact his life years after the couple's divorce. Perhaps it is testament to the fickleness of love and lovers. Joe DiMaggio is interred in a single crypt mausoleum in Colma, California, just south of San Francisco. There are often balls, bats, and gloves lovingly placed on his grave. Cemetery officials report that, every now and then, a veiled platinum-haired woman places a single red rose on his grave.

Burns and Allen

One of the most successful and longest-lived comedy duos was husband-and-wife team George Burns and Gracie Allen. They met in 1922 and married in 1926. Like many entertainers, they played the vaudeville circuit; then, when talking pictures entered the scene, they easily got jobs since they were adept at performing onstage. Some of their first roles were as fill-ins, or what was called "disappointment acts," so called because producers and directors were disappointed when an actor got sick or didn't show up and someone else was called up to take their place. Burns and Allen appeared in a number of one-reel Paramount comedies, often written by Burns in the early 1930s. Their breakthrough performance was in a musical comedy, *The Big Broadcast* (1932), where they played themselves, along with other celebrities like Bing Crosby, Kate Smith, The Mills Brothers, and Cab Calloway. By 1934, Burns and Allen had their own radio show, *The Adventures of Gracie*, that became highly rated. The show's title was changed to *The Burns and Allen Show* in 1936 and ran until 1950. It was originally a standard-issue variety show, then moved to a situation comedy format in 1941. The show debuted on CBS television on October 12, 1950, as *The George Burns and Gracie Allen Show*. The couple's comedic banter was a perfect fit for the small tube, and the show was an immediate success. One of the most successful aspects of the show was breaking what is known as the fourth wall (the wall between the audience and the performers), when George would step outside his role and make comments directly to the audience. He first did this by literally stepping to the side and saying something like

"Let's see what Gracie will do now." As the show progressed, the fourth-wall sequences were accomplished by George retreating to his study and turning on the television to see what the show's characters were doing. There was a continuity to the show, accomplished with running gags and themes such as announcer Harry Von Zell getting fired every week and George saying goodnight to Gracie at the end of each show. It is commonly thought that her response was "Goodnight, Gracie," but all she said was "Goodnight." Gracie retired at the end of the 1958 season. Burns tried to do the show the following season with the same cast minus Gracie, but it simply didn't have the same energy and was cancelled after one season.

George Burns

January 20, 1896–March 9, 1996
✪ 34 07 20 N 118 14 04 W (mausoleum entrance)
Forest Lawn Memorial Park-Glendale
Freedom Mausoleum, Sanctuary of Heritage

George Burns (Nathan Birnbaum) was born in New York City to Louis and Dorothy Birnbaum, the ninth of twelve children. His father died of influenza in 1903 when young "Nattie" was seven. To earn money for the struggling family, he took on a number of jobs, most notably as a syrup maker in a candy shop. All in all, not a bad job for a 7-year-old. To pass the time, some of the children who worked at the candy shop sang in harmony, and one time a passerby actually threw a few pennies their way. According to Burns, at that point he said, "The show business life is for me." He quit school in the fourth grade to pursue his goal fulltime, trying his hand at all types of entertainment. Around that time, he also changed his name to George Burns. Accounts differ, but either he chose the name because two popular baseball players were named George Burns, or he combined his brother George's name with the name of the Burns Brothers Coal Company. Burns found modest success, but his real ticket to the road of stardom happened in 1923 when he met a nice Catholic girl—Gracie Allen. Burns often said that he had talent, and that talent was Gracie. Until Gracie's retirement in 1958 and death in 1964, the names Burns and Allen were virtually inseparable.

Although Burns had amassed a small fortune through smart investments and lucrative contracts, show business was the only life he truly enjoyed; and after Gracie's death, he embarked on a solo career. Burns coproduced the television series *No Time for Sergeants*, did a number of nightclub performances with other stars, and spent time in solo appearances. He did always have one companion, even during his solo performances—his ever-present cigar. Burns' star never really faded. In 1975, he got an enormous boost when he won the Best Supporting Actor Academy Award for his performance of aging vaudeville star Al Lewis in *The Sunshine Boys*. All of a sudden, at age 80, George Burns was a big-time movie star. In 1977, Burns secured the role of God in the movie *Oh, God!* and reprised his role of the Almighty in *Oh God! Book Two* (1980) and *Oh, God! You Devil* (1984). Burns continued performing well into his 90s and was scheduled to make a number of appearances celebrating his 100th birthday, but after a fall and then a bout with the flu, he finally succumbed less than two months after his centennial birthday. According to his obituary in the *New York Times*, he was "buried in his best dark blue suit, light blue shirt and red tie along with three cigars in his pocket, his toupee, his watch that Gracie gave him, his ring, and in his pocket, his keys and his wallet with 10 hundred dollar bills, a five and three ones." His estate willed substantial sums to Cedars-Sinai Hospital in Los Angeles and Ben-Gurion University in Israel.

Gracie Allen

July 26, 1895 (or maybe not, see below)–August 27, 1964
✳ **34 07 20 N 118 14 04 W (mausoleum entrance)**
Forest Lawn Memorial Park–Glendale
Freedom Mausoleum, Sanctuary of Heritage

While it's reasonably clear than Grace Allen (Grace Ethel Cecile Rosalie Allen) was born in July in San Francisco to George and Margaret Allen, the year of her birth has been the subject of some discussion. Gracie claimed she was born in 1906, that her birth certificate was destroyed in the 1906 San Francisco earthquake. However, when it was pointed out that she claimed she was born in July and the earthquake occurred in April, she remarked, "Well. It was an awfully big earthquake!" The lettering on her crypt says 1902. However, census records from 1900, indicated Grace Allen was born in 1895, and the 1910 census indicated she was born in 1896. All this is somehow fitting for a woman who made her living playing a scatterbrained housewife. Young Gracie was a talented dancer and performed Irish folk dances with her three sisters as "The Four Colleens." After meeting George Burns, the couple started an act together with Gracie as the "straight man," but soon Burns realized that audiences were laughing more at Gracie, so they switched the roles around to George as the straight man and Gracie as his ditzy girlfriend (later, wife). In real life, Gracie was a bit self-conscious because of a scar on her arm that was the result of a scalding accident as a child, and because she had one green eye and one blue eye. Because of the scars on her arm, she always wore long or three-quarter sleeves, and the three-quarter sleeve became something of a trademark.

In the 1930s, Gracie and George adopted two children. Sandra Jean and Ronald "Ronnie" John were raised as Catholics but told they could make a choice when they got older. Both children tried their hand at acting, with Ronnie having more success. He appeared in a number of Burns and Allen television programs and starred in a 1960–61 television series titled *Happy*. Sandra played in a few episodes with her parents but eventually became a teacher.

The words "Together Again" are lettered on the couple's crypt. The inscription replaced the previous one, "Good Night, Gracie," which appeared on the crypt prior to George's death. Say goodnight, Gracie.

Others who played on the Burns and Allen Show:

Bea Benaderet (Blanche Morton)

April 4, 1906–October 13, 1968
Valhalla Memorial Park, North Hollywood
(see page 109)

Hal March (Harry Morton)

April 22, 1920–January 19, 1970
Hillside Memorial Park, Culver City

Fred Clark (Harry Morton)

March 9, 1914–December 5, 1968
(cremated, ashes scattered at sea)

Harry Von Zell (announcer)

July 11, 1906–November 21, 1981
(cremated, ashes scattered at sea)

Pickfair

✳ **34 05 25 N 118 25 09 W**

When social commentator Will Rogers, who served as honorary mayor of Beverly Hills, was asked what his most important job was, he quipped, "Telling tourists where to find Pickfair," the mansion owned by Hollywood's golden couple Mary Pickford and Douglas Fairbanks Sr. Silent film star Fairbanks purchased the property, which was originally a hunting lodge, for his bride Mary Pickford in 1919. Fairbanks converted it into a 22-room Tudoresque mansion complete with swimming pool, said to be the first private property in Los Angeles to have one. In 1932, fabled architect Wallace Neff was hired to do a major makeover. His creation featured ceiling frescoes, top-of-the-line furnishings, and high-priced art. Pickfair, which was located at 1143 Summit Drive in San Ysidro Canyon, became the destination for Hollywood royalty and other luminaries. To be invited to Pickfair was a sign of acceptance to the higher echelons of Hollywood society. Alas, the usual pressure of a Hollywood marriage and the industry's move to "talkies," which neither actor successfully transitioned to, put a strain on the relationship, and Pickford and Fairbanks divorced in 1936. Pickford wound up with the home and lived there with her third husband Charles "Buddy" Rich until her death in 1979.

850—Residence of Mary Pickford, Beverly Hills, California

Pickford became a recluse, and as her life waned so did the grounds and the condition of Pickfair. In the early 1980s, the property was purchased by Los Angeles Lakers owner Jerry Buss, who subsequently sold it in 1988 to much-maligned actress Pia Zadora (she received two non-coveted Razzies) and husband Meshulam Riklis, who was 32 years her senior when she married him at age 17. The couple, who eventually divorced in 1993, unceremoniously tore down Pickfair (citing termite problems) and built a large mansion with 15 bedrooms and 21 bathrooms on the site. The only thing remaining from the original Pickfair are the large iron gates with the "P" monogram and the short street that leads up to the house: Pickfair Way.

Douglas Fairbanks Sr.

May 23, 1883–December 12, 1939

✳ **34 05 16 N 118 19 02 W**

Hollywood Forever Cemetery, Los Angeles
(reflecting pool to the right of the Cathedral Mausoleum)

Douglas Fairbanks (Douglas Elton Thomas Ulman) was born in Denver, Colorado, to prominent New York attorney Hezekiah Charles Ulman and Ella Adelaide Marsh (it was Ella's third marriage). Ulman abandoned the family when Douglas was five, and he was raised by his mother, taking the last name of his mother's first husband, John Fairbanks.

Young Douglas found an outlet for his feelings of abandonment by taking up acting and, by all accounts, was a natural. Unfortunately, his theatrical bent got him expelled from high school for dressing up some statues, then he was asked to leave college after another prank. He eventually made his way to New York and Broadway. By 1915, he had signed a contract with Triangle Pictures and began working with legendary Hollywood director D. W. Griffith. In 1919, Fairbanks, Griffith, Mary Pickford, and Charlie Chaplin formed United Artists to wrestle control of distribution of their films from the other big studios. Fairbanks' qualities of athleticism and a buoyant on-screen persona were best showcased in a series of "swashbuckling" films, most notably in *The Mark of Zorro* (1920) and *Robin Hood* (1922).

In 1907, he was married to Anna Beth Sully; and in 1916, he began an affair with starlet Mary Pickford, eventually obtaining a divorce from Sully in 1919. Pickford was still married to actor Owen Moore and was concerned that a divorce from Moore and remarriage to Fairbanks would result in bad publicity. However, Fairbanks pressed the issue, and Pickford obtained a quickie Nevada divorce; Fairbanks and Pickford were married on March 28, 1920, in Los Angeles. Rather than become scandalous, the couple became Hollywood royalty, a status they nurtured throughout the 1920s with lavish parties at Pickfair. However, Fairbanks began an affair with Lady Sylvia Ashley in 1933, which led to a divorce from Pickford in 1936 and his subsequent marriage to Ashley later in 1936. Fairbanks dabbled in a few talkies but essentially retired after the 1934 British film *The Private Life of Don Juan*. He began having health problems in the mid-1930s and died of a heart attack in his Santa Monica home. After a funeral at the Wee Kirk o' the Heather Chapel in Forest Lawn–Glendale, his body was placed in a crypt in the Great Mausoleum. Two years later, Lady Ashley commissioned a substantial memorial with a reflecting pool at Hollywood Memorial Park (now Hollywood Forever Cemetery). He shares the space with his son from his marriage to Anna Sully, Douglas Fairbanks Jr. (December 9, 1909–May 7, 2000).

MARY PICKFORD

Mary Pickford

April 8, 1892–May 29, 1979

✳ 34 07 31 N 118 14 23 W

Forest Lawn Memorial Park–Glendale

Garden of Memory (east wall, sculpture with many figures; locked area)

Mary Pickford (Gladys Louise Smith) was born in Toronto, Canada, to John Charles Smith and Charlotte Hennessy. Her alcoholic father left the family when Mary was three, and he died in 1895 of a cerebral hemorrhage. Charlotte was a dancer but earned extra money by taking in boarders. One of the boarders got 7-year-old Mary a bit part in a play, which led to other roles. The whole family (her mother and a younger brother and sister) eventually got involved in various acting roles. In 1907, Mary went to New York City, vowing to get a leading role in a Broadway play that summer or start looking for a new career. She didn't get a lead part but got a supporting role along with a young man named Cecil B. DeMille. She floundered for a couple years, then met D. W. Griffith and began to get film roles. The first roles were just uncredited small parts, but she got moviegoers' attention, and they started looking forward to seeing pictures featuring the "girl with the golden curls."

From the beginning, Pickford was an astute businesswoman who exploited her attributes, demanding more and more creative control and more and more money. The studios were happy to comply, since it seemed every movie she appeared in turned to gold. By 1916, she convinced producer Adolph Zukor to pay her the record-breaking salary of $10,000 a week. By the early 1920s, her movies were grossing over a million dollars each. Like most artists, she eventually needed to stretch her repertoire and image. She did the unthinkable in 1928 when she cut her trademark curls and adopted the bob cut that was popular at the time. Fans shrieked. The *New York Times* featured her haircutting exploit on the front page. Pickford pleased the critics though, and her curl-less role in *Coquette* in 1929 earned her an Academy Award. Pickford didn't transition to the talkies well and retired from acting roles after her last film, *Secrets*, debuted in 1933.

Some say her most notable achievements were where she used her stardom to promote various causes both inside and outside the film industry. The Mary Pickford Institute for Film Education in Los Angeles and the Mary Pickford Theater at the Library of Congress in Washington, D.C., are named after her. In later years, Pickford became more and more reclusive, eventually falling victim to the alcoholism that claimed her father and mother, two siblings, and first husband. With the exception of visits by friend Lillian Gish and stepson Douglas Fairbanks Jr., she only communicated by phone. She didn't even leave Pickfair when she received a Lifetime Achievement Academy Award, preferring to give a brief acceptance speech from Pickfair. The American Film Institute has named Mary Pickford the 24th greatest female American Screen Legend of all time. She succumbed to a cerebral hemorrhage at age 87. Her grave at Forest Lawn–Glendale is behind a locked gate and is available for viewing only by those with a special key.

Cemetery Architecture & Monument Styles

C emeteries are a vast treasure trove of art and architecture. The fact is, cemeteries are America's most unspoiled resource of historic architecture. It would take many hours of strolling around Los Angeles to find the number of styles of architecture that one can find in a few minutes' walk in one of the area's historic cemeteries.

Most cemetery architecture is a mirror of the urban architecture of the time. Gothic cathedrals, Classical Revival city halls, Art Deco theaters, and rustic cast-iron garden furniture can all find their counterpart in the cemetery. And there are some styles of architecture that can be found only in cemeteries; we'll call this architecture "uniquely funerary."

Up until the Reformation in the sixteenth century, most cemeteries consisted primarily of randomly placed headstones. Wealthy folks purchased their way into being buried within the walls and floors of their church. But a series of edicts and a slowdown of church construction during the Reformation essentially put an end to burial within the church. Moneyed types started looking outside the walls of the church to erect a suitable memorial to themselves and their families. Elaborate statuary, tombs, and monuments slowly began to find their way into formerly stark churchyards and city cemeteries. When garden cemeteries with vast landscaped expanses began to be developed in the early nineteenth century, they became a new architectural frontier for America's architects, artists, designers, and builders.

Although the dominant memorial theme in Los Angeles–area cemeteries is the humble flat marker, most major architectural styles are represented in the form of mausoleums, chapels, and monuments. As a rule of thumb, the older the cemetery, the more diverse the architectural style.

Cemetery Architecture

The Tumulus and Grottos

The tumulus is one of mankind's oldest burial monuments, dating back 4,000 to 5,000 years BC. Examples of tumuli can be seen peppering the landscape all over Western Europe. Many large cemeteries will have a tumulus or two. When found in modern American cemeteries, they are often used for members of fraternal societies or military organizations because of their association with warriors. There are also a number of

Facing: Home of Peace Memorial Park, Los Angeles

Grotto, Holy Cross Cemetery, Los Angeles

rock assemblages in cemeteries known as grottos. These tumulus-like monuments are miniature cave-like chapels containing small altars and religious statuary. Grottoes are often seen in large Catholic cemeteries. Most of them are an homage to the most famous grotto in the world, the Grotto of Lourdes in France.

Egyptian Architecture

Egyptian Revival Architecture, Inglewood Park Cemetery, Inglewood

While it's debatable if grottos can really be called architecture, another tomb style of antiquity, Egyptian, is perhaps the most funerary of all architecture. After all, almost all architecture in ancient Egypt had something to do with death and the afterlife. American cemeteries have often had a schizophrenic attitude toward Egyptian Revival architecture because of its pagan roots. However, with the diverse population in the Los Angeles area, there doesn't seem to be any particular aversion to the Egyptian Revival Style.

Egyptian Revival architecture is the easiest architecture to identify. Almost every tomb of that style is adorned with a pair of vulture wings sprouting from a circle (symbolizing the sun) and flanked by twin Egyptian cobras, or asps (symbolizing death). Often a pair of male sphinxes (female sphinxes are Greek) guard the entry to the tomb. Above the entry to the tomb, and usually circling the entire tomb, is an architectural element called a cavetto cornice (flared with curve). Other hallmarks of Egyptian Revival architecture are the tapered (battered) entry and hieroglyphics. Since Egyptian architecture doesn't make use of the strength of arches or tapering columns, its dimensions are quite massive.

To provide strength, the walls of the Egyptian temple-style mausoleums taper in at about 70 degrees.

To soften the pagan demeanor, designers of Egyptian Revival tombs have often added selected Christian symbols and statues in front of or on the tomb and religious-themed stained glass windows.

Obelisk

Another very popular form of Egyptian architecture in the cemetery is the obelisk, which is representative of a ray of sunlight. Obelisks were first seen in Egypt during the time of the Old Kingdom, approximately 2650–2134 BC. The earliest excavation of an obelisk, dated around 2500 BC, is at Abu Ghurob. It was a massive, fairly squat pyramidal structure set upon a high plinth and was the focal point of the sun temple. During the time of the Middle Kingdom, approximately 2040–1640 BC, obelisks made of single slabs of Aswan granite became much taller and slimmer. They

Obelisk, Inglewood Park Cemetery, Inglewood

were typically erected in pairs in front of selected temples as part of a celebration of a Royal Jubilee. The sides of the obelisk were often inscribed, and the pyramidal top was sheathed in gold to radiate the light of the sun.

Classical Architecture

The most common type of cemetery architecture is Classical Revival. It is easy to identify by its columns and column capitals, which are classified into "orders," generally recognized as Doric, Tuscan, Ionic, Corinthian, and Composite. Doric architecture can be divided into Grecian Doric and Roman Doric. The best-known Doric building is the Parthenon, built in Athens around 450 BC. Doric architecture is identified by its tapering fluted columns that rise directly from the base (stylobate) and are crowned by plain capitals. Roman Doric columns are also fluted and crowned by plain capitals, but they have a base. Tuscan architecture is a stripped-down form of Doric architecture. The columns on a Tuscan building are smooth with a notable absence of ornamentation. Ionic architecture, which was developed around 600 BC, is characterized by relatively slender fluted

Greek Revival Architecture, Inglewood Park Cemetery, Inglewood

Classical Revival Architecture, Inglewood Park Cemetery, Inglewood

**Classical Revival Architecture (with Ionic capitals),
Mountain View Cemetery, Altadena**

columns that have a molded base. The column capitals are surmounted by a volute (a spiral scroll-shaped ornament). Architects assign more feminine characteristics to the Ionic form. The most ornamental of all of the orders is Corinthian and its hybrid cousin, Composite. The Corinthian order was an Athenian invention from around 500 BC, but the Romans developed it into its full ornamentation. In pure examples of Corinthian columns, the capitals are carved representations of leaves of the acanthus, one of the plants most often associated with funerary architecture. Its leaves represent overcoming the trials of life and death. Caught up in the allusions to nature in the Corinthian capitals, designers and carvers often added chirping birds, flowers, ferns, and other assorted flora and fauna to the acanthus leaves. When Ionic volutes are added to the design, the capitals officially cross the line from Corinthian to Composite.

Islamic Architecture

Islam originated with the prophet Mohammed, who lived from AD 570–632. During the next few centuries, Islamic architecture developed gradually. The style has never really died out and variations of it continue to be used to this day. Developed in Arabia, the architecture spread to North Africa, Spain, India, and much of the rest of Asia. Even though there was not a very large Islamic population when many of America's large mausoleums were built, many fine examples can be found in our cemeteries. Look for onion domes, horseshoe arches, and surfaces adorned with mosaics, carvings, and inlays.

**Islamic Architecture,
Home of Peace Cemetery, Los Angeles**

Modern Eclecticism, Calvary Cemetery, Los Angeles

Modern Eclecticism

Starting in the 1930s, architectural styles essentially became devoid of ornament. However, clever architects who wanted to put their individualized stamps on their designs often blended some of the emerging styles and sometimes borrowed from the past. This community mausoleum, constructed in 1936, is a blend of the clean lines of Art Deco, Moderne, and Stripped Classicism, and also a nod to Byzantine Revival, as evidenced in the petite domes.

Romanesque Architecture

A few centuries after Byzantine architecture was developed, Romanesque architecture appeared. It is most widely characterized by rounded arches and intricately carved but judiciously used ornament, which is primarily seen on column capitals, around doors and windows, and

Romanesque Architecture, Inglewood Park Cemetery, Inglewood

on moldings. Near the end of the nineteenth century, American architect Henry Hobson Richardson modified the Romanesque form by using rough rather than smooth stones. This "rusticated" Romanesque architecture, now called Richardsonian Romanesque, has a heavy authoritative look. It was widely used in buildings that demanded respect, such as courthouses, schools, churches, and mausoleums. In the cemetery, many Romanesque structures will have a few gothic details such as modestly pointed arches.

Gothic Architecture

Perhaps no style of architecture is so closely associated with cemeteries as Gothic. Its towers, spires, and buttresses are the stuff of ghost stories, dark and stormy nights, and evil sorcerers. The structural advantages of the Gothic style over other types of architecture enabled architects and designers to construct buildings and cathedrals of just about any size that their time and budgets would permit. Because Gothic architecture did not borrow heavily from any of the pagan Classical styles, it

Gothic Architecture, Calvary Cemetery, Los Angeles

is most closely associated with Christianity. It is, in fact, the first purely Christian architecture. The style is easy to identify by its vertical emphasis, pointed arches, and heavily ornamented spires. The All Souls Chapel (pictured) is a sympathetic adaptation of the parochial church in the rural district of Stoke Poges, Buckinghamshire, England.

Uniquely Funerary Hybrid Architecture

Not all architecture fits into the customary architectural styles. Architects often blended totally unrelated styles and sometimes created styles of their own. At the end of the nineteenth century, modern architecture was making its first beginning, but not before an architectural free-for-all

Uniquely Funerary, Calvary Cemetery, Los Angeles

known as Eclecticism burst upon the scene. Nowhere is this architectural grab bag more apparent than in the cemetery. Indeed, many mausoleums and funerary structures are a triumph of form over function. The closest type of architecture that these whimsical structures can be compared to is the "follies" of Victorian architecture. *The Penguin Dictionary of Architecture* defines a folly as "a costly but useless structure built to satisfy the whim of some eccentric and thought to show his folly."

Modern Classicism Architecture

In the early twentieth century, influential architects advocated a return to Classical architecture. Various forms of Classical Revival architecture exist to this day. Some types almost exactly mirror their two-millennium-old cousins, but most are sleeker and more stripped down. In the cemetery, look for buildings that appear to be scaled-back versions of Classical architecture. There is an absence of or a spartan use of ornament. Columns are modestly scaled or engaged (attached to the structure).

Modern Classicism,
Forest Lawn Memorial Park–Glendale

Art Deco Architecture

The Exposition Internationale des Arts Décoratifs et Industriels Modernes, held in Paris in 1925 as a showcase for "new inspiration and real originality,"

Art Deco, Inglewood Park Cemetery, Inglewood

introduced a new architectural and decorative style called Art Deco. This style would soon permeate designs in fabrics, automobiles, appliances, office buildings, and even mausoleums. Architects used a combination of Art Deco and International Style for many mausoleums built in the 1930s. Look for mausoleums that have a streamlined look—not the severe lines we associate with modern architecture, but the softer lines we think of when we think of an appliance such as a toaster in a 1930s kitchen.

Modern Architecture

With the modern age has come a lack of ornament and hard, clean lines. By now, the age of ornament has passed (although, from time to time, a few adventurous architects advocate its return). The range of modern architecture extends from tilt-up concrete buildings to massive glass, steel, and stone structures that look like they belong on a *Star Wars* set. In the cemetery, some of these structures are very utilitarian looking, while others seem to be ready to blast off from Earth. Modern manufacturing techniques have made it fairly easy to build mausoleums that are just about any shape, enabling architects to design some pretty far-out-looking structures. With

Modern,
Inglewood Park Cemetery, Inglewood

the assistance of lasers, elaborate designs can be etched into the surfaces, but there is usually an absence of external ornament since there are few craftspeople today who can execute such fine work.

Monument Styles

Community Mausoleums

Around the beginning of the twentieth century, community mausoleums started springing up in America. Cemeteries were rapidly becoming sculptural and architectural wonderlands, filled with elegant private mausoleums and artistic statuary. The time was ripe to offer aboveground burial to the masses. Cemetery promoters touted aboveground burial in a community

Risen Christ Community Mausoleum,
Holy Cross Cemetery, Culver City

mausoleum as cheaper than a private mausoleum and much easier on the grieving family than having shovelfuls of dirt tossed on loved ones'

Garden Crypts, Valhalla Memorial Park, North Hollywood

remains. The introduction of the outdoor garden crypt in the 1920s lowered costs even more. Because of increasing land prices in the Los Angeles area, community mausoleums have become very popular. Most community mausoleums also have cremation niches; however, some have stand-alone structures used solely for cremains. These buildings are called columbariums.

Garden Crypts

A somewhat more economical alternative to those desiring aboveground burial are garden crypts, which are essentially community mausoleums without a roof or any significant architectural features. They are quite popular in the Los Angeles area, partially because of the relatively benign weather, which makes visitation easy all year round.

Columbariums

Although cremation has been around for eons (ashes to ashes/ dust to dust), it's a rather recent phenomenon in America. However, in the last few decades, cremation has been on the rise. Rather than seeing business go out the window since cremains (cremated remains) can be easily cast to the winds, cemetery owners have adopted the columbarium, which is a building or structure designed to house urns and other receptacles containing cremains. In the multiethnic Los Angeles area, some of the best examples can be seen in cemeteries catering to those whose roots are with Far Eastern cultures and religions. The Vatican lifted the ban on cremation in 1963, and even Catholic cemeteries are building columbariums. Columbariums and niches are often constructed within community mausoleums.

Stupa Columbarium, Hollywood Forever Cemetery, Los Angeles

Scattering Gardens

Catering to the truly economical and environmentally conscious, many cemeteries are also building scattering gardens, which are landscaped areas, often with a memorial wall inscribed with names.

Sarcophagus

Besides mausoleums, the most abundant forms of architecture in the cemetery are the various interpretations of one of the oldest funerary monuments—the sarcophagus. The word "sarcophagus" is derived from combining the Greek words *sarco* (flesh) and *phagus* (eater), literally "a flesh eater," since the earliest types of these burial vessels, according to ancient scholars Theophrastus and Pliny, were made out of Assius stone from Assos in Asia Minor. Because of its caustic properties, this stone reduced the body to bone in a matter of weeks. In reality, most ancient sarcophagi were used to preserve bodies rather than dissolve them, but the term stuck.

Sarcophagus, Evergreen Cemetery, Los Angeles

In its simplest and most utilitarian form, the sarcophagus is a container for the body; but unlike a coffin or casket, it is designed to (more or less) last for eternity. It is rare to find a sarcophagus in a cemetery that actually contains a body, because most are ornamental; the body is usually buried in a vault beneath the sarcophagus. Whether the sarcophagus contains a body or not, it looks like it could contain a body. One of the most popular styles of the sarcophagus is made out of bronze and looks like a heavily decorated claw-foot bathtub with a cover. Most sarcophagi in cemeteries are made of stone. Aside from its need to look like it could house a body, the sarcophagus is really a piece of sculpture. Much of what is included in the broad description of sarcophagi has actually evolved into other forms, and sometimes it's hard to say where the line is between a sarcophagus and an ornamental tomb.

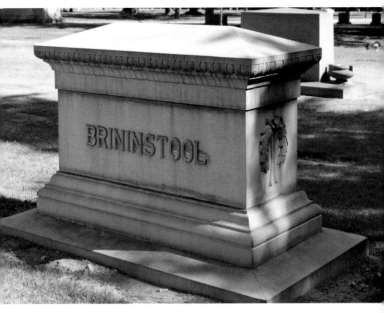

Pedestal Tomb, Mountain View Cemetery, Altadena

Pedestal Tomb

To give sarcophagus-like tombs a more imposing look, designers place them on pedestals. The pedestal tomb also may sport an array of attachments such as urns, draped urns, crosses, and obelisks. Angels and female figures, often depicting one of the Virtues, can be found leaning or standing around the tomb.

Tablet

The most common type of traditional grave marker is the tablet. Ask someone to draw a cemetery, and they'll depict a field jam-packed with stone tablets. They come in all shapes and sizes, from a simple stone to elaborately ornamented stele.

Above: Tablets,
Home of Peace Cemetery, Los Angeles

Right: Scrolled Tablet,
Mountain View Cemetery, Altadena

Zinc Tombstone

One of the most curious types of grave markers is made of metal. The Monumental Bronze Company of Bridgeport, Connecticut, and its subsidiaries manufactured zinc tombstones (which they called white bronze) from the late 1870s until the mid-1930s. The light blue-gray material (or brown if they have not been cleaned) is very similar to the color of gray granite but, unlike granite, is almost impervious to aging. The gravestones were available in a variety of designs and had interchangeable panels. They are fairly easy to spot because of the clean look of the lettering; rapping on them will reveal they are hollow.

Exedrae

These monuments are usually shaped like a curved or rectangular bench, but there are also many examples where the bench is straight.

The ancient Greeks constructed public shelters known as *stoa*. In their simplest form, these structures consisted of a colonnade, walled on one side and roofed. At intervals along these shelters were recesses with seats carved into them. The seating areas were known as *exedrae*, the Greek word for "out of a seat." These structures were frequently used in gymnasiums and public squares. Curved exedrae in public squares were

Above: Exedrae, Forest Lawn Memorial Park-Glendale
Facing: Zinc Tombstone, Mountain View Cemetery, Altadena

favorite gathering spots for philosophers and teachers since their students could gather around the conveniently placed seats. In private homes and gardens, exedrae were also used for entertaining and seating guests.

When designing exedrae for American cemeteries, architects used semicircular, rectangular, and straight forms. Typically, a statue or architectural feature with the family name is at the center of the exedra, and bench seats are on either side, although there are some examples that are simply a bench or have a statue off to the side. The heyday of the exedra was from the late nineteenth century until the 1920s. They are still popular today but are usually used in public areas rather than as monuments for individuals or families.

Treestones

Treestones, or tree stumps, are some of the most curious varieties of funerary art. They were derived from the Victorian rusticity movement, the most common example of which is cast-iron lawn furniture that looks like it's made of twigs. Any decorative art that was popular outside the cemetery in Victorian times eventually made it inside the cemetery. The heyday of treestone monuments was a quarter-century span from the 1880s to around 1905. Where one treestone is seen, often many will be found, suggesting that their popularity may have been tied to a particularly aggressive monument dealer in the area or a ready local supply of limestone, which was the carving material of choice. Treestones could also be ordered from Sears Roebuck, which may explain why they seem to be more popular in the Midwest, where more people read the catalog and became acquainted with the style. Treestones provide a ready canvas for symbols because so much symbolism is closely tied to nature. Treestones are a popular funerary motif for members of the Woodmen of the World (see page 211).

Flat Markers/Pillow Markers

Flat markers have become the dominant grave marker in today's cemeteries. Cemetery explorers deride them as having little artistic or architectural integrity, but cemetery superintendents and groundskeepers love them, touting their easy maintenance and, in the case of bronze, the longevity of the lettering. While most are rather pedestrian, there is still ample room to make a personal statement, especially on some of the larger styles. Pillow markers project slightly above ground level.

JEFF MORRIS
FINE ACTOR
"WEATHER PERMITTING"

Facing: Treestone,
Mountain View Cemetery,
Altadena

Above: Flat Marker (granite)
Westwood Village Memorial Park,
Los Angeles

Right: Flat Marker (bronze)
Westwood Village Memorial Park,
Los Angeles

Secret Societies, Clubs & Organizations

We are a nation of joiners. Sociologists say that we humans are herd animals; if enough of us are thrown together for any length of time, sooner or later we'll form a club or start a competition and appoint leaders. We do this for companionship as well as for protection and security. Many of us belong to some club or organization, whether it's the PTA, Rotary, or a softball team. Nowadays, however, most of us have little if any contact with so-called secret societies. At most, we'll recall seeing men in funny hats, skittering along in parades in miniature cars (Shriners) or see an emblem on a sign welcoming us to a town. We may have heard of the Masons or Odd Fellows, but we really aren't sure what they are. However, if we dig just a bit into our personal genealogy it's likely one or more of our grandparents or great-grandparents was a member of a secret society. Baby boomers may recall seeing episodes of *The Honeymooners*, where Ed Norton and Ralph Kramden, outfitted in their International Order of Loyal Raccoon regalia, trundled off to the Lodge (Kramden was the treasurer), or their African-American counterparts Amos Jones and Andy Brown shown being squeezed by the Kingfish in *Amos 'n' Andy* to participate in one of his schemes as the Great Supreme Kingfish, the leader of Mystic Knights of the Sea.

We like to poke fun at the antics, secret handshakes, and initiation ceremonies, but the truth is, these organizations were very powerful social and political forces just a few decades ago. A presidential candidate had a hard time getting elected without the endorsement of the Grand Army of the Republic. Many of the Founding Fathers of the

George Washington in Masonic regalia

United States, including our first president, George Washington, were Freemasons. The organizations were so powerful that many religious organizations railed against them, saying the secret aspect of them was the work of the devil. Members of the Catholic Church were forbidden to join secret societies, although the Church did allow participation in the Knights of Columbus.

A Dictionary of Secret and Other Societies, edited by Arthur Preuss and published in 1924, lists hundreds of societies that Catholics were forbidden to join. The book also provides statistics on various organizations. The Freemasons, the largest organization, had over 2.8 million members. Even lesser known organizations like the Improved Order of Redmen, which professed to follow the ways of Native Americans (although Native Americans were excluded from membership), had over a half million members. The heyday of the secret societies and clubs was in the years after the Civil War until the Great Depression. Many were born in the economically depressing times right after the Civil War, when individuals grouped together to provide companionship and security (many had health and life/death insurance benefits). Membership declined rapidly during the Great Depression of the 1930s, when the government stepped in to provide many of the social welfare benefits the secret societies provided.

There were also a number a number of African-American secret societies, many modeled on the structure of their Anglo-American counterparts and some directly copying the rituals and symbols of the Anglo-American societies (most societies neglected to copyright or trademark their symbols, making them available to all). The African-American secret societies were even more of a threat to churches since they drew what disposable income African-Americans had away from churches and towards the secret societies. The September 1890 issue of *The American Missionary* makes its case by describing the siphoning off of funds by the secret societies: "We unite with the *Congregationalist* and other influential religious journals in deprecating the increase and the dominating influence of secret societies. We recognize the evil especially among the colored people of the South, to whom the tinsel, the parades the ceremonies and the secrecy of these orders are very attractive. In most cases, these people spend time and money that are needed for their families and for the support of their churches; and the danger that the lodge usurp the place in their confidence that is due God and his ordinances. The evil grows, and where is the remedy? This Association uses all the legitimate influence it can exert to discourage secret societies in its schools and churches in the South."

Anglo members of secret societies fared no better in the eyes of some religious writers. In a lengthy discourse published in 1867 titled *Secret Societies: A Discussion of Their Character and Claims*, author Rev. David MacDill (among others) writes: "'I am afraid of these secret societies; they have sucked the spirituality out of all the members in our church who have joined them.' Young, promising Christians have often been blighted by them. The fervor of piety, interest in the church and its work, interest in Christ and his people, interest in God's Word and Spirit, all the various elements of an earnest life of faith and heavenly-mindedness have been blighted in these lodges."

Conspiracy theorists love to point to George Washington's Masonic background, citing the Freemasons' input on the layout of Washington, D.C., its influence in politics, and its mysterious symbols on the dollar bill. What is known for sure is that Washington was a Freemason, as were 33 of his generals, the Marquis de Lafayette, Ethan Allen, Benjamin Franklin, John Hancock, John Paul Jones, Paul Revere, 10 signers of the Articles of Confederation, 9 signers of the Declaration of Independence, and 13 signers of the Constitution.

The population boom in Los Angeles didn't occur until the early twentieth century, which was after many of the societies were established. However, many immigrants to Los Angeles brought their ties to organizations with them. Owing to the diversity of the area, a number of organizations sprang up that catered to particular ethnic and racial groups. Although many of the organizations are now defunct, a surprising number are still active. The best place to find evidence of both the active and extinct societies is in the cemeteries. You'll probably find entire sections devoted to some of the larger organizations, like the American Legion, Grand Army of the Republic, Freemasons, Elks, and Odd Fellows. In Los Angeles County, there are some smaller cemeteries devoted to only members of specific organizations.

✺ The Grand Army of the Republic (GAR)

The GAR was an organization with built-in extinction, since membership was limited to honorably discharged veterans of the Union Army, Navy, Marine Corps, or Revenue Cutter Service who had served between April 12, 1861, and April 9, 1865. Benjamin F. Stephenson founded it in Decatur, Illinois, on April 6, 1866. Many of the ceremonies and rituals of the GAR were based on Masonic principles, including the infamous "black ball" method of voting, except the GAR required more than one black ball to be denied membership. Although California was not directly engaged in the Civil War, many veterans moved there after the war, and GAR chapters were established. Some of those chapters purchased space in cemeteries and set aside burial plots for members. The GAR sections are often marked with a substantial monument.

The main activities of the GAR were to provide companionship through organized Encampments and, more importantly, to establish soldiers' homes, and to lobby for soldiers' pensions. The organization grew to 409,000 members by 1890 and was a political force to be reckoned with. Five U.S. presidents were GAR members, and any Republican candidate who had any hope of becoming president needed an endorsement of the GAR. This organization was also instrumental in establishing Memorial Day, May 30, as a national holiday and day of remembrance.

Alas, the GAR is no more. The final Encampment of the Grand Army of the Republic was held in Indianapolis, Indiana, in 1949, and the last member, Albert Woolson, died in 1956 at the age of 109 years.

In 1881, the GAR formed the Sons of Veterans of the United States (SV), better known as the Sons of Union Veterans of the Civil War (SUVCW). There is also a women's auxiliary, the Daughters of Union Veterans of the Civil War (DUV or DUVCW). Both organizations are still active today.

✺ Woman's Relief Corps (WRC)
Ladies of the Grand Army of the Republic (LGAR)
Loyal Ladies League (LLL)

The Woman's Relief Corps was the official female auxiliary of the Grand Army of the Republic (GAR). The organization was founded in July 1883

Woman's Relief Corps

in Denver, Colorado. On gravestones, the emblem is a Maltese cross with the letters W, R, and C embossed on three arms or the cross. The monogram is an abbreviation of the Woman's Relief Corps badge, which is a Maltese cross that displays "Womans" on the left arm, "Relief" on the top arm, "Corps" on the right arm, and "1883" (the year of their incorporation) on the bottom. In the center of the emblem is a scene with a Goddess of Liberty, a soldier ("fraternity with the GAR"), a boy ("youth, strength and the future of the Nation"), a woman ("motherhood, mercy, kindness and charity"), and a child ("the hope of the world who will be taught the virtues of loyalty to the nation's laws, and pass on the teachings of freedom and justice to the unborn generations to follow"). Emblems and badges also contain the letters F, C, and L, which signify Fraternity, Charity and Loyalty. The organization is still active today, concerning itself mostly with helping veterans, although it is far from its peak of 225,000 members in 1923. Membership is open to all women who pledge loyalty to the United States.

Another organization, the Ladies of the Grand Army of the Republic (LGAR), which was originally called the Loyal Ladies League, has a friendly rivalry with the Woman's Relief Corps. It accepts only blood relatives of honorably discharged Union soldiers, sailors, and Marine or Army nurses who served during the Civil War. The WRC narrowly beat out the LGAR as the *official* auxiliary to the GAR in an 1883 convention held in Denver of all auxiliaries to the GAR. Still active today, the LGAR claimed over 60,000 members in 1910. The LGAR and the WRC share the Fraternity, Charity, Loyalty motto, although the Web page for the LGAR clearly states that "the Loyal Ladies League was the first love of the GAR." The LGAR also claims to be the oldest women's hereditary organization in the United States.

✺ Women's Christian Temperance Union (WCTU)

The Women's Christian Temperance Union was organized in the summer of 1874 in Chautauqua, New York, in response to the perceived ravages alcohol was having on individuals and families. It was an offshoot of the Women's Crusade, which was organized in 1873. The organization, which is still quite active today, preaches total abstinence from alcohol and temperance in all things. Its definition of temperance is derived from a quote from the Greek philosopher Xenophone, circa 400 BC: "moderation

in all things healthful; total abstinence in all things harmful." Although most people define temperance as abstinence, The Order of Temperance founded by the Holy Roman Empire's Duke of Hesse in 1600 had a different opinion of what constituted temperance and limited its knights to no more than "seven goblets of wine at a meal and not more than twice a day."

The WCTU uses a white bow to signify Purity. The organization's "watchwords" are "Agitate, Educate, Legislate." The WCTU was kicked into high gear when Frances E. Willard became president in 1879. Her influence went beyond temperance, and she was a vigorous advocate for many women's issues, in particular as a suffragist. The WCTU lobbied strongly and was influential in including rights for women in the interpretation of the Fourteenth Amendment to the Constitution.

⊛ Brotherhood of Locomotive Firemen (B of LF)
Brotherhood of Railroad Trainmen (B of RT)

The Brotherhood of Locomotive Firemen was one of many railroad unions of the 1800s. The organization was founded on December 1, 1873, at Port Jervis, New York. Like most organizations,

Railroad Organizations

insurance benefits were the primary incentive for membership, but by the late nineteenth century, "The Brotherhood" had branched out into labor-management relations. The organization changed its name to the Brotherhood of Locomotive Firemen and Enginemen (BLF & E), which enabled engineers to join. In 1969, the union merged with the Order of Railway Conductors and Brakemen (ORC & B), the Brotherhood of Railroad Trainmen (B of RT), and the Switchmen's Union of North America (SU of NA or SU) to form the United Transportation Union (UTU). As of 2009, the United Transportation Union has about 125,000 members.

⊛ Young Men's Christian Association (YMCA)

The Young Men's Christian Association, often known simply as the "Y," was founded in London, England, in 1844 by George Williams, who noted that many young men who came to London to work were forced into living in less-than-desirable conditions. His intent in organizing the YMCA was to open a safe, clean haven for all Christian men, regardless of race, sect, or nationality. Initially, the YMCA was open to women and children, but after the Young Women's Christian Association (YWCA) was founded in 1855, most women drifted into that organization. The YMCA has become a worldwide organization and has about 45 million members. (Despite its size, many people are most familiar with the name YMCA when associated with the 1978 song by the Village People, "Y.M.C.A.") The YMCA symbol is an inverted triangle. The three sides represent the YMCA mission to "build a healthy SPIRIT, MIND and BODY for all."

⊛ Gold Star Mothers (GSM)
American Gold Star Mothers (AGSM)

Gold Star mothers was founded in 1918 by Grace Darling Seibold of Washington, D.C. Seibold had lost a son in aerial combat over France during World War I and wanted a lasting way to honor his memory. On July 4, 1928, the Gold Star Mothers became a national organization. The name came from the tradition of hanging a banner known as a "Service Flag" in their window, noting members of the family who were serving in the military. A blue star signified a living serviceman and a gold star signified one who had died in service to his country. To qualify for a Gold Star, a mother must have lost a son or daughter during a time of official war activities involving the United States.

Croatian Fraternal Union of America (CFU of A)

The Croatian Fraternal Union of America was founded in 1894 by Zdravko V. Muzina. The organization was chartered in 1895. Like many organizations of the time, its primary interest was to provide health care for ailing members. However, because it was formed by new immigrants, it also had a strong social element. By the time the organization was founded, Muzina had dropped out of sight. He died in 1908 at age 39. His obituary may provide some illumination on why he disappeared: "Muzina was morally weak, but otherwise a very gifted and talented man who [was] degraded by men of limited intelligence, but whenever and whoever writes a history of the Croatians in America, he must pause when he comes to the name of Zdravko Valentin Muzina, and let us hope that the writer will give him credit for the great good which he accomplished for our people and for which they will forever be proud." The Croatian Fraternal Union of America continues to be a very active organization and has 178 lodges in 32 states. Responding to the war in Croatia in 1991, the Croatian Fraternal Union of America established the Croatia Humanitarian Fund. Los Angeles has a significant and politically active Croatian population.

The Supreme Royal Circle of Friends of the World (SRCFW)

The Supreme Royal Circle of Friends of the World was founded in Forest City, Arkansas, in 1909 by Dr. Richard A. Williams. The fraternal organization was for black men. Its stated goals were "promoting the moral, physical, intellectual, and material welfare of its members." By 1911, the organization had grown to more than 9,000 members in 300 lodges, mostly in rural communities in Arkansas, Mississippi, Oklahoma, Tennessee, and Texas. As African-Americans migrated to California, chapters were established there. Much of the success of the RCF can be attributed to blacks' mistrust of government and white-owned banks. The Royal Circle of Friends offered fair returns for modest investments. The fee for joining the Royal Circle, including a medical examination, was $2.50. Members then paid $1 per quarter. When a member died, $300 was paid to the beneficiary. The acronym for the organization is RCF around the number 9, which was the founding date (1909) and the letters SRCFW.

Daughters of the American Revolution (DAR)

The Daughters of the American Revolution was founded on October 11, 1890, by a group of women who wanted to acknowledge their patriotism but had a hard time doing it because they weren't allowed into male-only patriotic organizations. Since its founding over a century ago, it has expanded to all 50 states and a number of foreign countries. Although the DAR's publicly stated eligibility requirements now emphasize "Membership in DAR is open to women at least eighteen years of age who can prove lineal bloodline descent from an ancestor who aided in achieving United States independence," and included Revolutionary War veterans, local militias, French and Spanish soldiers and sailors, partici-

pants in the Boston Tea Party, and other patriots, the organization had a thinly veiled segregationist policy. The organization finally amended its constitution to bar discrimination on the basis of race and creed after a highly publicized 1984 incident when Lena Lorraine Santos Ferguson was denied membership in the Washington, D.C., chapter because she was black. Ferguson eventually became a very active member of that chapter.

The organization is very active in genealogy and children's education, offering a number of scholarships. The DAR houses an extensive genealogy archive in its one-square-bock building in Washington, D.C., which also contains a theater, offices, a library, and a museum. As of 2008, the organization had about 170,000 members.

The DAR utilizes a seal, an emblem, and a ribbon as symbols of the organization. The insignia is most commonly used to mark the graves of DAR members. The primary part of the insignia consists of a spinning wheel mounted over a distaff—homage to Abigail Adams, who told her husband, John Adams, that the best way for her to help the revolutionary cause was to work with wool and flax. On the wheel's edge is the society's name, Daughters of the American Revolution, surrounded by 13 stars representing the 13 original colonies.

Sons of the American Revolution (SAR)

The Sons of the American Revolution has almost identical membership requirements as the Daughters of the American Revolution except that members are males. The organization traces its roots to 1876 in San Francisco, where a group of men who were descendents of Revolutionary War veterans wanted to celebrate the country's centennial. The group called itself the Sons of Revolutionary Sires, which sounded more like a radical horse-breeding club than a patriotic organization. The name was changed to the Sons of the American Revolution in 1889.

Although the majority of U.S. presidents have been members (Theodore Roosevelt signed the formal incorporation papers in 1906), it has never attained anything close to the membership figures of the Daughters of the American Revolution (26,000 members vs. 170,000 members).

In the cemetery, SAR graves are usually marked with a variation of the obverse side of the SAR badge. The marker consists of a laurel wreath topped by a Maltese cross with eight points, the acronym SAR, and a minuteman at the center. The SAR badge and grave marker are loosely based on the Military Order of Saint Louis (founded by Louis XIV in 1693) and the Legion of Honor (founded by Napoleon in 1803).

✵ Order of the Owls (OOO)

The Order of the Owls (not to be confused with the Independent International Order of Owls, a Masonic group) was founded by John W. Talbot and some associates in South Bend, Indiana, in 1904. The Owls was primarily a social and benevolent club with no apparent ties to insurance companies or a religion. Like other social clubs of the time, it provided its members a forum to discuss business and employment opportunities, and assisted the widows and orphans of fallen Owls. The Owls had four degrees and the usual assortment of secret rituals, passwords, oaths, and handshakes. At its peak in the early 1920s, the Order of the Owls had about 600,000 members who met in 2,148 lodges that they called "nests." Although there is evidence that small groups of Owls continue to meet, the membership numbers are now in the dozens rather then hundreds of thousands. This decline in membership may or may not be attributed to the founder of the order being sentenced to five years in Leavenworth prison in 1921 for morals charges involving a nurse at an Owls hospital.

✵ Elks (BPOE)
Emblem Club (EC)
Black Elks (IBPOEW)

Tombstones of Elks are easy to identify. They have an emblem with an elk in the center surrounded by a clock with Roman numerals and the letters BPOE (Benevolent Protective Order of Elks). Sometimes the words "Cervus Alces," which is a large extinct European elk, are also on the emblem. There is always a clock or the hands of a clock on the emblem. The clock's hands are frozen at eleven o'clock, a sacred time to all Elks. At eleven

| Elks | Emblem Club | Black Elks |

o'clock during any Elks ritual, an "Eleven O'Clock Toast" is read. There are a number of variations, the most common one being "My Brother, you have heard the tolling of the eleven strokes. This is to remind us that the hour of eleven has a tender significance. Wherever Elks may roam, whatever their lot in life may be, when this hour falls upon the dial of night, the great heart of Elkdom swells and throbs. It is the golden hour of recollection, the homecoming of those who wander, the mystic roll call of those who will come no more. Living or dead, Elks are never forgotten, never forsaken. Morning and noon may pass them by, the light of day sink heedlessly in the West, but ere the shadows of midnight shall fall, the chimes of memory will be pealing forth the friendly message, 'to our absent members.'"

The Elks were an offshoot of a drinking club called the Jolly Corks (JC), which was formed by actors in 1866. The purpose of the club was to avoid a New York law that prohibited the sale of spirits on Sundays. Gatherings of the Corks became very popular, and it was deemed necessary to formalize the club. The name Jolly Corks must have seemed a bit too explicit, so a search was conducted to find a more suitable name. It's said that the name Elks came from a stuffed head one of the members saw on display at the P. T. Barnum Museum (some say it was actually a moose head; but after all, it was a drinking club and mistakes do happen). The Elks became much more than a drinking club, and with over 1,500,000 members, it is now one the largest of the "animal clubs." The Elks are very strong on patriotism, public service, and caring for Elks who have fallen onto hard times.

The Emblem Club is the ladies auxiliary of the Elks. It was started in 1917 by a group of Elks' wives who made bandages for the World War I effort. The Emblem Club was officially chartered in 1926. According to the Emblem Club's Web site, "The insignia of the organization, an Elk's head surrounded by a wreath, is used on pins, stationery, publications and banners. This insignia shows that our members are related to or sponsored by members of the Benevolent and Protective Order of Elk's of the United States of America, and cooperates in their endeavors, when invited to do so." The Emblem Club's colors are purple (the color of royalty, denotes the highest standards and principles and is used by the Elks with whom our relationship or sponsorship establishes eligibility for membership in the Emblem Club) and gold used to signify quality or great value and symbolizes the rich blessings and material means, which we Share with those less fortunate than ourselves").

In early 1898, two African-Americans, B. F. Howard and Arthur J. Riggs, tried to join the all-white organization of Elks. After being denied membership, they formed the Improved Benevolent Protective Order of the Elks of the World (IBPOEW) on November 17, 1898. The organization found out that the Elks' ritual had not been copyrighted and adopted it, but not before securing their own copyright on the ritual. The IBPOEW currently claims a membership of approximately 500,000.

✸ International Order of Twelve, Knights and Daughters of Tabor (777 333)

The Knights of Liberty was a secret African-American organization organized by Moses Dickson and 11 black men in St. Louis, Missouri, in August 1846. Their goal was the destruction of slavery. The Knights claimed a peak membership of nearly 50,000, and they estimated that over a 10-year period, they helped some 70,000 slaves escape from slavery via the Underground Railroad.

Moses Dickson was also the author of the book *International 777 Order of Twelve 333 of Knights and Daughters of Tabor*. The International Order of Twelve, Knights and Daughters of Tabor, is the successor to the Knights of Liberty. The Knights took the name Tabor from the Bible. Tabor is a mountain in northern Israel where an army of Israelites won a decisive victory over their enemies, the Canaanites. The 777 is the biblical prophecy number of perfection; the 333 is the biblical prophecy number for the Trinity and the Resurrection. The number 12 either represents the number of original members or the 12th of August, when the society was formed.

✸ Rotary International (RI)

Rotary International, unlike many other organizations that were founded in the early twentieth century, was not a quasi-insurance company. Founded in 1905, Rotary was one of the first pure service organizations. It is comprised primarily of business owners and city officials. Its members participate in community service at both local and international levels. The organization claims 1.2 million

members in 170 countries. The name Rotary was derived from rotating meetings between its various members' offices.

✸ Fraternal Order of Eagles (FOE)
Ladies Auxiliary of the Eagles

The Fraternal Order of Eagles, originally named "The Order of Good Things," was founded in Seattle, Washington, in 1898 by a group of theater owners. According to the Eagles, its first organizational meetings

revolved around a keg of beer; before long, the wishy-washy name, the Order of Good Things, was changed to the more authoritarian Fraternal Order of Eagles. A constitution and bylaws were drawn up, and the name "Aerie"

Eagles   Ladies Auxiliary of the Eagles

was adopted as the designation for their meeting places and groups. The Eagles were originally composed of people working in the theater business (actors, stagehands, playwrights, etc.), and word of the organization spread rapidly because of the mobile nature of its members. Although the organization was like many others of the time in providing brotherhood, health benefits, and a funeral benefit ("no Eagle was ever buried in a Potter's Field"), the Eagles went farther by providing an "Aerie physician." The order also had its own stirring Eagle-appropriate script for a funeral service.

The Eagles still thrive. Much of their work revolves around lobbying for improving workman's compensation and social security, and sponsoring a number of health-related charities.

✸ Knights of Pythias (KP)
Colored Knights of Pythias (CKP)

If you see a heraldic shield coupled with a suit of armor on a tombstone, chances are it marks the spot of a fallen Knight of Pythias. Usually the letters F, C, and B (Friendship, Charity, and Benevolence) accompany the shield. It has been said that the Pythians have used upwards of 20,000 different symbols, so it's not unusual to find an array of symbols on one of their tombstones.

The Knights of Pythias was officially founded in 1864 as a secret society for government clerks. The name Pythias is a misspelling of the Greek name Phintias, a Pythagorean philosopher from Syracuse whose

Knights of Pythias   Pythian Sisters

story dates to the fifth century BC. Evidently, the infamous tyrant Diony-sius was about to put Phintias to death for questioning his rule. Phintias's friend Damon requested that he be held as a hostage so Phintias could go out and say goodbye to his friends and put his house in order before he died. At the appointed time of execution, Phintias was nowhere to be found, so Damon offered himself in Phintias's stead. But Phintias arrived at the last minute, prepared to accept his fate. Dionysius was so impressed with the trust and loyalty of these two men that he stayed the execution and asked both of the men to join him in friendship.

One Justus H. Rathbone was so favorably influenced by the tale, which he had seen as a play, that he formed a fraternal society (albeit misspelled) based on the traits of friendship, benevolence, and charity. It took a while for the Knights of Pythias to get started, including the expulsion (on two occasions) of Rathbone. At its peak in 1923, the society boasted over 900,000 members, but the Great Depression took its toll, and by the end of the twentieth century, membership had dropped to less than 10,000.

In 1869, a group of blacks in Philadelphia petitioned the Supreme Lodge to be admitted to the society, but they were rejected a number of times and formed their own order, the Colored Knights of Pythias (CKP), in 1875. The CKP was a popular society among Southern blacks. In 1920 in Georgia, it had over 30,000 members.

✸ Pythian Sisters (PS)

The female auxiliary of the Knights of Pythias is the Pythian Sisters. Their symbol is a Maltese cross embossed with the letters P (Purity), L (Love), E (Equality), and F (Fidelity).

✸ American Legion (AL)

The American Legion was founded in Paris, France, in 1919. It is primarily an association for ex-servicemen, and it works especially hard for veterans' rights for the wounded, infirm, and elderly. Because of its substantial member-ship, it also exercises quite a bit of political clout. The American Legion has gone to great lengths to explain the symbolism of their emblem. Here is the official explanation:

The Rays of the Sun form the background of our proud Emblem, and suggest that the Legion's principles will dispel the darkness of violence and evil.

The Wreath forms the center, in loving memory of those brave comrades who gave their lives in the service of the United States, that liberty might endure.

The Star, victory symbol of World War I, signalizes as well honor, glory and constancy. The letters U.S. leave no doubt as to the brightest star in the Legion's star.

Two Large Rings, the outer one stands for the rehabilitation of our sick and disabled buddies. The inner one denotes the welfare of America's children.

Two Small Rings set upon the star, the outer pledges loyalty and Americanism. The inner is for service to our communities, our states and the Nation.

The words American Legion tie the whole together for truth, remembrance, constancy, honor, service, veteran's affairs and rehabilitation, children and youth, loyalty, and Americanism.

✳ Boy Scouts of America (BSA)

The Boy Scouts were founded in 1910 by a group of five like-minded men who extolled the virtues and simple values of outdoor skills and public service. The Boy Scouts were inspired by similar groups in England and have spawned a number of imitators. At the beginning of the twenty-first century there were more than 3.3 million youth members and 1.2 million adult members of the Boy Scouts.

The fleur-de-lis on the Boy Scout emblem was adapted from the north point of a mariner's compass; the three points are reminders of the three parts of the scout's oath. The two stars symbolize the outdoors as well as the attributes of truth and knowledge. At the bottom of the emblem is the well-known Boy Scout motto, "Be Prepared." According to official Boy Scout literature, the upward swoop of the banner "hints that a Scout smiles as he does his duty." This particular example is the Americanized version that was adopted in 1911, which includes the addition of the eagle and shield, standing for "freedom and readiness to defend that freedom." Most Boy Scout emblems also have a small knot at the bottom, which is a reminder to "do a good turn daily."

✳ Loyal Order of the Moose (LOOM)
Women of the Moose (WOM) (WOTM)

Dr. John Henry Wilson founded the Loyal Order of the Moose (now known as Moose International) in 1888 in Louisville, Kentucky, apparently on little more than a whim. Wilson's plan was to establish a fraternal organization loosely based on other animal fraternities. Membership in the Loyal Order of the Moose didn't exactly skyrocket, but in a few years, there were about 1,000 members who met in lodges called "watering places," a reference, no doubt, to the alcoholic beverages that were consumed. Wilson's initial enthusiasm must have waned, because in a few more years, there were only several hundred loyal members.

Enter one James J. Davis, who was a government clerk from Elwood, Indiana. In 1906, he attended a rather grim Moose convention (at this point, there were only 246 active members) and was sworn in as member 247. Davis, who in today's world would have been labeled a "self-starter," saw hidden potential in the Moose world and, in short order, talked the struggling society into bestowing him with the title of Supreme Organizer. Davis came up with the idea of providing a "safety net" for working-class families as the benefit of Moose membership. For $5 to $10 a year, a member could buy protection for his wife and children if he died or became disabled. For the next 20 years, Davis toured the country, extolling the virtues of membership in the Loyal Order of the Moose. His proselytizing paid off: there were more than 650,000 members by 1928.

Today, membership hovers around 800 thousand. Two of Moosedoms proudest achievements are Mooseheart (a campus-like environment that provides care for the families of fallen Moose) and Moosehaven (a retirement community in Florida). The Moose emblem usually contains the letters P.A.P. (Purity, Aid, Progress). The female auxiliary, the Women of the Moose, was established in 1913 and has about 400 thousand. Its emblem is essentially the same but contains the letters H.F.C. (Hope, Faith, Charity).

✳ Woodmen of the World (WOW)

Treestones, also known as "tree-stump tombstones," often mark the resting place of a Woodman of the World. Joseph Cullen Root, a native of Lyons, Iowa, founded Woodmen of the World in Omaha, Nebraska, on June 6, 1890. Root was an inveterate joiner and, at various times, had been a member of the Odd Fellows, Freemasons, Knights of Pythias, and others. Root's organization was originally open to white males aged 18 to 45 from the 12 healthiest states, and it specifically excluded men in hazardous vocations like train brakemen, gunpowder factory employees, bartenders, and even professional baseball players. Eventually, Woodmen of the World relaxed most of its restrictions and today totals more than 800,000 members. It is now known as the Woodmen of the World Life Insurance Society/ Omaha Woodmen Life Insurance Society.

Although its membership is modest compared to other insurance-like organizations, it is one of the best-represented organizations in the cemetery. Why? Because up until the 1920s, membership in the Woodmen of the World provided each member with a tombstone. Even today, the insurance company claims that "no Woodmen shall rest in an unmarked grave." At first, the Woodmen of the World supplied the tombstone designs directly to local manufacturers but soon found that it was best to have local suppliers handle the design, manufacturer, and setting of the tombstones. Rustic treestones were already a popular style of tombstone and, with their woodsy name, the Woodmen of the World popularized treestones even more.

Although Woodmen of the World was primarily an insurance company, Root established a variety of ceremonies and rituals, and adopted a number of symbols because of his history with other fraternal organizations. Many of the symbols were formalized at the Woodmen Sovereign Camp in 1899, when the tree stump was officially adopted to symbolize equality and commonwealth. On tombstones, there are usually the Latin words *Dum Tacet Clamet*, roughly translated as "Though Silent, He Speaks," or in popular language as "Gone but Not Forgotten." Also embossed on the tombstone are usually a dove with an olive branch (peace), along with an axe, beetle, and wedge that, according to Root, symbolize workmanship and progress of culture.

Like many organizations, the Woodmen had internal problems, and a number of schisms and splinter groups developed. Some of them are Neighbors of Woodcraft (NOW), Woodmen Circle (WC), Royal Neighbors (RN), Supreme Forest Woodmen Circle (SFWC), Modern Woodmen of the World (MWW), and Woodmen Rangers and Rangerettes (WRR).

✺ Women of Woodcraft (WOW)

The Women of Woodcraft was a female auxiliary organization to the Woodmen of the World. Organized in 1897, they covered nine western states, and for a time their headquarters were in Leadville, Colorado. Their officers had titles such as "Guardian Neighbor," "Captain of the Guards," "Inner Sentinel," "Outer Sentinel," and "Magician." Unfortunately, it is not known what the duties of the Magician entailed. In 1917, the Women of Woodcraft changed their name to Neighbors of Woodcraft. From a distance, the emblem looks identical to the Woodmen of the World, but close inspection reveals that besides the different name, the motto *Dum Tacet Clamet* has been replaced with "Courage, Hope, Remembrance," and the tree stump is often broken, symbolizing the end of life.

✺ Modern Woodmen of America (MWA)

The Modern Woodmen of America was the original name of the Woodmen of the World. It is still an active organization and, with more than 750,000 members in 2003, it claims to be the country's fifth-largest fraternal life insurance company. Although most of the symbolism has been abandoned or toned down, up until the 1950s, members could purchase various items like cuff links and rings to identify them as Modern Woodmen of America. This jewelry featured the axe, wedge, and beetle (industry, power, and progress); the log and maple leaf (protection and brotherhood); and a palm, five stars, and a shield (peace, light, and safety). Modern Woodmen used the color red to signify life and action, white to signify innocence and purity of intention, and green to signify immortality. Employing a Victorian funerary tradition, some necklaces and watch fobs used braided human hair.

Neighbors of Woodcraft (NOW)

The Women of Woodcraft, also known as the "Pacific Circle, Women of Woodcraft" (covering the states of Colorado, Montana, Wyoming, Utah, Idaho, Nevada, Washington, Oregon, and California) moved to Portland, Oregon, in 1906, where articles of incorporation were filed with the state of Oregon. In 1917, the Women of Woodcraft changed its name to Neighbors of Woodcraft to reflect the organization's acceptance of both men and women for membership. On July 1, 2001, the 7,000 Neighbors of Woodcraft merged with the Woodmen of the World.

Freemasons (many acronyms; see Masonic Keystone on page 214)
Prince Hall Freemasons (PHF) African-American Society

The primary symbol of the Freemasons is the square and compass. Often found inside the symbol is the letter "G," which some say stands for *geometry* while others say it stands for *God*. Sometimes the symbol also contains clasped hands. The square and compass represent the interaction between mind and matter, and refer to the progression from the material to the intellectual to the spiritual. The Freemasons have a gift for clouding the origins of their organization, but historians say the roots of Freemasonry were among the stonemasons who built the great cathedrals in Europe. Since they went from job to job and were essentially self-employed, they were free masons. When they worked on a large job, they banded together to form lodges. The Masons have grown to

become the largest fraternal organization in the world. They are noted for their wide use of symbols and secret handshakes. A free black named Prince Hall started the black equivalent of the Freemasons in 1775 after being refused membership in the Masons. That organization, which is still quite active, is known as the Prince Hall Freemasons.

Besides the square and compass, also be on the lookout for other Masonic symbols such as the all-seeing eye, often with rays of light, an ancient symbol for God. Although many cultures have eye symbols, some good and some evil, when seen in a cemetery it usually means that the person was a Mason. This symbol is familiar to us as one of the mysterious images on the reverse of the dollar bill. Its placement on the dollar bill is largely the result of America's Founding Fathers, among them George Washington, Benjamin Franklin, Alexander Hamilton, Paul Revere, and John Paul Jones, who were Masons. In fact, one scholar describes Washington's Continental Army as a "Masonic convention."

✳ Shriners (Mystic) (AAONMS)

The Imperial Council of the Ancient Arabic Order of the Nobles of the Mystic Shrine, better known as the Shriners, was founded in 1872 by Freemasons Walter M. Fleming (a medical doctor) and William J. Florence (an actor), who apparently weren't having enough fun at Freemason functions. The Shriners were only open to 32nd-degree Master Masons and Knights Templar. They adopted many of the symbols of Islam but in a parody form, which, understandably, has irritated followers of that religion. They routinely wear amusing garments, including fezzes, give themselves titles like Most Illustrious Grand Potentate, engage in questionable antics, and have rather boisterous conventions. At one time, the Freemasons considered banning any member who was also a member of the Shriners.

Even though they still engage in their antics, most notably driving miniature cars and scooters in parades, Shriners are very well known for giving large sums of money to hospitals that care for badly burned and crippled children and to a number of other causes. Famous Shriners include Harry Truman, Barry Goldwater, J. Edgar Hoover, Chief Justice Earl Warren, and Red Skelton. The emblem of the Shriners contains a scimitar, from which hangs a crescent, "the Jewel of the Order." In the center is the head of a sphinx (not always seen in simple emblems) and a five-pointed star. On elaborate renditions of the emblem, the crescent contains the motto *Robur et Furor* ("Strength and Fury"). Also, when the letters of the Ancient Arabic Order of the Nobles of the Mystic Shrine are rearranged, they spell "A MASON."

✳ Masonic Keystone (HTWSSTKS)

The letters HTWSSTKS, arranged in a circle and usually within a keystone, are known as the Masonic Mark of an Ancient Grand Master. They are an abbreviation for "Hiram The Widow's Son Sent To King Solomon." Sometimes the center of the keystone contains a sheaf of wheat.

The Freemasons are not only big on symbols; they also have a multitude of degrees and attributes that they abbreviate on tombstones. Some of the most often seen include the following:

AAONMS Ancient Arabic Order of Nobles of the Mystic Shrine
AASR Ancient and Accepted Scottish Rite
AF&AM Ancient Free and Accepted Masons
F&AM Free and Accepted Masons

✳ Knights Templar (KT)
Social Order of the Beauceant (SOOB)

In cemetery symbolism, the Knights Templar is part of the convoluted Freemasons structure. The Knights claim to have been founded by a group of warrior monks in 1118, whose job was to keep the roads safe for pilgrims traveling to Jerusalem. They eventually grew very wealthy and were overthrown in 1307 by King Phillipe le Bel of France, who desired their income. Many of them escaped to England, Portugal, and Scotland, where they are said to have formed the Freemasons in the late 1700s. So many of their affairs have been shrouded in secrecy that it is impossible to put together an accurate history, except to say that in the cemetery, the Knights Templar emblem is almost always seen in its Masonic form, which is the symbol for York Rite Templarism: a cross with a crown enclosed in a Maltese cross, often containing the phrase *In Hoc Signo Vinces* ("In This Sign Conquer"), mistakenly thought to be the origin of the Christian monogram IHS.

Knights Templar

Social Order of the Beauceant

The female auxiliary of the Knights Templar is the Social Order of the Beauceant. The organization, which was founded in 1890, was originally named "Some of Our Business Society," a reference to the help the ladies were going to provide at the Knights Templar Grand Encampment in 1892. The organization grew to more than 15,000 members, a set of rituals was established, and a more flowery name—the Social Order of the Beauceant—was adopted in 1913. The emblem of the SOOB, a cross and a crown, is the same as the Knights Templar except it has the letters S, O, O, B around the outside.

✸ Eastern Star (OES) (ES)
Prince Hall Eastern Star (PHES) Black Women's Organization
Prince Hall Grand Chapter (of the) Eastern Star (PHGCES) Black Women

The Order of the Eastern Star has a convoluted history, but simply put, it is the female counterpart to Freemasonry. There are three organizations that use the name Eastern Star: the General Grand Chapter, Order of the Eastern Star; the Prince Hall–affiliated Eastern Stars; and the Federation of Eastern Stars. The original group, the General Grand Chapter, Order of the Eastern Star, was formed in 1876. It has been in decline in recent years, no doubt because of its powerful patriarchal rules. All degrees must be administered by a Master Mason (male).

A five-pointed star, usually with the tip pointing down, marks the grave of a member of the Eastern Star. Each symbol within the star points represents a heroine: Adah, Ruth, Esther, Martha, and Electa. They also

Eastern Star

Eastern Star

Prince Hall Eastern Star

symbolize the tenets of the Eastern Star: fidelity, constancy, loyalty, faith, and love. On tombstones, sometimes between the points of the star and other times in the center of the star, are the letters F.A.T.A.L. This refers to a double meaning of an oath taken by a member of the Eastern Star when a degree is bestowed on her. The first meaning is simply the word "FATAL," which means that it would be fatal to the character of a lady if she disclosed any of the secrets of the order. The other meaning of FATAL is an acronym meaning "Fairest Among Ten-thousand Altogether Lovely."

The Prince Hall Eastern Star emblem often has the tip on the top of the star pointed up.

✸ Eastern Star Past Matron

The emblem of an Eastern Star Past Matron has the Eastern Star symbol with a gavel suspended on a link of chain (or sometimes a gavel mysteriously levitating on a link of chain). Occasionally, a laurel wreath circles the star and a gavel is attached to the wreath by a chain.

✸ International Order of the Rainbow for Girls (RG) (IORG)

The meaning of the letters BFCL on the organization's emblem stands for Bible, Flag, Constitution, and Linen (or List of Masonic Leaders). When superimposed over an R with a pot of gold, it becomes the symbol for the International Order of the Rainbow for Girls (DeMolay is for boys). A clergyman, William Mark Sexton, founded the club in 1922 as a fraternal and social club for girls aged 11 to 20 who are related to members of the Freemasons or Eastern Star. Although all of the Masonic organizations profess to be nonsectarian, the Rainbow for Girls is strongly associated with the Bible and Christian beliefs. Rainbow Girls are encouraged to follow the seven-step path of 1) effective leadership, 2) church membership and active participation in the church of their choice, 3) patriotism, 4) cooperation with equals, 5) love of home, 6) loyalty to family, and 7) service to humanity. The completion of these seven steps results in the pot of gold (charity).

It is relatively rare to find this symbol in the cemetery because of the narrow age group of its members and the relatively low mortality rate of teenage girls.

✸ Knights of the Maccabees (KOTM)

The Knights of the Maccabees was one of the more successful mutual assessment fraternal societies that sprang up after the Civil War. Although they took on many of the trappings of other societies, such as the establishment of lodges, which they called Subordinate Camps (a Supreme Tent was the highest level), the KOTM was basically a pass-the-hat organization. When a member of the society died, each member was assessed 10 cents, which was given to the widow. The name of the organization was changed to the Maccabees in 1914, and it became more like a regular insurance company, although some of its older members insisted that its rituals and ceremonies remain. At its peak, the Maccabees boasted more than 300,000 members. But the Great Depression took its toll, and there are few members today.

The name Knights of the Maccabees refers to a Jewish tribe of the second century BC that revolted against Antiochus IV of Syria in the name of religion. The tribe was lead by Judas Maccabeau, who eventually secured a Jewish state, Judea. The founders of the Maccabees were impressed by Maccabeau's feats, especially his instruction to his soldiers that they reserve a portion of their spoils for the widows and orphans of their fellow comrades in arms. At the center of the Maccabees' emblem are often three small tents containing the letters O, T, and W, which refer to the Old Testament Wisdom the organization embodies.

✳ Ladies of the Maccabees of the World (LOTM)

There was also a female counterpart to the Maccabees known as the Ladies of the Maccabees of the World. It became a national auxiliary in 1892 that was known as the Supreme Hive of the Ladies of the Maccabees of the World and is said to be the first fraternal benefit group run by women. This particular tombstone is inscribed with the Latin phrase *ad astra per asperi* ("toward the stars [heavens] through adversity").

✳ Knights of Columbus (KC) (K of C)

The Knights of Columbus, founded in 1882, has often been described as the "Catholic Masons," because Catholics were forbidden by a Papal edict from joining the Freemasons. The purpose of the fraternal organization, which was originally open to Catholic men over the age of 18, was

to provide assistance to widows and orphans of the parish. It had close to 1.7 million members in 2009. Although it has many similarities to the Freemasons, including degrees and rituals, it is mainly an insurance company. In recent years, it has become more active in community affairs and politics.

The emblem of the Knights of Columbus was designed by Supreme Knight James T. Mullen and was officially adopted on May 12, 1883. The emblem incorporates a medieval knight's shield mounted on a formée cross, an artistic representation of the cross of Christ. Mounted on the shield are three objects: 1) a fasces, an ancient Roman symbol of authority composed of a bundle of rods bound together around an axe; 2) an anchor, the mariner's symbol for Columbus; and 3) a short sword, the weapon of the knight when engaged in an "errand of mercy."

⚜ The Society of Mary (SM or AM)

The Society of Mary is a Roman Catholic religious congregation comprised of priests and brothers. Fr. John Claude Colin and 11 of his companions founded the congregation in 1836 while they were attending seminary in Lyon, France. It considers Mary, the Mother of God, to be its first and perpetual superior. Because they bear the name of Mary and are called "Marists," the members of this congregation try to imitate Mary's life and virtues. In the words of their founder, they strive to "think as Mary, judge as Mary, and feel

and act as Mary in all things." They are now an international congregation, and Marist communities are found worldwide. In Catholic cemeteries, the emblem of the Society of Mary is found in areas where priests are buried, often called Priest's Circles. The circle of 12 stars probably represents the 12 founders of the school. The banner at the bottom reads *Sub Mariae Nomine* ("under Mary's name"), the society's motto.

⚜ Independent Order of Odd Fellows (IOOF)
Grand United Order of the Odd Fellows (GUOOF) African-American Society

The primary symbol of the Independent Order of Odd Fellows is three links of a chain. They share this symbol and a number of other symbols, such as the all-seeing eye, with the Freemasons, but the Odd Fellows use

it as their dominant sign. Indeed, sometimes the Odd Fellows are known as the "poor man's Freemasonry." They are also known as the "Three Link Fraternity." The links represent Friendship, Love, and Truth. On tombstones, the letters F, L, and T are often enclosed within the links of the chain.

The IOOF is an offshoot of the Odd Fellows, which was formed in England in the 1700s as a working-class social and benevolent association. The United States branch was founded in Baltimore, Maryland, on April 26, 1819, when Thomas Wildey and four members of the order from England instituted Washington Lodge No. 1. By the Civil War, it had

more than 200,000 members, and by 1915, there were 3,400,000 members. The Great Depression and lack of interest in fraternal orders took their toll, and by the 1970s, there were fewer than 250,000 members. But, the society claims that there has been a resurgence of interest, stating that now it has 10,000 lodges in 25 countries. Death care, including funerals, was one of the major benefits of Odd Fellows membership. One of the first orders of business, after establishing a lodge in a new town, was to purchase plots in an existing cemetery or to establish a new cemetery where plots were sold to members at a modest fee. The Grand United Order of the Odd Fellows was the largest and wealthiest black fraternal order in Georgia by 1916, boasting over 1,100 lodges with 33,000 members.

⊛ Daughters of Rebekah (DR)

The Daughters of Rebekah were formed in 1851 as a female auxiliary of the Odd Fellows. Like other women's auxiliaries of fraternal organizations, they were subservient to the male organization and, understandably, their numbers have fallen off in modern times.

In the cemetery, look for a circular emblem with a half moon sometimes containing seven stars on the right, which, according to the Rebekahs, represents "the value of regularity in all our work." The emblem also consists of a dove (peace), a white lily (purity), and the intertwined letters D and R. Sometimes the emblem also contains a small beehive, which symbolizes "associated industry and the result of united effort."

⊛ Companions of the Forest of America (CFA)

This is the emblem of the Companions of the Forest of America, a women's auxiliary of the Ancient Order of Foresters (AOF). In addition to the letters C of F of A on the emblem, there are the letters S, S, and C, which stand for Sociability, Sincerity, and Constancy.

⊛ The Improved Order of Red Men (IORM)
The Degree of Pocahontas (DOP)

In the cemetery, the initials T. O. T. E. (Totem of the Eagle) indicates a member of the Red Men, which traces its origin (although no direct evidence can be found) to certain secret patriotic societies founded before the American Revolution, such as the Sons of Liberty (SL). In 1813, the Society of Red Men was officially founded but was dissolved shortly thereafter, apparently because of its reputation for drunkenness. It was re-formed as the Improved Order of Red Men, and its stated aim is "to perpetuate the beautiful legends and traditions of a vanishing race and keep alive its customs, ceremonies, and philosophies." Interestingly, until recently, American Indians were banned from admission. The female auxiliary of the Red Men is the Degree of Pocahontas, which was organized in 1885.

⊛ Salvation Army

The Salvation Army is best known nowadays as a place for the downtrodden and disadvantaged to get help. It is well known for its drug and alcohol rehabilitation centers, its thrift stores, and its yuletide bell-ringing Santas. The quasi-military Christian organization (its leader is addressed as General, employees are known as Officers, and volunteers are known as Soldiers) was founded in 1865 by Englishman William Booth. It was officially named the Salvation Army in 1878.

Salvationists wore metal shields as badges in the early 1880s. The

Salvation Army

1886 Orders and Regulations for Field Officers implored every Soldier to wear a uniform, "even if it be but the wearing of a shield," so that they could be identified as Salvationists. The first shields were white with red lettering, but this was soon changed to red with white lettering, the one most recognized today.

A more complex formal shield with abundant symbolism is sometimes seen. According to the Salvation Army, the symbolism is thus:

(a) The round figure "the sun" represents the light and fire of the Holy Spirit.

(b) The cross in the center represents the cross of our Lord Jesus Christ.

(c) The letter "S" stands for salvation.

(d) The swords represent the warfare of salvation.

(e) The shots represent the truths of the gospel.

(f) The crown represents the crown of glory, which God will give to all his soldiers who are faithful to the end.

❀ Fraternal Brotherhood (FB)

The Fraternal Brotherhood was a secret beneficial society, with all the usual passwords and symbols, that was organized in 1896. They had a substantial building constructed in 1904 on Figueroa Street in Los Angeles that was featured on postcards. The name was changed to Golden West Life Insurance Association in 1931, and in 1948, it became the Homesteaders Life Company.

❋ B'nai B'rith (IOBB)

The Independent Order of B'nai B'rith (Children of the Covenant) is one of the few Jewish fraternal organizations. It was formed in New York in 1843, partly because Jews were denied membership in the more mainstream fraternal organizations like the Freemasons. Eventually, Jews were admitted into organizations like the Freemasons and the Odd Fellows, and those organizations are surprisingly well represented in Jewish cemeteries. B'nai B'rith has evolved into a huge charitable organization (it gives out and receives significant donations). Today, the B'nai B'rith is most well known through its Anti-Defamation League, which serves to combat anti-Semitism.

❋ Native Daughters of the Golden West (NDGW)
Native Sons of the Golden West (NSGW)

The Native Daughters of the Golden West, which was founded in 1886 (the Sons of the Golden West was founded in 1875) maintains records of California Pioneers who resided or were born in California before December 31, 1869. To date, they have compiled information on more than 33,000 pioneers. The "PP" on the emblem stands for Past President.

In Summary

There are literally hundreds of secret societies, clubs, and organizations. Many no longer exist while others remain strong. When you see an emblem with an acronym that you aren't familiar with or simply find an acronym without an emblem, try matching up the acronym with the list in this book. Then enter the name you find into an Internet search engine. You may be pleasantly surprised with how many results you get.

Cemetery Symbolism

emeteries are virtual encyclopedias of symbolism. The symbols on a person's tomb may help to tell us something about the life of its inhabitant. Dead men may tell no tales; but their tombstones do. Besides informing us of people's names and birth and death dates, their tombstones often tell us their religion, their ethnicity, their club memberships, their occupations, and what their thoughts were on the afterlife.

Most symbols in a cemetery have some connection with a religion, but many are overwhelmingly religion-specific, like the cross for Christians and the Cohanim (or Kohanim) hand sign for Jews. Generally, these symbols are associated with some sort of religious ritual.

Before we present our guide to cemetery symbolism, we must issue a small caveat—people may have requested something on a tombstone simply because they liked the way it looked, and it may have had absolutely nothing to do with their life. This is especially true with flower symbols. But, as a rule of thumb, the older the tomb, the more likely the symbolism had something to do with the person's life and their thoughts on the afterlife. For an in-depth examination of funerary symbols, consult the author's book *Stories in Stone: A Field Guide to Cemetery Symbolism and Iconography*.

Mortality Symbols

✳ Hands Together

Hands that appear to be shaking are usually a symbol of matrimony. Look carefully at the sleeves. One should appear feminine and the other masculine. If the sleeves appear to be gender-neutral, the hands can represent a heavenly welcome or an earthly farewell.

✳ Anchor

The anchor is a symbol of hope. The reason for this symbolic meaning comes from the passage in the Epistle to the Hebrews 6:19–20: "Which hope we have as an anchor of the soul, both sure and stedfast, and which entereth into that within the veil; Whither the forerunner is for us entered, even Jesus, made an high priest for ever after the order of Melchisedec."

In memory of the
2425 Native Americans
who were interred
in this cemetery of
San Fernando
Rey de España
between 1797 and 1852
anno domini 1997

Another type of anchor is the *crux dissimulata*. This anchor is actually a cross in disguise (the bottom open curve represents receptivity to spiritual matters). When Christians first started practicing their religion, they had to do it under a veil of secrecy lest they be persecuted for their beliefs. The anchor cross was one way Christians could broadcast their religion to other followers without being discovered. It is, understandably, a more popular symbol in cemeteries in coastal cities, but it has no direct link to the seafaring life.

✸ Hourglass (usually with wings)

The symbolism is clear: time is passing rapidly, and every day, everyone comes closer to the hour of death. A bolder interpretation of the hourglass suggests that since it can be inverted over and over again, it symbolizes the cyclic nature of life and death, heaven and earth.

✸ Torch, Inverted

The inverted torch is a purely funerary symbol. It is unlikely that it will be found anywhere but the cemetery. The inverted torch comes in two forms. The most common is the inverted torch with flame burning, which, while symbolizing death, suggests that the soul (fire) continues to exist in the next realm. The other version is an upside-down torch without a flame, which simply means life extinguished.

✸ Urn, Draped

The draped cinerary urn is probably the most common nineteenth-century funerary symbol. Some nineteenth-century cemeteries appear to be a sea of urns. The drape can be seen either as a reverential accessory or as a symbol of the veil between earth and the heavens. The urn is to ashes as the sarcophagus is to the body, which makes the urn a very curious nineteenth-century funerary device since cremation was seldom practiced. Nowadays, the word "ashes" has been replaced by "cremated remains" (abbreviated to "cremains" by the death-care industry). But in the nineteenth century, urns seldom contained ashes;

rather, they were used as decorative devices, were perched on top of columns, sarcophagi, and mausoleums, and were carved into tombstones, doors, and walls. The urn and the willow tree were two of the first funerary motifs to replace the death's heads and soul effigies when funerary symbolism started to take on a softer air after the Revolutionary War.

Nature Symbols

✹ Buds and Seedpods

Seedpods and small buds serve to remind us of the fragile beginnings of life, all too often cut tragically short. Buds, especially those that are broken, almost always decorate the grave of a child. The buds can be almost any flower, but rosebuds are the most commonly used.

Buds and Seedpods   Calla Lily

✹ Calla Lily

With its broad leaves and huge vase-like flowers, the calla lily is one of the most stunning flowers. On tombstones, it symbolizes majestic beauty and marriage. The South African calla lily was introduced in the United States during the second half of the nineteenth century, which coincided with the beginning of the golden age of the American cemetery. Soon after it was imported, it started to appear in mainstream American art as well as funerary art.

✹ Rose

The rose has become the queen of flowers because of its fragrance, longevity, and beauty. It has inspired lovers, dreamers, and poets for countless generations. Venus, the goddess of love, claimed the rose as her own. Cleopatra stuffed pillows full of rose petals. Nero arranged for rose petals to rain down upon his guests. But the early Christians were reluctant to use the rose as one of their symbols because of its association with decadence. However, people's love of the rose was strong and long-lived, so the Christians made some tactical adjustments and adopted the rose as one of their own symbols.

In Christian symbolism, the red rose became a symbol of martyrdom, while the white rose symbolized purity. In Christian mythology, the rose in Paradise did not have thorns but acquired them on Earth to remind man of his fall from grace; however, the rose's fragrance and beauty remained to suggest to him what Paradise is like. Sometimes the Virgin Mary is called the "rose without thorns" because of the belief that she was exempt from original sin.

✸ Ivy

Because ivy is eternally green even in harsh conditions, it is associated with immortality and fidelity. Ivy clings to a support, which makes it a symbol of attachment, friendship, and undying affection. Its three-pointed leaves make it a symbol of the Trinity.

✸ Weeping Willow Tree

Although the form of the weeping willow certainly suggests grief and sorrow, in many religions it suggests immortality. In Christianity, it is associated with the gospel of Christ because the tree will flourish and remain whole no matter how many branches are cut off. The willow and urn motif was one of the most popular gravestone decorations of the late eighteenth and early nineteenth centuries.

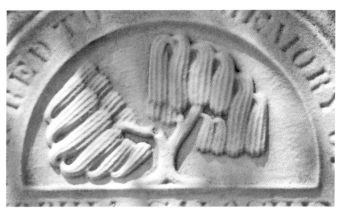

✸ Palm Fronds

Romans used palm fronds as a symbol of victory. Christians adapted them to symbolize a martyr's triumph over death and, by extension, any believer's triumph over death.

A staff made out of a palm tree is an attribute of Saint Christopher. In Christian mythology, he carried Christ across the river and then thrust his palm tree staff into the ground, where it grew and bore fruit.

Christian Symbols

Symbols of the Eucharist

The chalice with wafer, grapes, and wheat combined into a single scene are collectively a symbol of the Eucharist. The use of all of these elements together is usually restricted to religious orders. Grapes and wheat together are also a symbol for the Eucharist and are usually found on the graves of everyday folk.

Holy Ghost

A dove dive-bombing from the heavens, with an olive branch or a cross in its beak, is the symbol for the Holy Ghost. This representation of a dove comes from St. John 1: 32–34: "And John bare record, saying, I saw the Spirit descending from heaven like a dove, and it abode upon him. And I knew him not: but he that sent me to baptize with water, the same said unto me, Upon whom thou shalt see the Spirit descending, and remaining on him, the same is he which baptizeth with the Holy Ghost. And I saw, and bare record that this is the Son of God."

A similar-looking tableau, but with the dove holding the earth in its beak, is a symbol for the fourth, or highest, degree of a Knight of Columbus, a fraternal organization for Catholics.

Dove and Olive Branch

The dove is the most frequently seen animal symbol in the cemetery. It is portrayed in a number of poses, but most frequently it is seen holding an olive branch, a reference to the dove sent out by Noah to search for land as explained in Genesis 8:10–11: "And he stayed yet other seven days; and again he sent forth the dove out of the ark; And the dove came in to him in the evening; and, lo, in her mouth was an olive leaf pluckt off: so Noah knew that the waters were abated from off the earth." The dove then became a symbol of purity and peace because God had made peace with man.

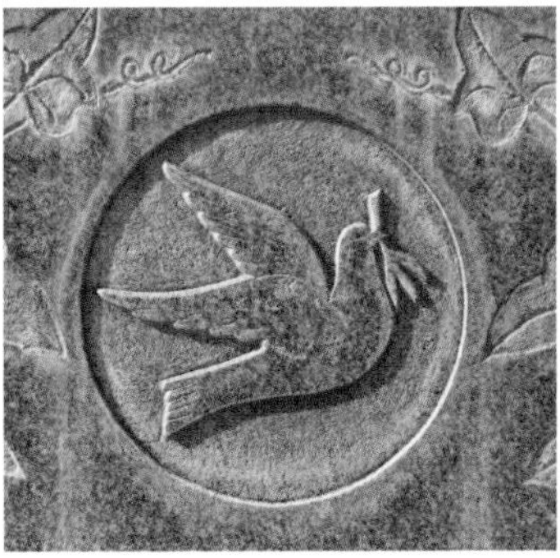

✸ Lamb

In funerary art, lambs usually mark the graves of children and particularly infants, symbolizing innocence. The lamb is one of the most frequently used symbols of Christ in all periods of Christian art. Christ is often depicted as a shepherd, but he is also referred to as the Lamb of God, as in St. John 1:29: "Behold the Lamb of God, which taketh away the sin of the world!"

Baby Lamb   Agnes Dei–Lamb of God

✸ Agnes Dei–Lamb of God

A lamb with a cross and usually also with a banner and a halo is the symbol for the Lamb of God. Christ is the Lamb of God as referenced in St. John 1:29 (see above).

In addition to the cross, banner, and halo, there are a number of other accessories that may be portrayed with the lamb. Among these are shepherds crooks, Chi-Rho crosses, and the Alpha and Omega symbols. If the lamb is portrayed without any additional items, it is a symbol of innocence and is frequently found on children's graves. Accessorized, the lamb is almost always the Agnes Dei.

✸ Chalice Cup

In the cemetery, the chalice is seen as the human heart's yearning to be filled with the true spirit of the Lord, as symbolized by wine. It is one of the strongest symbols of Christian faith. Its most vivid biblical reference is in St. Mark 14:23–25: "And he took the cup, and when he had given thanks, he gave it to them: and they all drank of it. And he said unto them, This is my blood of the new testament, which is shed for many. Verily I say unto you, I will drink no more of the fruit of the vine, until that day that I drink it new in the kingdom of God."

In paintings, the chalice is often depicted as a vessel used for gathering the blood from the dying Christ on the cross. In this context, the chalice symbolizes the Eucharist and the redemption of mankind. A chalice and a wafer are attributes of Saint Barbara.

✳ Alpha and Omega

Alpha and Omega are the first and last letters of the Greek alphabet. In Christian iconography, the Alpha and Omega emblem relates to three similar passages in the book of Revelation. The most expansive of the three passages, found in Revelation 21:5–7, reads: "And he that sat upon the throne said, Behold, I make all things new. And he said unto me, Write: for these words are true and faithful. And he said unto me, It is done. I am Alpha and Omega, the beginning and the end. I will give unto him that is athirst of the fountain of the water of life freely. He that overcometh shall inherit all things; and I will be his God, and he shall be my son."

It is quite common to see the Alpha and Omega symbols in all sorts of religious art, especially on books and clothing. As a symbol, the letters are frequently seen dangling from a Latin cross or incorporated in a Chi-Rho emblem.

✳ IHS

This symbol is often seen emblazoned on crosses. Often the letters are overlaid on each other, which, curiously, looks a lot like a dollar sign. Popular belief says that IHS (or sometimes IHC) is an abbreviation of the Latin phrase *in hoc signo*, which is a shortened version of a banner with the words *in hoc signo vinces* ("in this sign you will conquer"), seen in a vision by the Emperor Constantine before he went into battle—a good story, but not the origin of IHS. Another puts the origin as an abbreviation of the Latin phrase *Iesus Hominum Salvator* ("Jesus, Savior of Men")—another good story, but also not the origin. In fact, the origin is rather pedestrian. IHS, or IHC (derived from the lower-case Greek letters for iota, eta, and sigma), is an abbreviation of Jesus' name in Greek: *Ihsus, Ihsoys,* or *Ihcuc.*

✳ INRI

This symbol is very straightforward. It's the first letters of the Latin words *Iesus Nazarenus Rex Iudaeorum,* meaning "Jesus of Nazareth The King of the Jews." According to St. John 19:19–20, after Jesus was crucified, Pilate mockingly wrote these same words on the cross in Hebrew, Greek, and Latin.

❀ RIP

The most common letters seen on tombstones in cartoons are RIP. Even schoolchildren are familiar with this abbreviation, and it may be their first experience with cemeteries. RIP is an abbreviation for the Latin words *Requiescat In Pace*, which translates nicely to the English words "Rest in Peace."

❀ Lamp

The lamp is a symbol of wisdom and piety. When a person has a bright idea, it is often depicted as a lightbulb (lamp). Lamps light our way through the darkness to a better world. The symbolism of the lamp is well explained in Revelation 21: 22-24: "And I saw no temple therein: for the Lord God Almighty and the Lamb are the temple of it. And the city had no need of the sun, neither of the moon, to shine in it: for the glory of God did lighten it, and the Lamb is the light thereof. And

the nations of them which are saved shall walk in the light of it: and the kings of the earth do bring their glory and honour into it."

❀ Gate

In Christian funerary symbolism, gates represent the passage from one realm to the next. In scenes of the Last Judgment, gates are always central in the picture. Christ is often seen breaking through these dividing barriers between the damned and the righteous.

The Cross

I t's hard to think of a symbol more closely associated with a religion than the cross is with Christianity. But the use of the cross as a symbol predates its association with Christianity by thousands of years. In fact, the cross may be humankind's oldest symbol. In its simplest form of two intersecting lines of the same length, it makes an X, as in "X marks the spot." The circle, the X-shaped cross, and the cross that looks like a plus (+) sign are used by all cultures. The ancient + cross took on many meanings among pagan cultures, most notably as a symbol signifying the division between Heaven and Earth. This + cross was eventually adopted by Christians and is now known as the Greek cross.

But long before Christians utilized the cross as their supreme symbol, other cultures were employing it and modifying it to fit with their cultures. The ancient Druids were known to cut off all the branches of a giant oak tree except for two branches on either side of the trunk, thus forming a huge natural cross. Other cultures took the basic cross form and added to it. One of the earliest modifications of the + cross was by Eastern civilizations who added arms to the end of the cross to form a swastika, or fylfot, cross. The original swastika cross was a symbol of good fortune and has decorated ancient pottery, jewelry, and coins. It also became a power symbol among ancient fire-worshiping Aryan tribes because the arms of the

swastika resembled the sticks with handles that the tribal members rubbed together to make fire. Its various forms often represented the highest attainment possible, and it was used to represent both spiritual and worldly pursuits. Unfortunately, the swastika was also used by power-hungry rulers such as Charlemagne and Hitler, and is now associated with evil.

Another type of cross that has its roots in ancient civilizations is the Tau cross, which is shaped like a capital "T." This cross has frequently been referred to as the Old Testament cross because it was often used by Jewish tribes. The Tau cross was probably derived from the cross of Horus, known as an ankh, which looks like a Tau cross with an elongated O attached to the top. The ankh is often seen in hieroglyphics, most often held in the hand of a god or person of power.

The Christian cross was eventually adopted by adherents of that religion, but it wasn't Christendom's first symbol. Most scholars agree that, despite popular mythology that says early Christians scratched crosses everywhere they went, the first symbol Christians actually used was a fish. The use of a fish as a symbol may be because Christ is often portrayed as instructing his disciples to be fishers of men, or some even say that the word for fish in Greek contains the first letters of the phrase, Jesus Christ, the Son of God, Savior. But, whatever the reason, within a few centuries, Christians tossed aside the fish as their prime symbol and adopted the cross.

It's quite amazing that any form of the cross was adopted by Christians as their prime symbol, since crosses had been used for centuries to punish and persecute Christians as well as common criminals. In early Christian literature, the cross on which Christ was crucified is referred to as the "accursed tree." Nevertheless, the story goes that around the year AD 320, the Roman Emperor Constantine couldn't make up his mind whether he should continue practicing paganism, which had served his predecessors well, or embrace Christianity, which many of the Roman citizenry (including his own mother) were either following or exploring. The situation at hand for Constantine was a huge battle he was about to engage in with Maxentius, who was apparently enlisting the aid of supernatural and magic forces; so Constantine decided to pray to the God of the Christians to help him defeat his foe. During a midnight prayer, Constantine gazed toward the heavens and saw a grouping of stars that looked like a huge, glowing, luminous cross. After he fell asleep, Constantine had a dream in which he saw Christ holding the same symbol and instructing Constantine to affix it to his standards. This dream of Christ appearing to Constantine is, to many Christians, the source of the monogram IHS, which often appears on Christian tombs. The IHS is supposed to be an abbreviation of the words *In Hoc Signo Vinces* ("in this sign conquer"). A nice story but, unfortunately, not true. In reality, the source of the monogram IHS is the first three letters of Jesus' name in Greek, *Ihsus, Ihsoys,* or *Ihcuc.*

IHS or not, Constantine defeated Maxentius. What Constantine more than likely saw (or thought he saw) was an intersection of the two letters X and P, which was a popular symbol used by the Christians and known as a Chi-Rho, or Labarum, cross. The Chi-Rho represents the first two letters of XPIETOE (*Christos*) in Greek. In short order, Constantine had the emblem applied to all of his standards and banners, and placed upon the altars of the church. Thus began the use of the cross as a Christian symbol. Although the Chi-Rho cross is seldom seen in modern times, it's basic meaning has been preserved in the abbreviated form of the word for Christmas: Xmas.

Although there are dozens of types of crosses in cemeteries and thousands of types of religious crosses, there are basically three types that others evolved from: the Greek cross, which looks like a + sign; the Latin cross, which looks like the letter "t"; and the Celtic cross, which has a circle (known as a nimbus) connecting the four arms of the cross.

❀ The Greek Cross

Greek-style crosses and other crosses with equidistant arms are more likely to appear as part of a decoration on a tomb rather than as freestanding crosses. The Saint Andrew's cross looks like an "X." When Saint Andrew was condemned to be crucified, the story goes that he requested to be nailed to a cross that was unlike the cross on which Jesus was crucified, because Saint Andrew thought he was unworthy to be put in the same category as Jesus. Thus, the Saint Andrew's cross has come to signify suffering and humility.

The Maltese cross looks like a + sign with flared ends that are usually indented to form eight points. These eight points represent the Beatitudes. This cross is often associated with such fraternal orders as the Knights Templar.

Many of the Greek-style crosses are associated with heraldry, and they were worn by many Christian warriors as they marched off to the Crusades. These crosses can often be seen in a cemetery gracing a family crest or as part of an emblem of a fraternal order. Best known among these are the floré (floriated) cross, which has arms that end in three petal-like projections, and the patté (broadfooted) cross, where the arms look like triangles with the tip of the four triangles pointed at the center. These rather broad arms represent the wings of a bird and symbolize the protective power of the cross.

❀ The Latin Cross

The cross most commonly associated with Christianity is the Latin cross. Some of its many variations are the Cross of Calvary, which is a Latin cross with a three-stepped base, representing the Trinity; the Cross of the Resurrection, which is a simple Latin cross with a spiked end; and the Crucifix, or Rood, that has Christ nailed to it. Cemetery wanderers will also spy many Latin crosses with more than one cross arm. The most common of these is the Cross of Lorraine, which has a shorter arm above the long one. It was applied to the standards of Godfrey of Lorraine, one of the first Crusaders, after he was chosen ruler of Jerusalem. This symbol is familiar to us as the cross that graces Easter Seals. A variation of the style of the Cross of Lorraine is the Russian Orthodox cross, or Eastern Orthodox cross. This cross has an angled crossbar below the main crossbar. Where one is seen, often many are seen, since they generally appear in ethnic cemeteries or in ethnic areas of large cemeteries.

Sometimes Latin crosses and Russian Orthodox crosses are seen with angled pieces on top of the cross that look like a little roof. These crosses are known as wayside crosses, which can be seen by roadsides all over Europe. They are usually simple wooden affairs and were erected by the thousands. Unlike American roadside crosses, which usually commemorate victims of automobile accidents, wayside crosses are erected for the convenience of travelers who may be compelled to stop and pray. The more repentant of these travelers may become quite emotional, which gives the wayside crosses their alternate name: weeping crosses. Despite their rather flimsy nature, wayside crosses can often be seen in American ethnic cemeteries.

✲ The Celtic Cross

Celtic crosses are, without a doubt, the most effervescent of all crosses. Entire books have been devoted to their history. In American cemeteries, they can be found as plain stone monuments, but more often they are embellished with intricate tracery and symbolism. Of the dozens of varieties of crosses, the Celtic cross is most intensely associated with a person's roots. A vast array of sizes and styles of Celtic crosses adorn the graves of Irish and Scottish families. In fact, most Scots have a cross that is particular to their clan. The basic form of a Celtic cross is one that is enclosed in a circle (nimbus).

The Celtic cross is pagan in origin and predates Christianity by a number of centuries. In its early form, it was devoid of decorations, and the top three arms of the cross (representing the male reproductive power) were totally enclosed within the circle (representing the female reproductive power). As Christianity was adopted by the Celts, the circle began to get smaller, symbolizing either the triumph of Christianity or the loss of the goddess influence, depending on how you look at it. The symbolism of the Irish cross is strongly tied to Mother Earth and national pride. The four arms can represent the four elements—air, earth, fire, and water. In some Celtic crosses, the four arms correspond with four provinces of Ireland, with the circle used in creating a fifth province by incorporating pieces of the other four.

✺ Fylfot Cross

The fylfot cross (swastika) has become one of the world's most hated symbols. This particular cross, known as a Buddhist swastika, is located on a Japanese grave. In seventeenth-century Japan, Christians who feared persecution for their beliefs used this symbol as a way of disguising the more identifiable Latin cross.

✺ Floré Cross

A simple version of the floré (floriated) cross has three-pronged tips that represent the Trinity of the Father, the Son, and the Holy Ghost.

Floré Cross   **Maltese Cross**

✺ Maltese Cross

This simple version of the Maltese cross has four flared arms.

✺ Cross and Crown

The cross with a crown is a Christian symbol of the sovereignty of the Lord. When the crown is combined with a cross, the crown means victory and the cross means Christianity.

    The one to the right is surrounded by the Latin words *In Hoc Signo Vinces* ("In this sign, conquer"), which Christian ideology says Roman Emperor Constantine applied to his standards before going into battle against Maxentius. The first three letters of *In Hoc Signo* (IHS) are often misinterpreted as the IHS monogram that is often seen on crosses. The IHS monogram is actually the first three letters of Jesus' name in Greek: *Ihsus.*

    The cross with a crown on the right, also denotes a member of the York Rite Masons. As with all types of crowns used by the Masons, it symbolizes the power and authority to lead or command. *See also* Knights Templar on page 214.

✸ Crusader's Cross

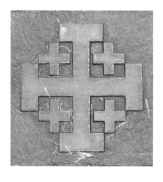

Greek Crosses are usually found applied to tombstones as a decoration rather than as freestanding crosses. When surrounded by four smaller crosses, the symbol is known as a Crusader's or Jerusalem cross. The four smaller crosses represent the four books of the Gospel or the four directions in which the Word of Christ spread from Jerusalem. All five crosses can also symbolize the five wounds of Christ during the Passion. When the tips of the main cross form a T as in this example, it is a cross potent (crutch), which is the logo for the Knights and Dames of the Holy Sepulcher of Jerusalem.

✸ Eastern Orthodox Cross

Hollywood Forever Cemetery has seen a dramatic increase in burials of people of eastern European descent. The Eastern Orthodox cross, also known as the Russian Orthodox cross, has a slanted bar underneath the main cross member.

Eastern Orthodox Cross   Latin Cross

✸ Latin Cross

The simplicity of the Latin cross makes it a blank canvas for adding symbols and inscriptions. It is one of the most recognized religious symbols.

✸ Latin Cross in "Glory"

A Glory combines a halo (a zone of light around the head) and an aureole (rays of radiating light surrounding the whole body). A Glory expresses the most exalted form of divinity. At the base of the cross is the monogram IHS, which is the first three letters of Jesus' name in Greek: *Ihsus*.

⊛ Wayside Cross

Wayside crosses are popular with eastern European ethnic groups. They are a reference to wayside, or weeping, crosses, where passersby are invited to stop and pray. Despite the fact that they are made out of wood rather than a more permanent material like stone, they are quite popular in American ethnic cemeteries.

Heavenly Messengers

Besides tombstones, the feature most often associated with cemeteries is angels. If you get a glimpse of an angel while driving down the road, it's likely you are driving by a cemetery. Wander into the cemetery and you'll likely see dozens of these heavenly messengers dotting the landscape. Despite their winged countenance, they are

tremendously variable in their posture and expression. While some are draped over tombs in grief, others seem ready to take flight with heavenly joy and aspiration. Tears stream from the eyes of one; another face is filled with adoration; another manages a wistful smile. Skilled sculptors have indeed brought cold stone and bronze to life.

Most angels in cemeteries are of a generic variety, but with a little sleuthing, a cemetery visitor can usually find an example of Gabriel, since he is portrayed with a horn; statues of Michael with his sword or shield are also fairly common. Cherubs are often found adorning children's graves.

Oftentimes, a cemetery has one particular angel that gets significantly more attention than others do. Hollywood Forever Cemetery is home to a rather sensuous statue of Eros (a sort of grown-up Cupid) and Psyche. Cemeterians tell us that people seem to adopt specific angels and call them their own. Certain angels seem to attract fresh-cut flowers; others attract toys and teddy bears.

Angels seem to have weathered well in America's cemeteries. They comfort us; they give us hope and sometimes even inspire us. There is no angel on the tomb of Tyrone Power in Hollywood Forever Cemetery, but there is an angelic verse from William Shakespeare (1564–1616), *Hamlet*, Act 5, Scene 2—"Now cracks a noble heart. Good night sweet prince: / And flights of angels sing thee to thy rest!"

Angels such as this one at the Home of Peace Cemetery are often depicted taking inventory of one's life.

In modern times, there has been a trend to occasionally depict angels with more butterfly-like wings. This flawless example is at Forest Lawn–Glendale.

An angel of the order of cherubim adorns the grave in Forest Lawn–Hollywood Hills.

A popular cemetery theme is angels assisting people on their heavenly ascent. This one resides at Inglewood Park Cemetery.

Hebrew Symbols

Jewish people have been memorializing their dead far longer than Christians. Jewish tombstones do not have nearly the vocabulary of symbols as Christian tombstones, but their brevity is deceiving. On many Jewish tombstones, the father of the deceased person is written on the tombstone. This piece of information gives genealogists a step back one generation.

✳ Dates

Dates are written in Hebrew according to the Jewish calendar, which starts with the Creation of the World. It was calculated by figuring the ages of people and events referred to in the Old Testament. That figure worked out to 3,760 years before the Christian calendar. Thus, the year 2000 in the Christian calendar would be 5760 (3760 + 2000) in the Hebrew calendar. Occasionally, the first 5,000 years are dropped. Thus, 5760 would be written as 760.

It should also be noted that, as a rule, headstones of Jews in Europe contain more symbolism than those in North America. European headstones will often have depictions of the tools of trade of the deceased as well as an array of plants and animals. Since the headstones in Europe are older, the wealth of symbols might point to lower literacy rates.

✳ Here Lies

This sign is found on almost every Jewish tombstone. It is the Hebrew words *po nikbar* or *po nitman* ("here lies").

✳ Menorah

The menorah is a seven-branched candelabrum. It is usually seen on the tombstone of a "righteous" woman. Its roots go back to the destruction of

Here Lies

Menorah

the Temple of Solomon. The most vivid account of the menorah in the Bible is in Exodus 25: 31–40, where the Lord explains the furnishings he wants Moses to make for the tabernacle.

Interestingly, the seven-branched menorah is rarely seen on European headstones (usually three or five branches are seen) because the seven-branched menorah was a symbol of the Temple and its use was prohibited as a headstone symbol.

✳ Star of David

The Star of David, a symbol of divine protection, is probably the most well known Jewish symbol, although it didn't become a major symbol until the late 1880s, when it was used by Zionists to identify themselves. Ironically, the Star of David symbol became a permanent identifier of Jews when Hitler ordered Jews to wear the symbol on their arms. When Israel put the star on its flag, the transition from minor symbol to the universal Jewish symbol was complete.

✳ Yahrtzeit

The *yahrtzeit* is an oil-filled basin with a floating wick. Nowadays, a yahrtzeit can also be a candle. It can also refer to an event as well as an object. Thus, during Yahrtzeit, a yahrtzeit candle is burned to commemorate the dead. The yahrtzeit is also called a *Ner Neshamah*, a "Lamp of the Soul," based on the verse in Proverbs 20:27—"The spirit of man is the candle of the LORD, searching all the inward parts of the belly."

Yahrtzeit   Levite Pitcher

✳ Ewer (Levite pitcher)

A pitcher signifies a Levite who, according to scripture, was responsible for cleaning the hands of the Temple priest (the Cohanim) prior to a religious service. Aside from these cleansing duties, Levites were also musicians, singers in choirs, and gatekeepers. In today's world, the Levites are the ones called on second (after the Cohanim) in the reading of the Torah.

✳ The Mosaic Decalogue

Thanks to Charlton Heston and Cecil B. DeMille, almost everyone knows these tablets as the Ten Commandments. In the cemetery, the two tablets are always joined. Sometimes they are seen with the Hebrew figures (five on each side) for the numbers 1–10, while other times the commandments are written out in an abbreviated form. Christians liked the idea of the tablets so much that they modified it with Roman numerals, and it has become a popular Christian symbol.

✳ Cohanim (Kohanim) Hands

These hands with thumbs, and sometimes forefingers, joined are a symbol of the members of the ancient priestly tribe of Aaron, who was a Levite. Nowadays, at certain services, the Cohanim raise their hands in the air to form an opening, which directs the radiance of God to stream down on the congregation. The Conanim hands usually mark the graves of fallen Cohns, Cohens, Cahns, Cowens, and their families.

✳ Pebbles

All cultures have ways of continuing to memorialize their dead by leaving something at the gravesite. Some of the more popular items include flowers (real and artificial), immortelles (ceramic flowers), food, pictures, toys, and notes. One of the most curious memorialization practices is the Jewish custom of leaving pebbles on and around the tombstone. The custom has become so well established that some Jews will bring pebbles and small stones from their travels to place on the tombstone. And, if pebbles are not available in the cemetery, coins and bits of glass are sometimes substituted. Nevertheless, the message is clear: at its most basic level, pebbles, like flowers, say that someone still cares and remembers. But why use stones? Like many folk customs, scholars say the origin of the practice is somewhat shadowy. What is clear is that using stones to memorialize a person or mark a place has gone on for thousands of years. In fact, because of the ready supply of durable materials, building rock cairns was one of the earliest methods man employed to mark important places.

Ultimately, the use of rocks and pebbles on graves is a practical matter. Graves in a rocky or sandy environment couldn't be dug very deep. Rocky ground is hard to excavate, and sand collapses before it can be dug very deep. Thus, graves were often quite shallow, and rocks and pebbles needed to be placed over the grave to prevent the remains from being disturbed by animals. These rock mounds became grave markers by default because of the nature of their form.

Jews were a nomadic people and, as such, traveled from place to place. When they passed the gravesite of a member of their tribe, it was entirely reasonable that they would do a bit of maintenance to that site, which, in an arid environment, would mean maintaining and, perhaps, adding to the stones. By extension, a nomadic people wouldn't leave fragile plants or flowers on a grave since they would soon be moving on and unable to care for them. Flowers, food, and other remembrances that are part of memorialization practices of other cultures were never part of early Jewish burial practices. Adding more rocks simply served the same purpose.

Asian Symbols

Although Chinese and Japanese tombstones do not have the vast repertoire of funerary symbols as do those from European cultures, they do have some interesting and significant symbols and traditions. The Los Angeles area has longtime populations of people with roots in Japan and China. In recent years, there has been an influx of immigrants from Southeast Asia and Korea.

Chinese symbolism is seen more in the funerary rituals than on symbols that appear on tombstones. The most significant Chinese tradition is the observance of Ching Ming, translated roughly as "pure brightness." Ching Ming occurs on April 5 (106 days after the winter solstice), but is sometimes moved to the first weekend if April 5 doesn't fall on a weekend. On the first day of Ching Ming, a priest conducts a 34-step ceremony called the "Three Presentations Ceremony" at the oldest grave in the cemetery. This ceremony's most memorable aspect is, no doubt, the 34th step, which is the lighting of more than 10,000 firecrackers.

Another name for Ching Ming is "tomb-sweeping (or cleaning) day" and refers to the cleaning and maintenance of the graves of one's ancestors. It is important to maintain and honor the graves of one's ancestors because of the Chinese belief that all fortune or misfortune stems from the reverence or lack thereof of one's ancestors. These departed ancestors still have similar physical needs (hence, the leaving of food, drink, and gifts) and can assist those still bound to the earth.

Like the Chinese, the Japanese also have a period of days for remembering the dead. This time is called Obon or Urabon (upside down), which refers to a Buddhist legend where a disciple of Buddha rescued his mother, who had been hanging upside down in hell because she had lied about eating some meat. Obon occurs in July and August, and has three parts: 1) visiting graves and leaving symbolic foods, which the dead "absorb"; 2) a community dance; and 3) a parade of floating lanterns, where the name of the deceased is written on a lantern and set off down the river, symbolizing the return to the underworld.

Japanese tombstones often have family crests called *mon* or *monsho*, not unlike European crests except they are more stylized. The tradition of heraldic crests started in the seventh century when the Chinese brought the designs to Japan. Soon, warriors were wearing these decorations on their armor to identify their allegiance. Through the centuries, thousands of patterns have evolved, and nowadays, almost every family has its own crest. Most crests are strongly tied to nature—the most popular designs are plants, flowers, and trees followed by birds and beasts. But there are many other designs representing the earth and sky, tools, geometric forms, and ideographs. The ideographs often symbolize attributes like chastity, good fortune, integrity, sincerity, perfection, peace, heaven, and many more. Examples of *mon* or *monsho* include the following:

✸ Tsumori Family Crest

This is the Tsumori family crest. It is in a circle design known as a *shippo* (seven treasures). The pattern of overlapping circles, called *shippo*, probably comes from *shi* (four) *ho* (directions), and the word evolved into *shippo*. The pattern symbolizes expansiveness. When the elements are more oval-like instead of perfectly round, it is a sign of maturity. The design appeared in the late Heian period (AD 794–1185). The overlap is exactly equal on all four sides.

✸ Tomoe Pattern

This *tomoe* pattern did not appear on Japanese family crests until the ninth or tenth centuries. Scholars differ on the origin of the pattern. Some say it is an adaptation of similar comma-like designs, like the yin-yang symbol, while others say it was derived from the shape of a leather guard worn on the left hand of archers to protect them from the snap of the bowstring. The guard is called a *tomo* and a graphic representation of a *tomo* is called a *tomo-e*.

✸ Crane

The crane is a popular Japanese symbol. It is associated with long life (more than 1,000 years). One Chinese and Japanese legend has hermit-sages riding on the backs of cranes. A number of different styles of cranes are employed in the Japanese art of paper folding, or origami.

Hishi Symbol

The diamond (*hishi*) is a textile design that appeared before the Heian period. Based on the water chestnut (*hishi*), the design was used by the court and warrior societies before the widespread adoption of family crests.

Hishi Symbol

Motoyama Family Crest

Motoyama Family Crest

The Motoyama family crest is a highly stylized goose (*kari*). Three goose heads are encircled with three Vs, which represent the flight of the goose.

Feather

Because of the association with warriors, family crests using various archery items are very popular. There are hundreds of variations and combinations. Arrowheads and bows are infrequently used on family crest designs, but complete arrows, feathers, and the notch on the feathers are frequently employed on the crests. Japanese literature refers to the life of a warrior as "the way of the bow and arrow."

Mulberry Leaf

This is a representation of a mulberry leaf (*kaji*). In ancient times, the kaji leaf, also known as the "paper mulberry," was used to fabricate representations of clothing left at Shinto shrines as an offering. The mulberry leaf was also used to make cups and plates for food offerings. More recently, during the Tanabata festival, ladies of the court write poems on the mulberry leaf. It has been incorporated into a number of family crests. This particular example is used by the Murata family.

Los Angeles Area Cemeteries

Web Sites

There are hundreds of Web sites that address various aspects of cemetery symbolism, religious beliefs and celebrity graves. As a starting point, try the following:

For cemetery history and information—
Association for Gravestone Studies (www.gravestonestudies.org)

For celebrity gravesites—
Find a Grave (www.findagrave.com)
Hollywood Underground (www.hollywood-underground.com)
Seeing Stars (www.seeing-stars.com/Buried/index.shtml)

For L.A. cemetery links—
www.archdiocese.la/directories/cemeteries/
calarchives4u.com/cemeteries/losangeles-cemeteries.html
home.earthlink.net/~nholdeneditor/jewish_cemeteries_in_los_angeles.htm
www.lafuneralguide.com/guide_categories/los_angeles_cemeteries
www.lagenealogy.com/langecem.htm
www.usc.edu/libraries/archives/la/cemeteries

Cemeteries

Abbey Memorial Park
1515 East Compton Boulevard
Compton, CA 90221
310-631-1141

Acton Community Cemetery
13900 Block of Aliso Street
Acton, CA 93510
661-269-1648

Acton Community Presbyterian Church
32142 Crown Valley Road
P.O. Box 177
Acton, CA 93510
661-269-1648 / 661-208-8032
www.actonpc.org/message.php
?topicID=7604&

Agudath Achim Cemetery
(Jewish cemetery,
founded about 1919)
1022 South Downey Road
Los Angeles, CA 90023
323-653-8886

All Souls Cemetery and Mausoleum
(Catholic cemetery, founded 1950)
4400 Cherry Avenue
Long Beach, CA 90807
562-424-8601
562-426-8065 fax
http://www.allsoulsmortuary.com/

Angelus Rosedale Cemetery
(Historic Cemetery, founded as
Rosedale Cemetery 1884)
1831 West Washington Boulevard
Los Angeles, CA 90007-1151
323-734-3155
323-734-3159 fax

Artesia Cemetery District
(founded 1884)
11142 East Artesia Boulevard
Cerritos, CA 90703
562-865-6300
artesiacemeterydistrict.com/

Avalon Cemetery
(founded 1967)
Santa Catalina Island
Avalon, CA 90704

Beth Israel Cemetery
(Jewish cemetery, founded 1907)
1068 South Downey Road
Los Angeles, CA 90023
213-653-8886
323-962-9652

Beth Olam Cemetery of Hollywood
900 North Gower Street
Los Angeles, CA 90038-3006
323-469-2322
323-962-9652 fax
www.betholam.com/hollywood.htm

Calvary Cemetery and Mausoleum
(Historic Cemetery)
(Catholic cemetery, founded 1896)
4201 Whittier Boulevard
Los Angeles, CA 90023-2017
323-261-3106
323-261-0420 fax

Chapel of the Pines
(founded 1905)
1605 South Catalina Street
Los Angeles, CA 90006
323-731-5734

Chinese Cemetery
    East 1st Street,
    at South Eastern Avenue
    East Los Angeles, CA 90022
    213-265-3709

Desert Lawn Memorial Park
    (founded 1950)
    2200 East Avenue "S"
    Palmdale, CA 93550
    661-947-7177
    www.desertlawnmemorialpark.com/

Downey Cemetery District
    (founded 1868)
    9073 East Gardendale Street
    Bellflower, CA 90242-4613
    562-904-7102 / 562-904-7236

Eden Memorial Park
    (Jewish cemetery, founded 1987)
    11500 Sepulveda Boulevard
    Mission Hills, CA 91345-1119
    818-361-7161

El Campo Santo (Historic Cemetery)
    (see Workman Cemetery)

El Monte Cemetery (Historic Cemetery)
    (Savannah Cemetery) (founded 1850)
    9263 Valley Boulevard
    at Mission Road
    Rosemead, CA 91770-1953
    626-287-4838

Eternal Valley Memorial Park
    23287 North Sierra Highway
    Santa Clarita, CA 91321
    818-365-3292

Evergreen Cemetery
    (aka Sunset Cemetery)
    (founded 1877; oldest existing
    cemetery in the City of Los Angeles)
    204 North Evergreen Avenue
    Los Angeles, CA 90033-3654
    323-268-6714

Evergreen Cemetery
    (see La Verne Cemetery)

Fairmount Cemetery
    (Historic Landmark)
    Glendora, CA
    Walk northwest from the south end
    of North Baldy Vista Avenue
    ✦ 34 08 26 N 117 53 21 W

Forest Lawn Memorial Park–
    Covina Hills (founded 1965)
    21300 Via Verde Drive
    Covina, CA 91724-3727
    800-204-3131
    626-339-5146 fax
    www.forestlawn.com/About-Forest-
    Lawn/Locations-and-Directions-
    Covina-Hills.asp

Forest Lawn Memorial Park–Glendale
    (founded 1916)
    1712 South Glendale Avenue
    Glendale, CA 91205
    800-204-3131
    213-344-9035 fax
    www.forestlawn.com/About-Forest-
    Lawn/Locations-and-Directions-
    Glendale.asp

Forest Lawn Memorial Park–
    Hollywood Hills
    6300 Forest Lawn Drive
    Los Angeles, CA 90068-1018
    800-204-3131
    www.forestlawn.com/About-Forest-
    Lawn/Locations-and-Directions-
    Hollywood-Hills.asp

Forest Lawn Memorial Park–
    Long Beach
    1500 East San Antonio Drive
    Long Beach, CA 90807-1233
    800-204-3131
    www.forestlawn.com/About-Forest-
    Lawn/Locations-and-Directions-
    Long-Beach.asp

Founders Memorial Cemetery
    (Historic Landmark)
    (Morningside Cemetery/
    Sylmar Cemetery/
    Pioneer Memorial Cemetery)
    14451 Bledsoe Street
    Sylmar, CA 91342

Glen Haven Memorial Park
    13017 North Lopez Canyon Road
    Sylmar, CA 91342-5698
    818-899-5211
    818-890-4606 fax
    www.interment.net/data/us/ca/
    losangeles/glenhaven/glenhaven.htm

Good Shepherd Cemetery
    (Catholic cemetery)
    43121 70th Street West
    Lancaster, CA 93536-7505
    805-722-0887

Grand View Memorial Park
    1341 Glenwood Road
    Glendale, CA 91201
    818-242-2697
    818-242-9438 fax
    grandviewmemorialpark.info/

Green Hills Memorial Park
    (founded 1948)
    27501 South Western Avenue
    Rancho Palos Verdes, CA 90275-1099
    310-831-0311
    310-519-7029 fax
    www.greenhillsmemorial.com/info.
    html

Harbor View Memorial Cemetery
(Historic Cemetery)
(founded 1883; formerly
San Pedro Cemetery)
2411 South Grand Avenue,
and West 24th Street
San Pedro, CA 90731
www.sanpedro.com/sp_point/
hrbrcemt.htm

Hillside Memorial Park
(Historical Cemetery)
(Jewish cemetery, founded 1946)
6001 Centinela Avenue
Culver City, CA 90045-0707
310-641-0707
800-576-1994
www.hillsidememorial.org/Home.
aspx

Hollywood Forever Cemetery
(Historical Cemetery)
(founded 1899;
formerly Hollywood Memorial Park)
6000 Santa Monica Boulevard
Los Angeles, CA 90038-1181
323-469-1181
www.hollywoodforever.com/
Hollywood/

Holy Cross Cemetery and Mausoleum
(Historic Cemetery)
(Catholic cemetery, founded 1939)
5835 West Slauson Avenue
Culver City, CA 90230-6500
310-836-5500
310-836-3560 fax

Holy Cross Cemetery
(Catholic cemetery, founded 1986)
444 East Lexington Avenue
Pomona, CA 91766
909-627-3602
909-465-0690 fax

Home of Peace Memorial Park
(Historical Cemetery)
(Jewish cemetery, opened 1855;
current location since 1902)
4334 Whittier Boulevard
Los Angeles, CA 90023-2090
323-261-6135
800-300-0223 toll free
323-261-2725 fax
www.homeofpeacememorialpark.
com

Inglewood Park Cemetery
(founded 1905)
720 East Florence Avenue
Inglewood, CA 90301-1482
310-412-6500
310-671-9440 fax
www.inglewoodparkcemetery.org/
home1.html

Joshua Memorial Park
808 East Lancaster Boulevard
Lancaster, CA 93535
661-942-8125

La Verne Cemetery
(formerly Evergreen Cemetery)
3201 "B" Street
La Verne, CA 91750-3904
909-593-1415

Lancaster Cemetery
(founded 1892)
111 East Lancaster Boulevard
Lancaster, CA 93535-2555
661-942-6110
www.lancastercemetery.com

Lincoln Memorial Park Cemetery
(founded 1930)
16701 South Central Avenue
Carson, CA 90746
310-635-7441

Little Lake Cemetery District
(founded 1843)
11959 Lakeland Road
Santa Fe Springs, CA 90670
562-944-6818

Live Oak Memorial Park
200 East Duarte Road
Monrovia, CA 91016-4646
626-359-5311
626-357-0013 fax

Long Beach Municipal Cemetery
1151 East Willow Street
Long Beach, CA 90806
562-570-6634
http://www.interment.net/data/
us/ca/losangeles/longbeach_mun/
index.htm

Los Angeles County Cemetery
(founded 1896)
3301 East 1st Street
Los Angeles, CA 90063
323-268-5111

Los Angeles National Cemetery
(dedicated 1989; former
Sawtelle Soldier's Cemetery)
950 South Sepulveda Boulevard
Los Angeles, CA 90049
310-268-4675/4494
310-268-3257 fax

Los Angeles Pet Memorial Park
5068 Old Scandia Lane
Calabasas, CA 91302
818-591-7037
www.lapetcemetery.com/

Morningside Cemetery
(Historic Cemetery)
(see Founders Memorial Cemetery)

Mount Carmel Cemetery
(Jewish cemetery, founded 1931)
6501 East Gage Avenue
City of Commerce, CA 90040
323-653-8886

Mount Olive Cemetery
(tombstones removed,
now "Founders Park")
Between 21100 and 12500 Whittier
Boulevard
Whittier, CA. 90601
562-945-3871
562-945-9106 fax
www.whittiermuseum.org/

Mount Olive Memorial Park
(Jewish cemetery, founded 1948)
7231 East Slauson Avenue
Commerce, CA 90040-3624
310-208-7514
www.mountolivememorial.com/

Mount Sinai Memorial Park–
Hollywood Hills
(Jewish cemetery, founded 1953)
5950 Forest Lawn Drive
Los Angeles, CA 90068-1099
213-469-6000
800-600-0076
213-469-2372 fax
www.mt-sinai.com/home/

Mount Zion Cemetery
(Historic Cemetery)
(Jewish cemetery, founded 1916)
1030 South Downey Road
Los Angeles, CA 90068
213-852-1234

Mountain View Cemetery
Pasadena Cemetery Association
2400 North Fair Oaks Avenue
P.O. Box 6069
Altadena, CA 91001
626-794-7133
626-794-2080 fax

Oak Park Cemetery
Sycamore Avenue at
East Oak Park Drive
Claremont, CA 91711-5314
909-399-5487
www.ci.claremont.ca.us/
ps.municipalservices.cfm?ID=1765

Oakdale Memorial Park
1401 South Grand Avenue
Glendora, CA 91740-5434
626-335-8834
626-335-4403 fax

Oakwood Memorial Park
(Historic Cemetery)
22601 Lassen Street
Chatsworth, CA 91311-2652
818-341-0344
818-341-6499 fax

Odd Fellows Cemetery
3640 Whittier Boulevard
Los Angeles, CA 90023-1789
213-261-6156

Olive Grove Cemetery
(founded 1896)
10135 South Painter Avenue
Whittier, CA 90605

Olive Lawn Memorial Park
13926 La Mirada Boulevard
La Mirada, CA 90638-3198
562-943-1718
www.olivelawn.com/

Pacific Crest Cemetery
(founded 1902)
2701 182nd Street,
at Inglewood Avenue
Redondo Beach, CA 90278-3993
310-370-5891

Paradise Memorial Park
11541 East Florence Avenue
Santa Fe Springs, CA 90670-4356
562-864-7316

Park Lawn Memorial Park
6555 East Gage Avenue
City of Commerce, CA 90040-3602
323-773-3220 / 562-806-0660
323-927-6269 fax

Pierce Brothers–Valhalla
Memorial Park
10621 Victory Boulevard
North Hollywood, CA 91606-3918
818-763-9121

Pierce Brothers–
Valley Oaks Memorial Park
(nonsectarian cemetery,
contains Jewish section)
5600 Lindero Canyon Road
Westlake Village, CA 91362
818-889-0902 / 805-495-0837

Pioneer Memorial Cemetery
(Historic Cemetery)
(see Founders Memorial Cemetery)
www.sfvhs.com/PC-main.htm

Pomona Valley Memorial Park
502 East Franklin Avenue
Pomona, CA 91766-5372
909-622-2029
909-622-4726 fax
www.pomonacemetery.com/

Queen of Heaven Cemetery
(founded 1957)
2161 South Fullerton Road
Rowland Heights, CA 91748-3598
626-964-1291
626-964-4325 fax
www.queenofheavenmortuary.com/

Resurrection Cemetery
(Catholic cemetery, founded 1952)
966 North Potrero Grande Drive
Montebello, CA 90640
323-887-2024
323-722-0874 fax

Roosevelt Memorial Park
(founded 1923)
18255 South Vermont Avenue
Los Angeles CA 90248
310-329-1113 / 323-321-0482
www.rooseveltmemorialparkand
mortuary.com/html/mortuary.htm

Rose Hills Memorial Park
(founded 1914)
3888 South Workman Mill Road
Whittier, CA 90601
562-699-0921
www.rosehills.com/

Rose of Sharon Cemetery (part of
Forest Lawn–Long Beach)
1500 East San Antonio Drive
Long Beach, 90807
800-204-3131

Rosedale Cemetery
(Historic Cemetery)
(see Angelus Rosedale Cemetery)

Russian Molokan Cemetery
Association
7201 East Slauson Avenue
Los Angeles, CA 90040
323-724-3984

San Fernando Mission Cemetery
(Historic Cemetery)
(founded 1797)
11160 Stranwood Avenue
Mission Hills, CA 91345-1120
818-361-7387
818-365-6187 fax

San Gabriel Cemetery
(founded 1872)
601 West Roses Road
San Gabriel, CA 91775-2236
626-282-2764
www.sangabrielcemetery.com/

San Gabriel Mission Cemetery
537 West Mission Drive
San Gabriel, CA 91775
626-457-7291

Santa Monica Cemetery
1847 14th Street
Santa Monica, CA 90401
310-458-8717

Sawtelle Soldier's Cemetery
(see Los Angeles National Cemetery)

Serbian United Benevolent Society
(Serbian cemetery)
4355 East Second Street
Los Angeles CA 90022
323-261-8033

Shalom Memorial Park
(Jewish cemetery, founded 1951)
13017 North Lopez Canyon Road
Sylmar, CA 91342
818-899-5216

Sierra Madre Cemetery
Sierra Madre Boulevard
and Coburn Avenue
Sierra Madre, CA 91024

Spadra Cemetery
57 Freeway and Overpass
(difficult access)
Pomona, CA 91768
✳ 34 03 05 N 117 48 03 W

Sunnyside Cemetery
1095 East Willow Street
Long Beach, CA 90806
562-595-9392

Sylmar Cemetery (Historic Cemetery
(see Founders Memorial Cemetery)

Valhalla Memorial Park
(see Pierce Brothers–
Valhalla Memorial Park)

Valley Oaks Memorial Park
(see Pierce Brothers–
Valley Oaks Memorial Park)

Verdugo Hills Cemetery
7000 Parsons Trail
Tujunga CA 91042

Western Memorial
401 South Prairie Avenue
Inglewood, CA 90301-5001
310-412-6850
www.westernsequoia.com/

Western Memorial Park
10841 Rush Street
South El Monte, CA 91733
626-453-0866

Westwood Village Memorial Park
(founded 1904)
1218 Glendon Avenue,
at Wilshire Boulevard
Los Angeles, CA 90024
310-474-1579
310-474-0917 fax

Wilmington Cemetery
(Historic Cemetery)
(founded 1857)
605 East "O" Street
Wilmington, CA 90744-1612
310-834-4442

Woodlawn Cemetery
1847 14th Street
Santa Monica, CA 90404
310-450-0781 / 310-458-8717

Woodlawn Memorial Park
(founded 1869)
1715 West Greenleaf Boulevard
Compton, CA 90220

Workman Cemetery
(Historic Cemetery)
(aka El Campo Santo / Little
Acre of God Cemetery)
15415 East Don Julian Road
City of Industry, CA 91746
www.homesteadmuseum.org
/ecsanto.htm

Young Israel Cemetery
(Jewish cemetery, founded 1938)
13622 Curtis at King Road
Norwalk, CA 90650
213-653-8886

Suggested Reading

Axelrod, Alan. *The International Ency-clopedia of Secret Societies and Fraternal Orders.* New York City: Facts On File, Inc., 1997.

Benson, George Willard. *The Cross: Its History and Symbolism.* Buffalo, New York: Hacker Art Books, 1983.

Bliss, Harry A. *Memorial Art Ancient and Modern.* Buffalo, New York: Harry A. Bliss, 1912.

Carmack, Sharon DeBartolo. *Your Guide to Cemetery Research.* Cincinnati, Ohio: Betterway Books, 2001.

Colvin, Howard. *Architecture and the Afterlife.* New Haven, Connecticut: Yale University Press, 1991.

Ferguson, George. *Signs and Symbols in Christian Art.* New York City: Oxford University Press, 1954.

Hancock, Ralph. *The Forest Lawn Story.* Los Angeles: Angelus Press, 1964.

Keister, Douglas. *Forever Dixie: A Field Guide to Southern Cemeteries & Their Residents.* Salt Lake City: Gibbs Smith, Publisher, 2008.

————. *Going Out in Style: The Architec-ture of Eternity.* New York City: Facts On File, Inc., 1997.

————. *Stories in Stone: A Field Guide to Cemetery Symbolism and Iconography.* Salt Lake City: Gibbs Smith, Publisher, 2004.

Memorial Symbolism, Epitaphs and Design Types. Olean, New York: American Monument Association, Inc., 1947.

Meyer, Richard, ed. *Cemeteries and Graveyards: Voices of American Culture.* Logan, Utah: Utah State University Press, 1989.

————. *Ethnicity and the American Cemetery.* Bowling Green, Ohio: Bowling Green State University Popular Press, 1993.

Pictorial Forest Lawn. Glendale, Cali-fornia: Forest Lawn Memorial-Park Association, 1970.

Preuss, Arthur, ed. *A Dictionary of Secret and Other Societies.* St. Louis, Missouri: B. Herder Book Co., 1924.

Ridlen, Susanne S. *Tree-stump Tombstones.* Kokomo, Indiana: Old Richardville Publications, 1999.

The Penguin Dictionary of Symbols. Lon-don, England: Penguin Books, 1996.

Willsher, Betty. *Understanding Scottish Graveyards.* Edinburgh, Scotland: Canongate Books Ltd, 1995.

Index